First World War
and Army of Occupation
War Diary
France, Belgium and Germany

57 DIVISION
Divisional Troops
502 Field Company Royal Engineers
1 February 1917 - 10 June 1919

WO95/2973/1

The Naval & Military Press Ltd
www.nmarchive.com
Published in association with The National Archives

Published by

The Naval & Military Press Ltd

Unit 10 Ridgewood Industrial Park,

Uckfield, East Sussex,

TN22 5QE England

Tel: +44 (0) 1825 749494

www.naval-military-press.com

www.nmarchive.com

This diary has been reprinted in facsimile from the original. Any imperfections are inevitably reproduced and the quality may fall short of modern type and cartographic standards.

© **Crown Copyright**
Images reproduced by permission of The National Archives, London, England, 2015.

Contents

Document type	Place/Title	Date From	Date To
Heading	WO95/2973/1 502 Field Company Royal Engineers		
Miscellaneous	502nd Field Coy R.E Feb 1917-Jun 1919		
Heading	War Diary Of 502nd. (Wessex) Field Co. R.E. From:- 1.2.17. To 28.2.17 Volume I		
War Diary	Blackdown	01/02/1917	12/02/1917
War Diary	Southampton	12/02/1917	12/02/1917
War Diary	Le Havre	13/02/1917	14/02/1917
War Diary	Baileul	15/02/1917	16/02/1917
War Diary	Vieux Berquin	15/02/1917	16/02/1917
War Diary	Sailly-Sur-La Lys	18/02/1917	18/02/1917
Heading	War Diary Of 502nd. (Wessex) Field Coy. R.E. From 1st March 1917 To 31st March 1917		
War Diary		01/03/1917	31/03/1917
Heading	War Diary Of 502nd (Wessex) Field Coy R.E. From 1st April 1917 To 30th April 1917 (Volume 3)		
War Diary		01/04/1917	30/04/1917
Heading	War Diary Of 502nd (Wessex) Field Coy. R.E. From 1st May 1917. To 31st May 1917 Volume 4		
War Diary	(Fleurbaix H.15.C.10 France 36 N.W.3 1/10,000	01/05/1917	31/05/1917
Heading	War Diary Of 502nd (Wessex) Field Coy. R.E. From 1st June 1917 To 30th June 1917 (Volume 5)		
War Diary	Fleurbaix France 1.10000 36N.W.3	01/06/1917	07/06/1917
War Diary	Fleurbaix	08/06/1917	30/06/1917
Heading	War Diary Of 502nd (Wessex) Field Co. R.E. From 1st July 1917 To 31st July 1917 (Volume 6)		
War Diary	Fleurbaix France 1:10,000 N.W.3.	01/07/1917	04/07/1917
War Diary	Fleurbaix	05/07/1917	31/07/1917
War Diary	War Diary Of 502nd (Wessex) Field Co. R.E. From 1st August 1917 To 31st August 1917 (Volume 7)		
War Diary	Fleurbaix France 36 N.W. 1/20000	01/08/1917	02/08/1917
War Diary	Armentieres	03/08/1917	20/08/1917
Heading	War Diary Of 502nd. (Wessex) Field Co. R.E. From 1st September 1917 To 30th September 1917 (Volume 8)		
War Diary	Armentieres Map. Ref. France 1.20000 36 N.W.	01/09/1917	05/09/1917
War Diary	Armentieres	06/09/1917	15/09/1917
War Diary	Wackland Camp B.136.4.9	16/09/1917	17/09/1917
War Diary	L.32 B.7.6 (France 36A.140,000)	18/09/1917	18/09/1917
War Diary	O.6.A.0.0	19/09/1917	19/09/1917
War Diary	Flechinelle M.33 B.3.3	20/09/1917	27/09/1917
War Diary	Flechinelle (France 36A.140000)	28/09/1917	30/09/1917
Heading	War Diary Of 502nd. (Wessex) Field Co. R.E. From 1st October 1917 To 31st October 1917 (Volume 9)		
War Diary	Flechinelle France 1/20,000 36A SW	01/10/1917	10/10/1917
War Diary	Flechinelle France 36A 120000 SW	11/10/1917	16/10/1917
War Diary	Campagne (Map Ref Hazebrouck 5A 1 100000)	17/10/1917	17/10/1917
War Diary	3 Miles S.E Of St Omer Portland Camp Near Crombeke N. Of Poper Inghe Map Ref	18/10/1917	18/10/1917
War Diary	Portland Camp New Crombeke X 28a.2.9	19/10/1917	22/10/1917
War Diary	Yser Canal Bank C.19.a.0.5 (28 N.W.2)	23/10/1917	25/10/1917
War Diary	Canal D'Yser C.19.H.0.5. (28.N.W.2)	25/10/1917	31/10/1917

Miscellaneous	502nd (Wessex) Field Co. R.E.		
Heading	War Diary Of 502nd (Wessex) Field Co. R.E. From 1st November 1917 To: 30th November 1917 (Volume 10)		
War Diary	Canal D'Yser C.19 A O.5 (France 28 N.W.2 1 10000)	01/11/1917	08/11/1917
War Diary	Hocquinghem 3 F 23.21. Sheet 13 Calans 1-100,000	09/11/1917	30/11/1917
Miscellaneous	Handing Over Notes. Appendix No.I	08/11/1917	08/11/1917
Heading	War Diary Of 502nd (Wessex) Field Co. R.E. From 1st December 1917 To 31st December 1917 (Volume 11)		
War Diary	Calais 13 1-100,000 3.F.3.2	01/12/1917	09/12/1917
War Diary	Proven Area	09/12/1917	09/12/1917
War Diary	Hazebrouck 5A-1-100,000 25.72.64	10/12/1917	10/12/1917
War Diary	Sheet 28 B 14 6.27 (Elverdinghe)	10/12/1917	14/12/1917
War Diary	Elverdinghe Sheet 28 B146.2.7	15/12/1917	17/12/1917
War Diary	Boesinghe Sheet 28 B 5.6. 5.3.	18/12/1917	31/12/1917
Miscellaneous	Appendix A		
Miscellaneous	To the Officers, N.C.O's and Men of the 502nd. Wessex Field Co.R.E. Christmas, 1917. Appendix "B"		
Heading	War Diary Of 502nd (Wessex) Field Co. R.E. From 1st January 1918 To 31st January 1918 (Volume 12)		
War Diary	Boesinghe Sheet 28 B56.5.3	01/01/1918	01/01/1918
War Diary	Proven Area 19/X 26 C 4 6	02/01/1918	02/01/1918
War Diary	36 LA Haye B 28.b.2.6	03/01/1918	03/01/1918
War Diary	Armentieres Sheet 36 B 29 B.5.2	04/01/1918	13/01/1918
War Diary	Pontde Nieppe 36.b123a 85.45	14/01/1918	25/01/1918
War Diary	Erquinghem H.8.b.9.2	26/01/1918	31/01/1918
Operation(al) Order(s)	C.R.E's Operation Order No. 14	20/12/1917	20/12/1917
Miscellaneous	March Table Issued With C.R.E's Operation Order No. 14		
Operation(al) Order(s)	C.R.E's Operation Order No. 15	30/12/1917	30/12/1917
Miscellaneous	March Table Issued With C.R.E's Operation Order No. 15		
Miscellaneous	502nd. (Wessex) Field Co.R.E. Work In Hand. Appendix B	05/01/1918	05/01/1918
Miscellaneous	Proceedings Of A Conference Held At Bde. H.Q. 22nd Jany. 1918. Appendix "D"	23/01/1918	23/01/1918
Heading	War Diary Of 502nd (Wessex) Field Company R.E. From February 1st 1918 To February 28th 1918 (Volume 13)		
War Diary	Erquinghem 36 4.8.b.9.2	01/02/1918	03/02/1918
War Diary	Erquinghem A.8.b.9.2	03/02/1918	05/04/1918
War Diary	Erquinghem 36 48.b.9.2	06/02/1918	10/02/1918
War Diary	Erquinghem 36 H8b 9.2	10/02/1918	13/02/1918
War Diary	Armentieres 36B30d00.30	14/02/1918	28/02/1918
Miscellaneous	502nd (Wessex) Field Co. R.E.	11/02/1918	11/02/1918
Heading	War Diary Of 502 (Wessex) Field Coy R.E. From 1/3/18 To 31/3/18 (Volume 14)		
War Diary	Armentieres Sheet 36 B30.d.00.30	01/03/1918	19/03/1918
War Diary	Bac St Maur Sheet 36 H13c60.90	20/03/1918	31/03/1918
War Diary	Estaires L.32.b7.6	31/03/1918	31/03/1918
Operation(al) Order(s)	57th Division. C.R.E's. Operation Order No. 18		
Operation(al) Order(s)	57th Division. C.R.E's. Operation Order No. 19	31/03/1918	31/03/1918
Miscellaneous	March Table To Accompany C.R.E's Operation Order No. 19		
Miscellaneous	502nd Wessex Field Co. R.E. Standing Orders		
Heading	57th Divisional Engineers 502nd (Wessex) Field Company R.E. April 1918		

Type	Description	Date From	Date To
Heading	War Diary 502 (Wessex) Field Coy.R.E.1 From 1/4/18 To 30/4/18 (Volume 15)		
War Diary	Estaires L.32.6.7.6 (Hazebruck) 100,000	01/04/1918	01/04/1918
War Diary	Steenbecque F.4.9.2	02/04/1918	03/04/1918
War Diary	(Sheet Lens 11) Warluzel 4 F.6.6	04/04/1918	07/04/1918
War Diary	(Lens.II) Warluzel 4 F.6.6	08/04/1918	08/04/1918
War Diary	Mondicourt 54.F.61	09/04/1918	09/04/1918
War Diary	Amplier 5 E.7.6	10/04/1918	10/04/1918
War Diary	Halloy 5F.18	11/04/1918	12/04/1918
War Diary	Sus St Leger 4F.2.8	13/04/1918	13/04/1918
War Diary	(57d.140000) Authie I10.a.9.3	14/04/1918	16/04/1918
War Diary	Sailly-Au-Bois J.16.d.8.5	17/04/1918	19/04/1918
War Diary	Couin J.1.b.7.5	20/04/1918	30/04/1918
Miscellaneous	Administrative Arrangements Reference 57th Divisional Order Number 77. Appendix A	31/03/1918	31/03/1918
Miscellaneous	Train Arrangements For Move Of 57th Division Less Artillery		
Operation(al) Order(s)	172nd Infantry Brigade Operation Order No. 45	01/01/1916	01/01/1916
Miscellaneous	Train Arrangements For Entraining Of 172nd Infantry Bde Station April 2nd & 3rd 1918	02/04/1918	02/04/1918
Operation(al) Order(s)	170th Inf. Bde. Order No. 115.		
Miscellaneous	170th Inf. Bde. Admin Instruction No.23 With Reference To 170th Inf Bde Order No 115	07/04/1918	07/04/1918
Operation(al) Order(s)	170th Inf. Bde. Order No. 116	08/04/1918	08/04/1918
Operation(al) Order(s)	170th Inf. Bde Admin Instruction No.24	09/04/1918	09/04/1918
Diagram etc	Method of Completing Red line Trenches. Appendix F		
Heading	War Diary Of 502nd (Wessex) Field Coy. R.E. From 1st May 1918 To 31st May 1918 Volume 16		
War Diary	Couin J.16.9.6 (57D)	01/05/1918	06/05/1918
War Diary	Coigneux J.3.b.3.6 Sheet 57 D	06/05/1918	31/05/1918
Heading	War Diary Of 502nd (Wessex) Field Coy. R.E. From 1st June 1918 To: 30th June 1918. Volume 17		
War Diary	Sheet 57 D Coigneux J.3.b.3.4 Trenches Referred To See Map Attached	01/06/1918	03/06/1918
War Diary	57D Coigneux J.3.b.9.4	03/06/1918	04/06/1918
War Diary	Gommecourt Wood E 28 C9.6	04/06/1918	30/06/1918
Operation(al) Order(s)	57th Division C.R.E's, Operation Order No. 21		
Miscellaneous	170th Infantry Brigade Instruction No.52	08/06/1918	08/06/1918
Miscellaneous	Work Programme Beginning 9th June 1918		
Miscellaneous	170th Infantry Brigade Instruction No.50	10/06/1918	10/06/1918
Operation(al) Order(s)	C.R.E's Operation Order No. 23	27/06/1918	27/06/1918
Map	Map		
Heading	War Diary Of 502 (Wessex) Field Coy R.E. Volume XVIII		
War Diary	Bus-En-Artois J.20. C3.9	01/07/1918	25/07/1918
War Diary	Sheet 57 D Bus-En Artois J.20.c.3.9	25/07/1918	28/07/1918
War Diary	(Sheet Lens II Bouque Maison 4.E.05.50	29/07/1918	31/07/1918
War Diary	Wanquentin 3H.30.jo	30/07/1918	31/07/1918
Miscellaneous	Company Sports	11/07/1918	11/07/1918
Operation(al) Order(s)	57th Division C.R.E's Operation Order No. 24	28/07/1918	28/07/1918
Operation(al) Order(s)	57th Division C.R.E's Operation Order No. 25	30/07/1918	30/07/1918
Heading	War Diary Of 502nd (Wessex) Field Company R.E. From August 1st 1918. To August 31st 1918. Volume: XIX		
War Diary	Sheet 51 To NW Arras	01/08/1918	06/08/1918
War Diary	Arras	06/08/1918	11/08/1918

War Diary	Arras G.22.C.7.9	12/08/1918	22/08/1918
War Diary	Wanquetin K32.6.5.0	23/08/1918	23/08/1918
War Diary	Warluzel Sheet Lens 11	24/08/1918	24/08/1918
War Diary	Basseux Lens 11.4.H	25/08/1918	26/08/1918
War Diary	Boisleux-Au-Mont J4.0.5	27/08/1918	28/08/1918
War Diary	St. Martin Sur Cojeul K.4 0 5.75	29/08/1918	31/08/1918
Operation(al) Order(s)	170th Inf. Bde. Order No. 145	18/08/1918	18/08/1918
Miscellaneous	Diary of Moves. 502 Wessex Field Coy. R.E. Appendix B		
Heading	War Diary Of 502nd (Wessex) Field Coy. R.E. From Sept 1st 1918 To: Sept 30th 1918 Volume XX		
War Diary	Sheet Lens II St. Martin Sur Cojeul K.4. 05.75	01/09/1918	02/09/1918
War Diary	Hendecourt 51e S.W U.17.a.0.3	03/09/1918	03/09/1918
War Diary	51.B SW.SE 57 S.N.E Hendecourt 51d SW. U.17.a.O.J	04/09/1918	06/09/1918
War Diary	Hendecourt U.17.a.0.3	06/09/1918	07/09/1918
War Diary	51B V.2.8.c.0.9	07/09/1918	07/09/1918
War Diary	Queant D.7.b.4.9	08/09/1918	10/09/1918
War Diary	57c N.E. Queant D7.b.4.9	10/09/1918	15/09/1918
War Diary	Croisilles T. 30.B.5.5	16/09/1918	16/09/1918
War Diary	Gouy En Artois 51c P 18 D.1.6	17/09/1918	20/09/1918
War Diary	Riviere Grosville	21/09/1918	21/09/1918
War Diary	R.25 D.65.15	22/09/1918	24/09/1918
War Diary	Riviere R 25 D 65.15	24/09/1918	25/09/1918
War Diary	57 C.N.W. Neroevil	26/09/1918	26/09/1918
War Diary	57C. N.E	27/09/1918	27/09/1918
War Diary	57 C.N.E. E 29 D.22	28/09/1918	29/09/1918
War Diary	57C N.E. Graincourt E29.d 2.2	30/09/1918	30/09/1918
Heading	War Diary Of 502nd. (Wessex) Field Company R.E. From October 1st 1918 To October 31st 1918 Volume XXI		
War Diary	57c N.E. Graincourt E29.b.2.2	01/10/1918	09/10/1918
War Diary	57 B.N.W. Proville A 20b.20.50	09/10/1918	09/10/1918
War Diary	57c N.E Fontaine F.21D.95.30	10/10/1918	10/10/1918
War Diary	D 29.e.50.30	11/10/1918	12/10/1918
War Diary	Marles Les Mines Hazebrouck 5A 66.2.1	13/10/1918	13/10/1918
War Diary	Bethune 1/40,000 R12A2.8	14/10/1918	16/10/1918
War Diary	N.24.b.2.7	17/10/1918	17/10/1918
War Diary	Sheet 36 Hallenes P13c5.7	18/10/1918	18/10/1918
War Diary	Hellemmes Q 18.a.2.8	19/10/1918	20/10/1918
War Diary	Sheet 37-140,000	21/10/1918	21/10/1918
War Diary	H27 Q.5.7	21/10/1918	22/10/1918
War Diary	Sheet 37-1-40,000 H27 A 5.7	22/10/1918	22/10/1918
War Diary	Cazeau H33.c.6.6	23/10/1918	26/10/1918
War Diary	Sheet 37 Cazeau H33 C 6.6	26/10/1918	29/10/1918
War Diary	Sheet 36 Lezennes R13d.05.45	31/10/1918	31/10/1918
Operation(al) Order(s)	170th Inf. Bde Order No. 158	10/10/1918	10/10/1918
Operation(al) Order(s)	170th Inf. Bde Order No. 159	11/10/1918	11/10/1918
Miscellaneous	Table "A" For Personnel Moving By Train No.4		
Miscellaneous	Table 'C' Detail Of Transport Proceeding By Train No.5		
Operation(al) Order(s)	170th Inf. Bde. Order No. 160	13/10/1918	13/10/1918
Miscellaneous	March Table To Accompany 170th Inf. Bde. Order No. 160		
Heading	War Diary Of 502nd. (Wessex) Field Company R.E. From November 1st 1918-To November 30th 1918 (Volume 22)		
War Diary	Sheet 36 & 37 1-40,000 Lezennes (Fine) R.13d.05.	01/11/1918	09/11/1918

War Diary	Templeuve 37.H.33	10/11/1918	15/11/1918
War Diary	Froyennes Sheet 37.O.14	16/11/1918	25/11/1918
War Diary	Lezennes Sheet 36	26/11/1918	26/11/1918
War Diary	R 13d 05.45	27/11/1918	30/11/1918
Heading	War Diary Of 502nd (Wessex) Field Coy. R.E. From December 1st 1918 To December 31st 1918. Volume XXIII		
War Diary	Carvin (Mine) Lens II IL 40.85	01/12/1918	01/12/1918
War Diary	Louez Lens 11 3. I 57.75	02/12/1918	11/12/1918
War Diary	Louez	12/12/1918	31/12/1918
Heading	War Diary Of The 505th (Wessex) Field Co R.E. From January 1st To 31st 1918 Volume Twelve		
Heading	War Diary Of 502nd. (Wessex) Field Coy. R.E. From 1st January 1919 To 31st January 1919 Volume 24		
War Diary	Louez Near Arras	01/01/1919	31/01/1919
Heading	War Diary Of 502nd. (Wessex) Field Company R.E. From Feb. 1st 1919 To Feb 28th 1919 Volume 25		
War Diary	Louez N Arras	01/02/1919	28/02/1919
Heading	War Diary Of 502nd (Wessex) Field Company R.E. March 1st 1919 To March 31st 1919 Volume 27		
War Diary	Louez In Arras	01/03/1919	10/03/1919
War Diary	Louez	11/03/1919	31/03/1919
Heading	War Diary Of 502 (Wessex) Field Company R.E. From 1st April 1919 To 30th April 1919 Volume No. 27		
War Diary	Louez	01/04/1919	30/04/1919
Heading	War Diary 502nd (Wessex) Field Company R.E. 1st May 1919 To 31st May 1919 Volume No.28		
War Diary	Lens II 3.I.61.78	01/05/1919	03/06/1919
War Diary	No.3 Embarkation Camp Dunkerque	04/06/1919	10/06/1919

WO95/2973/1
502 Field Company
Royal Engineers

57TH DIVISION

502ND FIELD COY R.E.
FEB 1917 - JUN 1919

C O N F I D E N T I A L

W A R D I A R Y

O F

502ND. (WESSEX) FIELD CO. R.E.

From:- 1.2.17.   To:- 28.2.17.

VOLUME 1.

Army Form C. 2118

WAR DIARY
or
INTELLIGENCE SUMMARY
(Erase heading not required.)

Instructions regarding War Diaries and Intelligence Summaries are contained in F.S. Regs., Part II. and the Staff Manual respectively. Title Pages will be prepared in manuscript.

Place	Date	Hour	Summary of Events and Information	Remarks and references to Appendices
BLACKDOWN	1·2·17	9 AM	LIEUT. W. J. M. DAVISON and 3 O.R. left for FRANCE as advance party.	
"	12·2·17	{3·30 AM / 4·45 AM}	Company (+2 Officers attached) left for FRANCE via SOUTHAMPTON entraining at FARNBOROUGH in half Companies at 5·35 AM and 6·50 AM.	
SOUTHAMPTON	12·2·17	{7·20 AM / 8·40 AM}	Arrived.	
"	12·2·17	6 pm	Embarked on MANCHESTER IMPORTER — 2 Officers and 81 O.R., 79 Animals, 19 Vehicles & 33 Cycles.	
"	12·2·17	6·30 pm	" " ARCHANGEL — 6 " 128 O.R.	
LE HAVRE	13·2·17	7 AM	Disembarked and proceeded to No. 5 REST CAMP.	
"	"	2 PM	" " " " " "	
"	14·2·17	8·30 AM	Left REST CAMP less 1 Sapper sent to No. 2 HOSPITAL, LE HAVRE and proceeded by Rail to	
BAILLEUL	15·2·17	6 pm	Arrived.	
"	15·2·17	8·30 pm	Left for VIEUX BERQUIN (Billets)	
VIEUX BERQUIN	15·2·17	MIDNIGHT	Arrived. Company occupied Barns in neighbourhood and left on 18·2·17. Two attached Officers left to rejoin their own Unit (421st Field Coy R.E.)	
"	16·2·17			
SAILLY-SUR-LA-LYS	18·2·17	1 PM.	Arrived and proceeded to take over and carry on the work of the outgoing Unit (1st FIELD COY. NEW ZEALAND ENGINEERS) Sections 2 & 4 occupying working billets at Barret Farm and Sections 1 & 3 at RUE-DE-QUESNE.	
	28-2-17.			

W. ___
Major,
Commanding 302nd FIELD CO. R.E.

CONFIDENTIAL

WAR DIARY

OF

502ND.(WESSEX) FIELD COY. R. E.

From: 1st.March 1917   To: 31st.March 1917.

Volume 2.

Army Form C. 2118

WAR DIARY
~~INTELLIGENCE SUMMARY~~
(Erase heading not required.)

Instructions regarding War Diaries and Intelligence Summaries are contained in F.S. Regs., Part II. and the Staff Manual respectively. Title Pages will be prepared in manuscript.

Place	Date 1917 MARCH	Hour	Summary of Events and Information	Remarks and references to Appendices
	1.		O.C. attended Conference with G.O.C. 170th Brigade and Battalion Commanders. No.1 Section moved from billets Rue de Quesne to billets G.24.a.5.1.	
	3.		O.C. attended Conference with C.R.E. and O.i.C. Field Coys. R.E. - principally with reference to arrangement of Infantry Constructional Parties in accordance with Notes on the Co-operation of Infantry and R.E.	App 1
	4.		Inspection of Subsidiary Line by C.R.E. and O.C.	
	5.		No.1 Section moved from billets at G.24.a.5.1 and Sections 3 & 4 moved to Sailly-sur-la-Lys from advanced billets at Rue de Quesne and Rue au Bassins to Headquarters billets at Sailly-sur-la-Lys. No.2 Section remaining at advanced billets at H.26.a.2.0.	
	6.		O.C. attended Conference with C.R.E. and O.i.C. Field Coys. R.E. - principally with reference to drainage and acceleration of work by adopting scheme of working by Platoons retained for 5 days.	
	11.		Permanent Constructional Parties first used - 20 Platoons employed, including 2 making hurdles at Coy Headquarters.	
	12.		O.C. visited Subsidiary Line and reported on Constructional Parties to C.R.E.	
	13.		O.C. attended Conference with C.R.E. and O.i.C. Field Coys. R.E. - principally with reference to drains, wiring, bridges etc. O.C. met G.O.C. Division on Subsidiary Line. The General expressed satisfaction at the amount of work done.	
	14.		1 N.C.O. & 24 men of 2/4th L.N.L.R. and 1 N.C.O. & 24 men of 2/5th L.N.L.R. attached to this Unit as permanent drainage men and to form Nucleus of Pioneer Coy.	
	16.		Cellar Farm Avenue bombarded	
	17.		O.C. inspected concrete M.G. Shelters Subsiding Line. Cellar Farm Avenue shelled and stoked for 50 feet. Lieut. French and 2 N.C.Os & 5 men from M & C Coy. at Company Headquarters with respect to lighting of V.C. Deep Dug Out.	
	18.		Bridge at Estaires - circuit tested with detonators - satisfactory result. Monthly report and Map sent to C.R.E.	

Army Form C. 2118

WAR DIARY
or
INTELLIGENCE SUMMARY

(Erase heading not required.)

Continued.

Page 2

Place	Date 1917 March	Hour	Summary of Events and Information	Remarks and references to Appendices
	20		Capt. Fox attended Conference with C.R.E. and O.C's Field Coys. Principal subject taking over additional line on East, the defences of which are now supervised by the 421st Field Coy.	
	21		O.C. visited Subsidiary, Support and Front Line on East from Rue de Bassiers to Rue David with a view to taking over defences from 421st Field Coy.	
	22		O.C. visited Headquarters 170th Brigade with respect to the formation of a Pioneer Coy.	
	23		Two Officers (Capt. Holme and Lt. Dickson) and 179 O.R. reported at 6 p.m. This party plus 50 O.R. already attached, (see 14.3.17) = 2 Officers and 127 O.R. forming the 170th Brigade Pioneer Company. 1 Lieut. West (the remaining Officer detailed) did not report until 28/3/17	
	25		Pioneer Company began work on Subsidiary Line – Drains and Tramways. Area Rue De Bassiers – Rue David taken over from 421st Field Coy R.E. 2nd Lieut. Dickson detailed as O.C. Drains and Tramways – 50 men detailed for drains 15 for tramways.	
	26		2nd Lieut. J. Stead left for duty at Divisional R.E. Park, Bas St Maur.	
	27		20 additional men detailed from Pioneer Coy. for drains.	
	28		O.C. attended Conference with C.R.E., O.C's Field Coys. and O.C. Pioneer Coy. principally with reference to organization and duties of Pioneer Coy.	
	29		Fleurbaix bombarded by enemy	
	31		Quiet Day. (no stoppage of work) Electric Lighting Installation tested at V.C Pump Bay Oui and inspected by O.C.	

White Major
Commanding 502nd Wessex Field Coy.
R.E.

CONFIDENTIAL

WAR DIARY

OF

502ND.(WESSEX) FIELD COY. R.E.

From: 1st.April,1917   To: 30th.April,1917.

(VOLUME 3)

[signature] Major
O.C. 502 Wessex Field Coy R E

WAR DIARY / INTELLIGENCE SUMMARY

Army Form C. 2118

Place	Date 1917	Hour	Summary of Events and Information	Remarks and references to Appendices
	April 1		No.1 Section relieved No.2 Section for work in Front and Support Lines - and went into forward billets at H.26.a.0.2. Officers - Lieut Jotman and J Lieut Fletcher, Front line and Support line sent with 7.M. Bacon Subsidiary Line - No.4 Section, under J Lieut T.W.V. Stuart for Back Area under C.R.E. Nos. 2 & 3 Sections in Subsidiary line. All Sections except No.1 billeted at Sailly-sur-La Lys.	Page 1
	" 2		A Sapper lost his way, did not report at Dead Body Dump on his way to meet Construction Party. Note for future, a few men of outgoing Relief must remain in Fwd Area to act as a Guide.	
	" 3		Construction Parties of the Liverpool Scottish were shelled East of Croix Blanche and were withdrawn by their Officer. All Construction Parties from this Battalion were withdrawn from their work on Subsidiary Line between 12 noon and 1pm. by order from their own headquarters. Note - Construction Parties must not be close together. Reported to C.R.E. Snow in morning, fine afternoon. Attended Conference with CRE and O's C. Field Companies. Principal Subject - Possible Offensive. R.E. and Construction Parties found as follows :-	
			LINE / RE Section / Infantry Battalion Front / 1 / 2/5 L.N.L.R. Subsidiary / 2+3 / 2/10 Liv'pl Scottish 2/3/ L.N.L.R Back Area / 4 /	
	" 4		O.C. with CRE and MO at Dept Dug Outs, VC and Cella Farm, re Gas protection, handrails, steps and fitprops etc. Construction Parties shelled East of Croix Blanche, and withdrawn to another part of line. 2/5 LNLR in the Front Line relieved by 2/6 LNLR tonight. This night Salker Indian slightly gassed in Devon Avenue and sent to Hospital. Capt Fox and 2 other Officers investigating Divisional Water Supply.	
	" 6		Inspection of Battering and Capt Pickl relief the Cookhouse and Q.M. Stove, suggested soup, pudding, broth O.C attended Conference with CRE and O.C. Field Amb. Road by 172 W Brigade at 10:35pm.	
	" 10		O.C. Called at Headquarters 171st Brigade and at HQ 2/5 KLR with reference to arrangements relating to Construction Parties. No Construction Parties this day.	
	" 12		Meeting of R.E. and Officers of 2/5 KLR at Croix Marechal with reference to work to be done etc. Capt Duhl inspected Animals and Cables.	
	" 13		Monthly Progress Report with Maps of Trenches, Dug Outs, Shelters, M.G Emplacements, Screens, Emergency Route Water etc and Report on Water Supply and Systems sent to H.Q. R.E.	
	" 15			

WAR DIARY or INTELLIGENCE SUMMARY

Army Form C. 2118

Page 2

Place	Date 1917	Hour	Summary of Events and Information	Remarks and references to Appendices
	Apl 19		Conference CRE and OC Field Coys. Barbed Wire only to be issued to Brigade for Front Line. No duck boards except for absolutely essential work. Gates in Communication Trenches not required.	
	" 20		Conference CRE and OC Coys re portable extension of Duraval Front. OC reported to Headquarters 170th Brigade, Fleurbaix and met OC 421st Field Coy re taking over billets.	
	" 21		Capt Fox inspecting line. Base Depot to N Eastern Brigade Boundary. Note: N Entanglements and Wire Entanglements completed and Wiped.	
	" 23		OC with CRE (Major Derry) and Col. Lowe of the 3rd Australian Divisional Engineers rec't S.E. portion of Armentières Defence.	
	" 24		Conference CRE and OC C Field Coys	
	" 25		OC reported at Headquarters 170th Brigade for instructions re moving into billets at Fleurbaix.	
	" 26		OC visited Supportline from City Poste to Belle Volere and called at Battalion Headquarters at Toney House. Eaton Hall and Brigade Headquarters.	
	" 27		Nos. 2 & 3 Sections moved from Sailly-sur-la-Lys to billets at Porté à Bleus Yarm, Fleurbaix. Company has No. 4 Section placed under command of G.O.C. 170th Infantry Brigade for work in Brigade Area, front line of which runs from E.31.D.2 to 7.8 central. Distribution of RE front and Support Line Area: No.1 Section Right half Brigade Sectr. No.3 Section Left half Brigade Sectr. Support to Subsidiary Line No.2 Section. Rear & Subsidiary Line No.4 Section.	
	" 28		CRE left on leave. Major Jones acting CRE, and built two acting OC 502nd Field Coy RE.	
	" 29		Nos. 1, 2 & 3 Sections working. half the men by day and half by night. Each Officer visited his Sappers and Carrying Parties by day and night.	
	" 30		Men considerably interfered with when at work by Machine Guns, Rifle Grenade, and Shell fire on night of 29th-30th.	

30-4-17.

a/ O.C. 502nd (Wessex) Field Coy RE.

C.A.M. Captain
Field Coy. R.E.

C O N F I D E N T I A L

WAR DIARY
OF
502ND.(WESSEX) FIELD COY. R.E.

From: 1st.May 1917.   To: 31st.May 1917.

(VOLUME 4)

Army Form C. 2118

WAR DIARY
INTELLIGENCE SUMMARY
(Erase heading not required.)

Instructions regarding War Diaries and Intelligence Summaries are contained in F. S. Regs., Part II. and the Staff Manual respectively. Title Pages will be prepared in manuscript.

Place	Date	Hour	Summary of Events and Information	Remarks and references to Appendices
Anstreuliers field (FLEURBAIX)	1.5.17		C.S.M. T.H. ROWE after application for Commission had been sent in, received orders and proceeded to E.Y.C. DEGANWY, NORTH WALES. Sergt. R.B. BARLOW made A/C.S.M. this day.	Ch. IV (CL)
H.15.C.1.O.	2.5.17		Divisional R.E. Headquarters moved to CROIX DU BAC. Captain CREGAN, R.A.M.C., moved to by. Headquarters Billet.	(CL)
FRANCE	3.5.17		A party of 4 to 10 Pioneers of Infantry daily making brushwood camouflage screens, which are in great demand. C.L.S.	
36 N.W.3	4.5.17		No.1 Section moved from H.26.a.0.2 to by. H.Q. Billet H.15.C.1.O. No.4 Section moved from Billet at SAILLY (G.22.a.4.3) to by. H.Q. Billet H.15.C.1.O. No.2 Section moved from by. H.Q. Billet H.15.C.1.Q. to SAILLY (G.22.a.7.3)	Ch.
1/10,000	5.5.17		Enemy shelling with 5.9 in. guns between Moyes East of this billet, fragments of shells falling through our R.E. now detailed:- Front and Support Line CORDONNERIE SECTOR - 2 Lieut. STREET and N° 4 Section. BOUTILLERIE SECTOR - 2 Lieut J.H. FLETCHER and N°3 Section. Between Support and LAVENTIE-ARMENTIERES Railway Lieut C.R. NORMAN and N° 1 Section. Rear of Railway Line Lieut DAVISON and N°. 2 Section. During this week 3 Pontoon Bridges have been formed across River LYS by night.	Ch.
	7.5.17		Enemy shelling back areas during the day - SAILLY and BAC-ST-MAUR.	Ch.
		8. 0 pm	Gas Alarm by Stromba Horn. Gust storm blown and men paraded with Respirators on for 20 minutes. Posted Special Gas Guards. No Gas reached billet.	
		8.30 pm	Heavy shelling on enemy back areas all along 2nd Army Front. In case enemy retaliated on our billet, moved men into trenches in field in rear. Stayed there 1½ hours.	
		11.0 pm	Heavy shelling by us again for 5 minutes. Men moved to field in rear for half an hour.	Ch.
	8.5.17		Conference at R.E. H.Q. Lt. Col. ALLANSON (G.S.O.) present. Chief subject - recommendations on weekly reports of good work done by Infantry. In future each field by. to recommend in this way not more than 4 Platoons.	(CL)
	10.5.17		Brigadier-General A. MARTYN relinquished command of 170th Infantry Brigade. Lt. Col. HICHENS acting temporarily.	
	11.5.17	3.30 am	N° 505 but Sapper F. NICHOLLS wounded by H.E. shell in hand. - Sent to Hospital. Gas Alarm by Stromba Horn. Blew Horn at this billet. Officers and N.C.O.'s out side, men kept in billet, all with Respirators on for half an hour. Posted Special Sentry, and Respirators worn in alert position for rest of night. No Gas eventuated.	
	12.5.17		Brigadier General F.G. GUGGISBERG (R.E.) arrived to take command of 170th Infantry Brigade.	Ch.
	13.5.17		A/C.L.S. reported to time (in the line).	Ch.
	15.5.17		Captain FOX with General GUGGISBERG and Brigade Major, along Subsidiary Line from CHARRED POST to CROIX MARECHAL. Inspection of by. animals by G.O.C. Division. Return from leave of C.R.E. Return to by. of O.C.	(CL)

Army Form C. 2118

WAR DIARY
or
INTELLIGENCE SUMMARY
(Erase heading not required.)

Instructions regarding War Diaries and Intelligence Summaries are contained in F.S. Regs., Part II. and the Staff Manual respectively. Title Pages will be prepared in manuscript.

Place	Date	Hour	Summary of Events and Information	Remarks and references to Appendices
FLEURBAIX H15.d.10 FRANCE 36.N.W.3 1/10,000	16/5/17		O.C. reported to G.O.C 170th Brigade at FLEURBAIX and to C.R.E at CROIX DU BAC- Consultation G.O.C- C.R.E + O.C. at Brigade Headquarters- 1 Platoon only will be available for Constructional parties. G.O.C explained what future work in intervening his He -	Capt Y.
	17/5/17		O.C. at ELBOW FARM and CHAPEL FARM O.C. spoke to G.O.C 170th Brigade and informed C.R.E that 10 elephant shelters were required for subsidiary line- O.C. met Brigade Staff Capt at MARE'S NEST re accommodation required to fit it up as Brigade Hd Qrs-	Capt.
	18/5/17		O.C. at COMMAND POST re additional shelters etc- FLEURBAIX stellet- Presentation of the Military medal to 19 N.C.O.s and men of the 57th Division. Capt Rundle broke his arm playing football- (Physical training) Acting Lce Capt (unproven) Threadborough wounded at ERQUINGHEM.	Rundle Vice + Capt Capt.
	19/5/17		O.C. at R.E. Park, Bac S. MAUR, Hd qrs R.E and O.C. Pioneer No 2 section taking down Heron Hut at Sailly for re-erection at Huclyn 170th Infantry Brigade- Revision work at Engineers New Hd qrs 170th Brigade begun.	Capt
	20/5/17		O.C. and Capt. Fox reconnoitring at Command Posts Chapel Farm, ELBOW FARM and CROIX MARECHAL Lt Norman and 2/ Lt Fletcher reconnoitring at CROIX BLANCHE JUNCTION POST, WINTERS NIGHT POST, WINDY POST and CHARD POST referenced work required to be done by Garrisons under R.E supervision- O.C. Reported to C.R.E that He was going to Hospital-	Capt.

Army Form C. 2118

WAR DIARY
or
INTELLIGENCE SUMMARY
(Erase heading not required.)

Instructions regarding War Diaries and Intelligence Summaries are contained in F.S. Regs., Part II. and the Staff Manual respectively. Title Pages will be prepared in manuscript.

Place	Date	Hour	Summary of Events and Information	Remarks and references to Appendices
(FLEURBAIX) 465 C10 FRANCE 36.N.W.3 M9.a.0.0.	21/5/17		O.C. spoken to G.O.C. 170th Brigade (Gen GUGGISBERG) that he was to be sent to hospital on the 23rd. The General very kindly informed the O.C. that in the circumstances and having regard to the O.C's age it would be advisable for him to be placed in some position where work was not likely to be so strenuous as in the case of O.C. Field Coy. – that L. and the General was good enough to say he would facilitate such a course.	C.D.
	22/5/17		New system of working parties organized by 170th Brigade came into force. R.E. Officers and eighties not to work in front and support line unless in exceptional circumstances. O.C. Field Coy to report at Brigade H.Q. daily. Subalterns i/c Right and Left Sectors (corresponding with Battalion Sectors) to report daily at their respective Battalion Headquarters and at Head.qs of Companies in the lines. In each Sector 3 Platoons available for work in front and support lines. These are not to be supervised by R.E.– 1 Platoon available for work behind Support this under supervision of R.E.	C.D.
	23/5/17		O.C. left for Casualty Clearing Station on sick leave – Sapper Hirst reported by 2/Lt Weare Ambulance as wounded on 18/5/17	C.D.
	25/5/17		Capt Dw with A/G O.C. R.A. C.R.E. + 2 Col Cooks commanding Right Group Artillery inspected sites at the full river R.E. DAVID for 2 new O.P.s to be built by Field Coy. Working party of 21 men being provided by Col. Cooks	C.D.
	26/5/17		Col. Dx inspected BEE POST (Right Sub Sector) with a view to improving defences, also V.C. Dugout which is not in use. But which needs Sandbag fatigue. Weather very fine	C.D.

WAR DIARY or INTELLIGENCE SUMMARY

Army Form C. 2118

Place	Date	Hour	Summary of Events and Information	Remarks and references to Appendices
FLEURBAIX H.15.c.1.0. FRANCE 36.N.W.3. 1/10,000	26/5/17	(Cont'd)	H.Q. of 170th Inf Bde moved to H.20.D.6.6.	weather fine & hot
	27/5/17		Work on O.P.s required by R.A. begun last night.	" " & hot
	28/5/17		Capt Dix attended Bde HQ received instructions from B.G.C. re proposed advance. Discussed work of R.E. & Pioneers. Received written General Preliminary Instructions from Bde. Pioneers to work with R.E. Men inspected by Dr O.R. Unit - all clean & satisfactory. Fine & hot	
	29/5/17		Clothing Board at SAILLY. Inspected SAILLY BRICKFIELDS R.E. (Corps) dump recently taken over by C.R.E. Weather cooler but fine & hot	
	30/5/17		Capt Dix with C.R.E. inspected O.P.s under construction. Rifles & Lewis cooler & cooler	
	30/5/17		Capt Dix & Lieut J.A. Welch reconnoitered with 2nd Lt "Patrol" Officer of 2/7th Bn in NO MANS LAND between our line of NG Central Lethbridge line of N.6.c.7.5. with a view to suitability of ground for O.T. in case of an advance. Left our line 11 p.m. returned 2. a.m. May 31 Enemy showing no M.M.G. fire 2nd Capt.	
	31/5/17		In both sides of objective where 2nd Lt ...... at 2.30 a.m Enemy attempted rain attempted on Central divisional line & we took three prisoners. Preparations for possible advance. Conference at Capt's Office. Main topics: preparations for possible advance, repair of roads.	

C.H. Dix Capt
502nd WESSEX FIELD Co. R.E.

CONFIDENTIAL

WAR DIARY

OF

502ND.(WESSEX) FIELD COY. R. E.

From: 1st.June,1917.   To: 30th. June,1917.

(Volume 5).

MAJOR
COMMANDING 502nd
WESSEX FIELD Co. R.E.

WAR DIARY
INTELLIGENCE SUMMARY
(Erase heading not required.)

Army Form C. 2118

Instructions regarding War Diaries and Intelligence Summaries are contained in F.S. Regs., Part II. and the Staff Manual respectively. Title Pages will be prepared in manuscript.

Place	Date	Hour	Summary of Events and Information	Remarks and references to Appendices
FLEURBAIX FRANCE 1:10,000 36.N.W.3.	1/6/17		Acting O.C. Capt Fox with B.G.C. 170th Inf. Bde. inspecting emplacement of R.E. dumps proposed advance & before preparation of Emergency Routes, R.E. dumps, Bridges &c. R.E. Engineers for all 2 C.T.s across N.M.L. on Bn. Bomb Scheme submitted approved by R.O.C.S. Also list of stores to be at R.E. dumps. All animals picketed in the open.	June CRS
	2/6/17		O/C inspected Pats in subsidiary line. Garrisons at work on covering line dug outs. Improving accommodation &c + trench repairs.	June C.R.S
	3/6/17		O/C inspected progress on two O.P.s under construction.	" June C.R.S
	4/6/17		O/C with B.G.C. 170th Inf. Bde. inspecting instructions for advance to enemy's front line.	June C.R.S
	5/6/17	12 noon	O/C + I.I. head I.W.S. Street reconnoitred Saps extending into N.M.L. from left of Princess Stop. If he arrived. The enemy appear to have pro-Strippers at work. It is possible to look over our front line parapet all along the Right Batt. Sector - Also I.C. Down Avenue to Forty Street - & to R.C.C. event on dawn of 3rd taub.	June C.R.S
	6/6/17	A.M.	Made considerable extensions into N.M.L in daylight	June C.R.S
		P.M.	30 Sappers +40 Pioneers practice extending on tape practice extending on tape. digging CT by night	June C.R.S
	7/6/17	P.M.	Some parties of Sappers + Pioneers practice carrying runching material + practice runching by night	June C.R.S

WAR DIARY
INTELLIGENCE SUMMARY

Army Form C. 2118

Instructions regarding War Diaries and Intelligence Summaries are contained in F. S. Regs., Part II. and the Staff Manual respectively. Title Pages will be prepared in manuscript.

(Erase heading not required.)

Place	Date	Hour	Summary of Events and Information	Remarks and references to Appendices
FLEURBAIX	8/6/17	11 p.m	Dug Sap + enlarged old sap leading out from Top of Bunnys Row - 30 saps to premises	free CRS
	9/6/17	11 p.m	Near white compound - (under convent Neuve bain) Enemy Dy⁰ of street but started work at night. #7 M⁰ Sap places a cement slab with 30 sapper & 30 pioneers into new sap previously enlarged - Poor trenches	free CRS
	10/6/17		General view of N Coy forged on increased night tapings. 5 of above referred to watch & making night. Past work washed out by rain - 5th Echelon of change showery	free CRS
	11/6/17		Sap cleared to enlarge 4. R. RAILES otherwise flying corps/air Photo to Lut Col Buller RE Lt Col for Division promised Corps Ammo to achieve Corps aim police attacked Lut Col Buller RE have transferred Capt. I approach communications employees of Engrs. N. have transferred	free CRS
	12/6/17		Lt B. Sap (and M.(6)/17) C.R.E Infy Dist⁰ inspected Coys ammo into new bunkers (the latter not ready)	free CRS
	13/6/17		Lieut H.T Tolman from Co. H.G.D Torres from 421 G. reported for duty. Capt Ely now inspects O.P.S. O.C. 11/4 R. E Col Riemann + A.M. Intelligence officer on RUE DU BOIS + at THE MILL (RUE DU MOULIN) R.G.C. 11 pm Dug Role returned, shown by	free CRS
	14/6/17	3 PM	Conference at PDH HQ. CO's retiring. Heavy shelling of railway nearby. Frisky bits dropping on billet, I constructor	free CRS
	15/6/17		Impact Jerry Boys trainees who are to aug. O.T.S. no 90. No one of aux for night. 13/16 hours (men trained in practical operation beg new by any any all 90's for same up front-line of research to W. Rainy fogs to aug. 2 cts T/2 O.B.Z. RJ.	June CRS
		11 AM	Classes on for tonight CHB - cancelled. 1/4 Col R Pegl to make job	
	16/6/17	11 AM	Conf - 4. C.O. of Div. HQ. New scheme of attack. 5 pub. + 9 CT's to throw objections 2/4 F. NF Ryal 2nd S/L S NF. to aug. CTS To Neil A.S. Ioward + Lieut H.T. Tolman. Each will form one of the new Balf B.O.C.T.S. recruits surveys reports.	

WAR DIARY
or
INTELLIGENCE SUMMARY
(Erase heading not required.)

Army Form C. 2118

Place	Date	Hour	Summary of Events and Information	Remarks and references to Appendices
FLEURBAIX	7/6/15		Heavy shelling throughout afternoon & night — shells dropping into White House to canal. O.C. inspected dump, also saddle posts. Transport of 2nd Coys 2nd & 4th Bn. 1 Corp. 2/6/7 N.Z. Reg. in dugouts CTS [?] Bryant & Wynn collecting them & consolidating parties (Frost Stephen L.R.)	Shelling C62
	18/6/15		Third Street reconnoitred. Preparations in BRISHONS CT. Training of reinf. & CT parties continued.	Shelling CK3
	19/6/15		Lieut. O'Hern & Lieut. Campbell appointed Ass't Transport Off. in Field. Marks & [?] Infantry Brigade respectively. Lieut [?] Jones in F. E. L with B6 Shovel [?] [?] & Bn Broadwood spent to 1 Coy of 2/5 R.W. digging C.T.S. (practice)	Shelling O60
	20/6/15		Lieut. Hinton assisting 2nd [?] Salient [?] E. placing men in place & time. Pressure & [?] of pontoons postponed.	Shelling Ox 2
	21/6/15		Lieut. R.C.L. Hinton [?] [?] [?] Ass't Returns Information Gen. Broadwood visited dug shovels rectum at HOEPLINES	Shelling Q 9
	22/6/15		Went round [?] dug post dispensed with of COCHIN VILLA RUE DAVID. WESSEX M.T.M. Emplacement, TINBARN & DEAD DOG DUMP Pc.	Shelling BX 8-7
	24/6/15		Sent Sarson hit by fragment of shell while dressing Lieut. A.R. Gath from Sothsmour Roy. Co. reported for duty O.C. with R.E.C. 170th Bde. & B. Mayr. & Col. Creagh to look in left sector confer. [?] unless said. two men who left our lines of 2 AM with a view to remaining in N.M.L. throughout day returned about 10AM & 2 PM both wounded McGuire shelling of billets in Rue Marie of men killed and many injured. Johnstone all from built.	C62

WAR DIARY or INTELLIGENCE SUMMARY

Army Form C. 2118

(Erase heading not required.)

Instructions regarding War Diaries and Intelligence Summaries are contained in F. S. Regs., Part II. and the Staff Manual respectively. Title Pages will be prepared in manscript.

Place	Date	Hour	Summary of Events and Information	Remarks and references to Appendices
FLEURBAIX	25/6/17	3AM	Two bombs dropped by aeroplane in field close to Officers Mess. Heavy shelling observed all day of batteries on either flank, seen flying through roof tiles of our huts + dugouts (up). 2 mm T mortar crenellated. O.C. inspected O.Ps at The Mill + Crokes House, also O.C. Sally Park on Right Sector; also H.T.M. Emp'l. "WAIT" "SEE" near CELLAR FARM TRAMWAY SUPPORT LINE. OP at the Mill ready for use.	cooler fine CAS
	26/6/17		O.C. visited M.G. and crews BLANCHE, practising working of C.T.N. training Reinforcements from A. Series + panels, very informative. Angle gun-picket banged my mixed grates + breechcasts, missiles enough but only during my visit - told her to keep on during in with enemy. Also visits VERDUN H.T.M. emplacement. Repairs by us (6ft WATLING ST) & Lieut Dolman laying out new Emergency route for forward and our extreme left. Common for barrage + and (by night) on Portuguese on our left. New ruin, nuisance caught.	fair CAS
	27/6/17		Lieut Davison appointed acting Captain & O.C. to-in Major Davys. Frank pending Gazette. OC with R.G.C. 170th Bde in line inspecting C.T. + screening necessary for battery driven up by day to fight time by HUDSON JAY, (also) Lapin with T.O.C.C. a at a very much F.M. said.	showery CAS
	28/6/17		O.C. marched HUDSON BAY POST, mining direction to III Dolman.	
	29/6/17		O.C. visited O.Ps with Major Winch, as temporary command R' Group artillery, also inspected flash posts screening but up on RUE DuBOIS by R.A. Walk on Sally Park MAROONS DAM POSTS, also screening S. CITY RD, HUDSON DAY POST, BAY AVENUE	showery CAS showery CAS

WAR DIARY
INTELLIGENCE SUMMARY

Place	Date	Hour	Summary of Events and Information	Remarks and references to Appendices
FLEURBAIX	30/6/17		Road repair has been carried on during past week with 2 to 3 loads slag ballast daily. Roads behind (NORTH of) RUE DU QUESNES were in worse condition than those in front, which we have to mend.	Pioneer Officers + 4 to 6 mins wet
			Health of Company during this month good. Discipline during this month good – only three or four small offences brought to orderly Room. Section of Mine Coy has been stationed at SAILLY for work up to 24/6/17 one section of Mine Coy – under O.C.E. is arranging work, only 10 men from this Coy in each area – under O.C.E. is arranging a composite section of 10 men from each Coy required for this in future. Being billeted at BAC ST MAUR for this work. During this month the 1/5th & 2/5th Ad. Pioneer Cos have been (except for 25 men on Trench Tramways) entirely under my orders. Their help is of great service: creating saying in nearly all work, carrying stores, undrawing & carrying transport at night 60 to 70 of them are available daily for these jobs. I could employ 100 more as there is a great shortage of staff eng. Previous Information in work, upkeep of C.Ts in rear of supports suffers neglect on this account.	C.M.S.

C.M. [signature]
COMMANDING 592nd
WESSEX FIELD Co. R.E.

CONFIDENTIAL

WAR DIARY

OF

502ND.(WESSEX) FIELD CO. R.E.

From : 1st. July,1917.   To: 31st. July,1917.

(Volume 6).

W.J.H. Douglas Capt
for MAJOR
COMMANDING 502nd
WESSEX FIELD Co. R.E.

WAR DIARY
or
INTELLIGENCE SUMMARY
(Erase heading not required.)

Army Form C. 2118

Instructions regarding War Diaries and Intelligence Summaries are contained in F.S. Regs., Part II. and the Staff Manual respectively. Title Pages will be prepared in manuscript.

Place	Date	Hour	Summary of Events and Information	Remarks and references to Appendices
FLEURBAIX FRANCE 1:10,000 N.W.3.	1/7/17	A.M.	O.C. visited Sally Ports (6) on our extreme left. Two night work shows little progress. Similarly with new C.T. to HUDSON BAY POST.	fine C.R.O
		7PM.	O.C. started party screening BAY AVENUE with screens rough bag work.	
		10PM.	O.C. also party on new C.T. & Sappers Pioneers on Sally Ports.	
	2/7/17	A.M.	O.C. with Lieut Garth to O.Ps at THE MILL & COOKE'S VILLA. also to Sally Ports on Right Sector & WAIT & SEE. H.T.M. Emplt. where Bomb Store has been completed. Also inspected gun position in GRANDE RUE (left sector) where R.A. require advice as where farm house has cracked owing to bad construction of position by previous R.A.	fine C.R.O
		10PM. 6.3AM.	Supervising work on new Sally Ports & new C.T. Getting A frames & panels in C.T. requires a large trench and is uneconomical of space. Started making bridges for raid - out 2. 3x2" bearers 3'x3" slab, & 2 3"x2" bearers.	fine C.R.O
	3/7/17		O.C. inspected laying out of replica of Roche trenches. This is being done by W.H. Welshes r10 another old rooms ESTAIRES. 5 men doing the same at ERQUINGHEM. O.C. at Sally Ports & new C.T. at night. Enemies very quiet another mining as it is "market forms" some built up & some old parapet, consequently contains old dugouts, revetting frames &	most fine C.R.O
	4/7/17		C.R.E. with Capt Davison inspecting building billets for possible Bn. HQrs. for Infy of Infantry mine. O.C. inspected W.F.M. Emplts. also posts in Subsidiary Line.	fine C.R.O

WAR DIARY or INTELLIGENCE SUMMARY

(Erase heading not required.)

Army Form C. 2118

Place	Date	Hour	Summary of Events and Information	Remarks and references to Appendices
FLEURBAIX	5/7/17		O.C. visited Sally Ports & new C.T. at night. O.P.s by day. E Lieut. Jackson reconnoitring land night & bright clothes in N.M.L. in front of BOUTILLERIE	cold C.h.d.
	6/7/17		O.C. to BAILLEUL re working-men to cement Capt. PERROTT R.E. & Major TINDALL re water supply night sector. This is apt to be very short in summer.	fine C.h.d.
	7/7/17	8.30 to 10.30 PM	Heavy Barrage of T.M. re by Boche in 2 hours. Sally Ports nearly finished. 22 trips forward man.	
			Road concealed. O.C. visited 25.2 N.Z. re water supply also V.O. Horrocks the same. – KILDARE O.P. re repairs.	fine C.h.d.
		P.M.	Conference at C.R.E.'s office re Pioneer Corps. Work & billets.	
	8/7/17	A.M.	O.C. visited O.P.s with Capt. COOKES, O.C. R.I. Group Artillery	
		P.M.	O.C. visited 3/4 L.N.L. & unfortunately	
			Lt. Hesker returned with him sick from ESTAIRES.	
	9/7/17		O.C. with F.H. Dobman inspected proposed H.T.M. Emplacement behind THE BREWERY (L/Cpl. Leaty), D.T.M.O. being present. Also saw 245 O.S.P. which is nearly complete. Sally Port nearly complete. Inspected O.P.'s Lewis at 3R.W.F.R.Y. which is in daily to be conducted. L/h T.E. PEARCE joined the Coy as reinforcement (Engineer unranimany Officer) in place of 2/Lt F. STEAD who took Rl. Park & seems likely to be away for the only in future. Proposed Plan of Ireland. Conference with R.S.C. 170 & 9th Div. re work in future. 170 & 9 Div. Pioneer Co. & attaching so run to this Coy, who has been attached. Present.	fine C.h.d

1875 Wt. W593/826 1,000,000 4/15 J.B.C. & A. A.D.S.S./Forms/C. 2118.

Army Form C. 2118

WAR DIARY
INTELLIGENCE SUMMARY
(Erase heading not required.)

Instructions regarding War Diaries and Intelligence Summaries are contained in F.S. Regs., Part II. and the Staff Manual respectively. Title Pages will be prepared in manuscript.

Place	Date	Hour	Summary of Events and Information	Remarks and references to Appendices
FLEURBAIX	10/7/17		O.C. with Lt Pearce inspected F. & G. Emergency Routes & Convent Villa O.P.	Fine & hot
	11/7/17		O.C. attended C.R.E.'s Conference - subjects - administration of Pioneer Coy., new scheme of defence at night. new boundary for road repair.	Fine & hot
	12/7/17		O.C. saw C.O. 2/4 & 2/5 L.N.L. Regt. re Water Supply to Huie Right Subsector.	Fine & hot
	13/7/17		O.C. inspected works at "VERDUN" H.T.M. Emplt. "WESSEX" WAIT & SEE T.M.T Emplt & O.P.s at DAVID HOUSE & COOKESVILLA. O.P. at last named completed. ½ Coy 10th & 9th No 8 Pioneer Co. moved to billet M15C52 (200 yds from two days billet) Officers of Coy messing with Officers of this unit.	Fine & hot
	14/7/17		O.C. inspected work on water Supply RUE DU BOIS, KILDARE O.P. RIFLE KILN Dump is nearly depleted of filled Sand Bags & is being given up. & men re to be returned for duty with their Pioneer Co.	Showery (?)
	15/7/17		O.C. inspected CITY ROAD & TIN BARN O.P.s & new Coy H.Q. being built at HUDSON BAY POST.	Fine & hot
	16/4/17		O.C. saw O.C. Right Artillery Group re O.P.s & men at work on same; also re M.T.M. Ammunition Store to be made in trenches. Visited attached men at SAILLY, preparing to move to another billet.	Fine & hot
	17/7/17		SAILLY detachment moved to new billet at G.17.C.99. O.C. inspected same. Construction of 10 concrete places for M.G.s together.	Showery (?)
	18/7/17		O.C. inspected Crotia Villa O.P. where dug out is being built. also O.T.s on left subsector.	wet & ?
	19/7/17		O.C. visited new work at HUDSON BAY POST, O.P. at the BREWERY & various other jobs. P.C.T.s on left	cloudy ?

1875 Wt. W 593/826 1,003,000 4/15 T.R.C. & A. A.D.S.S./Forms/C. 2118.

WAR DIARY
or
INTELLIGENCE SUMMARY

(Erase heading not required.)

Army Form C. 2118

Place	Date	Hour	Summary of Events and Information	Remarks and references to Appendices
FLEURBAIX	20/4/17		O.C. left this P.M for England in leave. Capt Davies acting O.C.	
"	21-7-17		Capt Davies with I.O. Thorpe inspected works & fuel in front of the "WESSEX" H.T.H. emplacement in ready for firing. "VERDUN" H.T.H.E repaired well.	
"	22-7-17		Capt Davies O.C. conference at Brigade H.Q. Rev. orders of warning R.E. instructions found but not cancelled later, and did not include C.R.E.'s approval.	Heavy rain 10 y m 81
"	23-7-17		Capt Davies & I. Lt Trotman served Light Railway Syst. N.E at BREWERY O.P & NEW COY H.Q. at HUDSON BAY and Ken. H.T.H.E in left centre. started manoeuvres.	Not so warm 70 y m 81
"	24-7-17		Lely Parts on left sector Junkers & blocked up. Capt D advised super the several 18 pr. gun emplacements until so near to Jerry gun trench more seen to enter, & no memory of Jerkies are of been.	Cloudy 67 y m 81
"	25-7-17		Capt Davies inspected work at Verdun Emplacement. Has more planks returning dome as part of city Road.	Rains 76 y m 81 early A.M.
"	26-7-17		Capt. Davies & I.O Thorpe inspected generally up to and in N.A.I.R. S.E.E. practically Junkers. Late too NEW COY H.Q. decided upon.	Cloudy in evening 70 y m 81
"	27-7-17		Capt Davies attended conference at C.R.E's C.R.E. laid observations and gave particulars of measures. C.R.E. & Sgt Skeh in left sector trenches.	Cloudy 72 y m 81

WAR DIARY
INTELLIGENCE SUMMARY
(Erase heading not required.)

Army Form C. 2118

Place	Date	Hour	Summary of Events and Information	Remarks and references to Appendices
FLEURBAIX	28.7.17		Brigadier 140th Bde and Capt. D Burrows left section working on scheme	Hunt 29/7/17
"	29.7.17		for defence of Left Flank. New orders continued. 2nd Lt. Y. Leslie with #3 section handed the pontoon bridge at Pondeau Marah. Very wet day.	29/7/17
"	30.7.17	10.0 am	Heavy shoot 10.0 am pontoon equipment. Pontoon equipment to landing stages. Key 10th Pontoon Park.	
			Brig. Gen. 1 Lieut. Two Sergts. 60 carrying Infantry to be in attendance of gas bombardment of Capt. D Burrows 9.II G.S. Ride to rear Flank before orders.	29/7/17
"		6.00 pm	G.O.C. 140th Inf. Bde. ordered R.E. Subs. and 2nd section to prepare to move. Before 10.00 as have all scheme of Left Flank to be handed over; work to be independence for 3 days.	30/7/17
			Section Officers lectured all men on use Rendez gas.	
"	31.7.17		Received orders from C.R.E. to move 3 section to Left section. Nos. 1 & 3 Section details to go.	30/7/17
		5.30 pm	General parade. D.G.O. lectures men on gas a manner all ranks.	

D. C. J. Laurels, Capt.
MAJOR
COMMANDING 522ND
WESSEX FIELD Co R.E.

CONFIDENTIAL

WAR DIARY

OF

502ND. (WESSEX) FIELD CO. R.E.

From: 1st. August 1917   To: 31st. August 1917.

(Volume 7)

MAJOR
COMMANDING 502'D
WESSEX FIELD Co. R.E.

WAR DIARY
or
INTELLIGENCE SUMMARY

(Erase heading not required.)

Army Form C. 2118

Place	Date	Hour	Summary of Events and Information	Remarks and references to Appendices
FLEUR-BAIX FRANCE 36 N.W.	1/8/17	1/20 0/00	O.C. returned from leave. 2 Sections proceeded to ARMENTIERES from LEUIS WELCH, Lothian. This Coy to take the place of 421 (W.L.) Field Coy temporary billets. 421 Coy casualties putting two sections out of action. W.L. which was supplied 500 cassualties.	w.l.o. C & O
	2/8/17		About 2 sections working on new Bde H.Q's Rue Sadi Carnot. O.C. visited them with O.C. 170 W Pioneer Coy O.C. 421 W Coy R.E. & Capt. Sowden Acts O.C. both on before from O.C. 421 W Coy R.E. Sections handed over view to Lieut Mclachrie.	Showers over.
ARMENTIERES	3/8/17		H.Q's remaining 2 Sections in ARMENTIERES - took up billets in 28, 30, 31, 33, 35 & 37 RUE SADI CARNOT together with 2 Sections 170 W. Inf. Bde Pioneers. Sleeping in cellars. Nos. 1 & 2 Sections proceeded HOUPLINES & occupied billets vacated by 421 Co.	w.l.o. C & O
	4/8/17		About 2 sections Pioneers proceed to HOUPLINES & Pioneers remaining 2 Sections occupied their billets R SADI CARNOT. R.E. Pioneer Officers mess together at both places. O.C. visited two work on strengthening billets.	w.l.o.
	5/8/17		O.C. & Capt. Selwin (O.C. Pioneers) in Turi. reconnoitre LOTHIAN AVE. Conference with C.O's at Bde H.Q. re artillery retaliation &c.	Fine C & O
	6/8/17		O.C. reconnoitres PLANK AVE & C.T.s right sector, many notice. Found neighing - Segment Blow in which seem to have had no attention	Fine C & O
	7/8/17		O.C. inspected bridges at ARMENTIERES.	Fine C & O

Army Form C. 2118

WAR DIARY
or
INTELLIGENCE SUMMARY
(Erase heading not required.)

Instructions regarding War Diaries and Intelligence Summaries are contained in F.S. Regs., Part II. and the Staff Manual respectively. Title Pages will be prepared in manuscript.

Place	Date	Hour	Summary of Events and Information	Remarks and references to Appendices
ARMEN-TIERES	8/8/17		O.C. inspected C.T.s LeMoulin- Transport at CROIX DU BAC. Tel' Pelichu attended Exhibition of Pack Tft. Lt. Steel left for England on leave.	Summary Ord.
	9/8/17		O.C. visited HAYSTACK FARM and proposed M.T.M Emplacement, also C.T.s on Nursery. HEADQUARTERS WALK TO CENTRAL AVENUE	Summary Ord.
	10/8/17		O.C. returning to C1 (nursery) route being constructed. Heavy shelling of ARMENTIERES all day. 1 Shell & bomb hit roof of Officers Billet. Detachment billet at HOUPLINES also hit	Summary Ord.
	11/8/17		O.C. saw C.R.E. re tools required on defectors. & debris in ARMENTIERES. Visited Transport lines. Intermittent shelling of A-	Summary Ord.
	12/8/17		O.C. inspected second important Emplt of FUSILIER AVENUE which no in bad state decided to take repairs in hand. A bomb burst during afternoon	Showing Ord.
	13/8/17		O.C. met R.G.C. 170th Inf. Bde. in Subs & Rein re trenches proposed connect LOTHIAN AVE. & BRICKSTACK LANE. Inspected drainage to Arbury. Showing A bomb burst fairly heavily throughout the day	C. Ord.
	14/8/17		O.C. visited Inf. "O.P.s at HOUPLINES with Bde. Intelligence Officer. saw C.R.E. re Bombardment of ARMENTIERES and so heavy before.	Showing Ord.
	15/8/17		O.C. inspected C1 + C2 Envy knocks. also gunpits where Artillery work got to clear in mud & hurried. Enemy artillery quiet.	Summary Ord.

Army Form C. 2118

WAR DIARY
or
INTELLIGENCE SUMMARY
(Erase heading not required.)

Instructions regarding War Diaries and Intelligence Summaries are contained in F.S. Regs., Part II. and the Staff Manual respectively. Title Pages will be prepared in manuscript.

Place	Date	Hour	Summary of Events and Information	Remarks and references to Appendices
ARMENTIERES	16/9/17		O.C. along Tram line between Lyster Ave & to reccno & support line East of FUSILIER AVENUE. This line much weaker than Tyster to be put also inspected F & X Emergency works & Trestle for bridge to be put across at C.26.A.7.1. Enemy artillery quiet, relieved by a whizz bang in LOTHIAN C.T. Relief of C. WENDOVER.	True Copy Cho.
	17/9/17		O.C. saw Bde Major, 172nd Inf Bde. + OC sewrights re Emergency works in their sector. On run N 1°180 170 16 Army. Going to ERQUINGHEM. Reconnoitred new Emergency Works and the ARMENTIERES-new system of working on the trench with Pioneer Bn very satis-factory. B E Battalions ought with Pioneer Bns making good progress, severed detachment at Ay H.Q'rs. RE working some progress or Pioneer Officer He reconnoitre in such work and draws Trams Enemy very quiet. Enemy artillery showed or in field between Officers very useful for reconnaissance & in many various trips. All ranks of both Companies work harmoniously together.	True Copy Cho.
	18/9/17		OC inspected OPs of HUPLINES. Inspected trenches. NEUVRY W. CANADA &c. Inspected vehicles stores at Q Bridge dressings by Sherjoe.	True Copy Cho.
	19/9/17		O.C. with Gen & Barnes & Genl Guggisberg inspected O. & W. Emergency Works & proposed extensions. Traces of awards.	True Copy Cho.
	20/9/17		O.C. inspected regimental Aerial ditch running from Chapelle d'Armentieres to Drainage Pump - SPAIN AVENUE. This with Clear so a most excellent Emergency route.	True Copy Cho.

1875 Wt. W3593/826 1,000,000 4/15 J.B.C. & A. A.D.S.S./Forms/C. 2118.

Army Form C. 2118

WAR DIARY
or
INTELLIGENCE SUMMARY
(Erase heading not required.)

Instructions regarding War Diaries and Intelligence Summaries are contained in F.S. Regs., Part II. and the Staff Manual respectively. Title Pages. will be prepared in manuscript.

Place	Date	Hour	Summary of Events and Information	Remarks and references to Appendices
ARMENTIERES 2018/17 (contd.)			O.C. also reconnoitred & reported on Routes for Bde HQrs. (Southern) at ERQUINGHEM - W.N. Hildwit Rides by motor which stabling outside	fine C.B.P
	21/8/17		Routes, O.- I.O. & Assembly Places South west of town being got on with. O.C. showed I.- & Places of on them.	fine C.B.P
	22/8/17		O.C. to R.E. Park re stores - had Col. Bell, B.G.R.E. + others turned out at ERQUINGHEM - O.C. reconnoitred N. of ONNEHO.	fine C.B.P
	23/8/17		O.C. to II Street reconnoitred ground to be cut by C.T. linking Bronker "THE CROSS CUT." O.C. visited Ry. Hd. Qrs. Re L. line, also I C.T.s - Due to be in much better condition.	fine C.B.P
	24/8/17		O.C. inspected work being done on O.R. UI. Emergency Routes, + at ASSEMBLY PLACES. These are all nearing completion. Check Standing work nearly cut at 4 AM one section of HOUPLINES over ARMENTIERES shelato of work done. O.C. writing reports most of day. Weekly reports sent in to Routes (W.) Pioneer Bn. & moving, re B.G.C. 176 IR. Bde.	fine C.B.P
	25/8/17		(?) Summary of work done. (W.) Pioneer Bn. & moving. Visited C.R.E. at Head Carts. Pioneer Bn's weekly work report. Says general work recd compliments re in weekly work report - Says general work had been done by R.E. Pnps. Since arrival in area. Decision - Visited Detachment HOUPLINES re work. Conference of C.R.E.'s - no more + Workshop where in Real - C.R.E. seems very much pleased with work of Wire Bny.	fine C.B.P
	26/8/17		Visited & hydrostatic Info of Officers Parties at work in early morning on THE CROSS CUT. Showed Lt. Scott securing regular as route - Reconnoitred clothing between Light Rail. HQrs. (Near GLOUCESTER AVE.) & BUTTERNE LANE.	fair C.B.P

WAR DIARY / INTELLIGENCE SUMMARY

Army Form C. 2118

Place	Date	Hour	Summary of Events and Information	Remarks and references to Appendices
ARMENTIERES.	27/8/17		O.C. at usual traffic "K1" C.C. 26 & 61 inspected & Y Engineer Route. Since gale of MOUPLINES received orders to send a section originally with Transport to COYECQUE (Map Ref. 1:100,000 HAZEBROUCK 5A.)	Ch/8
	28/8/17		11 o'Street left for new area with R.G.C. 79 & Bde. Men left in lorries. Transport left, taking two days. Stopping overnight at ST. VENANT. O.C. inspected work on "CROSS CUT".	Showery Cold.
	29/8/17		O.R's inspected trench. O.C. accompanied him round left sector - rup.TOWN HALL (O.P.)	Showery Cold.
	30/8/17		O.C. attended Conference of C.O.s N.W. with R.G.C. 170 & Bde. in "tin". Subject: Training & preparations for same when in sect. - also trench discipline	Showery C.O.
	31/8/17		O.C. inspected P. bridge site for proposed new truss	Showery Cold.

C.V. Ivy
MAJOR
COMMANDING 502nd
WESSEX FIELD Co. R.E.

CONFIDENTIAL

WAR DIARY

OF

502ND.(WESSEX) FIELD CO.R.E.

From 1st.September 1917. To 30th.September 1917.

- (Volume 8).-

30/9/17

MAJOR,
COMMANDING 502ND
WESSEX FIELD Co. R.E.

WAR DIARY
INTELLIGENCE SUMMARY
(Erase heading not required.)

Army Form C. 2118

Instructions regarding War Diaries and Intelligence Summaries are contained in F.S. Regs., Part II. and the Staff Manual respectively. Title Pages will be prepared in manuscript.

Place	Date	Hour	Summary of Events and Information	Remarks and references to Appendices
ARMENTIERES FRANCE (MAP REF. 1:20,000. 36NW.)	1/9/17		O.C. visited Detachmt. HOUPLINES, inspected K1 new bridge & screens being erected near Claria Bridge PK (C.19 C 7.3.) so that cops may keep shipping but across INGLIS TYPE bridge there. The O.C. visited O.C. 421 dilute re drainage schemes in HOUPLINES subsector.	at 026a61 showing Cmd
	2/9/17		Lt. TROTMAN proceded on leave to ENGLAND. Lt. PEARCE returning from Yc just section at HOUPLINES. Heavy work in section - had to practice march out how transport lines. Transport inspected by O.C. O.C. visited O.C. 2 wd field Co. near NIEPPE & obtained information respecting work done by that Coy (8th army) in advance from (YPRES SALIENT) (near WESTHOEK)	Fine Cmd
	3/9/17		Inspected HOUPLINES detachment built also "CROSS CUT" learned cubies in ARMENTIERES. Started Pier in making ducktrack none are obtainable from Rl Park. materials are valued Detachment (dismounted men & No.4 Sectn) returned from COYECQUE	Fine Cmd
	4/9/17		Gave instructions re learning O'rourke &c. Detachmt. transport (& Lt. Nut %c) returned from COYECQUE. mounted guard under BQC.5 men to prevent Canadian Heavy R.A. moving 8" How. into garage in yard. thro trout. Party on cross cut interfered with & Coy. he on factories.	Fine Cmd
	5/9/17		CRE. inspected work done near P. bridge (C.19.87.3) in screening river - OC went to work at junction for CROSS CUT & CHAPELLE D'ARMENTIERES road - 2 platoons 1st or 2nd Royal Scots Fusiliers (latter war.) Then to deceive Corporal line near FUSILIER AVE. which also have well repaired. Them to HOUPLINES heavy menu line. Attended re Conference re Recurring for COS & Conference re Recurring	Fine Cmd

1875 Wt. W593/826 1,000,000 4/15 J.B.C. & A. A.D.S.S./Forms/C. 2118.

WAR DIARY
INTELLIGENCE SUMMARY

Army Form C. 2118

Instructions regarding War Diaries and Intelligence Summaries are contained in F.S. Regs., Part II. and the Staff Manual respectively. Title Pages will be prepared in manuscript.

(Erase heading not required.)

Place	Date	Hour	Summary of Events and Information	Remarks and references to Appendices
ARMENT-IERES	6/9/17		Inspected field of 4/5 L.N.L. Regt. also cross cut wires shells yesterday. Called on C.R.E. re centering II. Garth to Rest Europe	pure Chr
	7/9/17		O.C. to B"HQ Left Sector, re wiring in front of Support Line. Support line badly damaged by minnie - fire held up.	pure Chr
	8/9/17		Lecture by C.R.E. 8th Divn on operations near WESTHOEK. O.C. inspected wire in front of Supports.	pure Chr
	9/9/17		O.C. with II Lt Stephen & 2nd Lt Hitchens (2/5-L.N.L. Regt) inspected damage to Support Line by CHICKEN FARM - Right Sector - men working in line disturbed at night by gas shells. C.R.E.'s conference re work in proposed sect' area. B.G.C. 170 th Inf Bde. left on leave. Lt Col. Merchant commanding Bde.	pure Chr
	10/9/17		Boring of 170th Inf. Bde Pioneers Coy. discussed today - this Coy has done very good work especially lately while they had been pulled wire & officers have masu'd with the Coy. The officers have been very useful for recommencing areas & they with some of them must have had special jobs given them - such as up on emergency Bombs, filling their holes, nestling notice boards, drainage (10/45 employed on this) &c. Remainder have been employed with sappers directly under R.E. Supervisors above to men leave forming nr. Prep. Rest Area for Bde Baths.	
	11/9/17		Inspected approach for field Switch revetin II Garth Left Post through WIMEREUX. II Pearse interview with by me. II Street Left with his Section for Bde Rest area. II Pearse taking charge of his Sector. C.R.E.'s Conference at Selot. Received orders to build Trestle Bridge near P. bridge at C.19.C.7°.45.	various Capt

WAR DIARY
INTELLIGENCE SUMMARY
(Erase heading not required.)

Army Form C. 2118

Instructions regarding War Diaries and Intelligence Summaries are contained in F.S. Regs., Part II. and the Staff Manual respectively. Title Pages will be prepared in manuscript.

Place	Date	Hour	Summary of Events and Information	Remarks and references to Appendices
ARMENTIERES	12/9/17		Making preparation for Inglis Bridge. A platform 20ft square of two lengths of baulks to be made at one end, and a tressel abutment the other end. Own work a bag necessary. Worked from 7.30 AM to 8.30 P.M. 8" x 8" square timber borrowed from R.E. Park for the purpose.	Fine Cloudy
	13/9/17		2/ worked 7.30 AM to 9.30 pm on bridge. Inglis preparations. 2/i Ditches 25 men went to AIRE (a trench in construction of bridge)	Fine Cloudy
	14/9/17	12 noon	25 motor lorries arrived at ERQUINGHEM with bridge park – ordered on as at a time. Parties arranged for construction. 76 Sappers from two Coys + 24 from Reserve Section. 20 Pioneers + 60 Infantry (relieved every four hours). Infantry parties did not all arrive, so to cover strength.	Fine Cloudy
		7.0	Bridge built	
		7.30	Cwry "in place" Bro marching covered on all through the night till 5.30 AM. Bridge completely planked. Completed then so work stopped – then dead tired.	Fine Cloudy
	15/9/17		Completed dismantling & camouflaging bridge, loading up stores &c. Capt Barnam handing over to 157 Coy R.E. Remainder of Pioneer Coy left. We taking over their tools - 2/i Ditches returned from leave	
MACKLAND CAMP B.13.b.4.9.	16/9/17		Moved to Nini Camp having after handing over documents, defends &c work in hand. British Trumps to 15/15 Division. (30th Div?)	Very hot Cloudy
	17/9/17		Practice route marches with packs	

WAR DIARY
INTELLIGENCE SUMMARY

(Erase heading not required.)

Army Form C. 2118

655

Instructions regarding War Diaries and Intelligence Summaries are contained in F. S. Regs., Part II. and the Staff Manual respectively. Title Pages will be prepared in manuscript.

Place	Date	Hour	Summary of Events and Information	Remarks and references to Appendices
L.32 D.7.6 FRANCE (36A.1/40,000)	18/9/17	10 p.m	Arrived at this billet. Packs were carried in lorries - No men fell out. Poor accommodation - Several men bivouacked	See CRD
O.6.A O.O.	19/9/17	1.30 p.m	Arrived at this billet. poor accommodation - Several men bivouacked overnight. No casualties on march - packs in bus	See CRD
FLECHIN ELLEGOA(F) M.33.b.3.3	20/9/17	2.0 p.m	Arrived at this village. Interpreter here. Fixed billets which are poor. One man fell out sick. packs carried in lorries.	See CRD
	21/9/17		O.C. visited village. LIGNY, WESTREHEM + FONTAINE-LES-HERMANS (Bde HQ). Men started training. Drill + Musketry - 7.30 to 1.30 AM football re. inf. bn	See CRS
	22/9/17	A.M. P.M.	O.C. with B.G.C. 170 & 172 of Bde inspected manoeuvre area near ENQUIN EG ATTE O.C. attended C.R.E's conference re spoils + training	See CRS
	23/9/17		Sunday - Church Parade - football match re. B.n.	See CRS
	24/9/17		O.C. at Manoeuvre Area.	
	25/9/17		O.C. at Manoeuvre area twice - Once with B.G.C. 170th & 172nd Inf. Bde. deciding sites of strongpoints. pill boxes &	See CRD
	26/9/17		Taping out trenches with tapes & pegs on Manoeuvre area -	See CRD
	27/9/17		4 Sections each constructing a strong point tonight	See CRD

Army Form C. 2118
657

WAR DIARY
INTELLIGENCE SUMMARY
(Erase heading not required.)

Instructions regarding War Diaries and Intelligence Summaries are contained in F. S. Regs., Part II. and the Staff Manual respectively. Title Pages will be prepared in manuscript.

Place	Date	Hour	Summary of Events and Information	Remarks and references to Appendices
FLECHIN ÉLLE	28/9/17		O.C. to C.R.E. re recommendations to honours re. Inspecting strong points constructed last night.	See C.R.2
(FRANCE 36.A.1.46.00)	29/9/17		Coy. Sports- Programme attached. Seut. R.E. Competition tonight No 2 Section made Storing Point for	See C.R.2
	30/9/17		B.G.C. 170th Inf. Bde. spoke to Coy. complimenting them on work done in the line	See C.R.2

Ch. [signature]
MAJOR
COMMANDING 502nd
WESSEX FIELD Co. R.E.

Vol 9

C O N F I D E N T I A L

WAR DIARY

OF

502ND. (WESSEX) FIELD CO.R.E.

From: 1st. October,1917   To: 31st. October,1917.

(Volume 9)

Ch.Dox Major.
Commanding 502nd.(Wessex) Field Co.R.E.

WAR DIARY
INTELLIGENCE SUMMARY
(Erase heading not required.)

Army Form C. 2118.

Instructions regarding War Diaries and Intelligence Summaries are contained in F. S. Regs., Part II. and the Staff Manual respectively. Title pages will be prepared in manuscript.

Place	Date	Hour	Summary of Events and Information	Remarks and references to Appendices
FLECHINELLE 1/10/17 FRANCE 36A 1/20.000 S.W.	1/10/17		170th Bde digging shallow trenches in Micmorne Area. G.O.C 171st + R.O.C. Bde patent inspecting work, + this Coy's stores/points.	fine CW4
	2/10/17		Training continued - work on Micmorne Area. Sent escort to BOULOGNE for Sapper J. OATES who has been absent since 28/9/17.	fine CW4
	3/10/17		Training continued - 57th Fush. Sports finished. Programme attached.	
	4/10/17		Training contd. Sapper J. OATES + escort arrived. O.C. attended conference at Bde H.Q. re Inspection by 2 M.C. Bde + re Manoeuvre.	dry CW4
	5/10/17		Coy training.	windy CW4
	6/10/17		Inspection in Bde groups by Sir A Haig C in C British Armies in France.	very hot CW4
	7/10/17		Coy with Bde in Manoeuvre area.	very hot CW4
	8/10/17		Coy training - use of weapons &c.	wet CW4
	9/10/17		Coy training.	wet CW4
	10/10/17		do. 3 Sections to Army Bridging School AIRE for practice in constructing light MG & S bridges	showery CW4

Army Form C. 2118.

WAR DIARY
— OF —
INTELLIGENCE SUMMARY.
(Erase heading not required.)

Instructions regarding War Diaries and Intelligence Summaries are contained in F. S. Regs., Part II. and the Staff Manual respectively. Title pages will be prepared in manuscript.

Place	Date	Hour	Summary of Events and Information	Remarks and references to Appendices
FLECHINELLE FRANCE 36A 1/20000 SW	11/10/17		Coy training. Coy to move (no practice move) by 6 p.m.	fine Cloudy
		3.6 p.m	Orders Coy paraded ready to move off	
		6.45 "	Coy paraded	
		6.30 "	Adjt moved off	
	12/10/17		Trained Sports Reg. Coy training	wet Cloudy
			DARS inspected arrivals. Musketry practiced with new Reg.	
	13/10/17		Received orders to move tomorrow to RENESCURE from 17th.	wet Cloudy
			At 10 p.m. more cancelled. Bde.	
	14/10/17		Rapid Sun. Musketry Competition	fine Cloudy
	15/10/17		3 sections to COYECQUE - inspected rice time with bombers once with trustees. O.C. also to Bde. Hdqrs. formation of Pioneer Co.	fine Cloudy
	16/10/17		Another Musketry Competition. N.C.O.s with compasses. Preparations for move.	fine Cloudy
CAMPAGNE (MAP REF HAZEBROUCK 5A 1/100,000 BruinsSE) St OMER	17/10/17		Arrived by route march from FLECHINELLE at 4 p.m. Not on route Section joined the Coy en route. Marched with 170 Bde War Group marched immediately behind Bde HQrs. No casualties. Weather fine fallen out. One mule very lame.	fine Cloudy
PORTLAND CAMP (near CROMBEKE N of POPERINGHE MAP REF (no column)	18/10/17		Transport left CAMPAGNE at 7 a.m. Marched with Bde. Bn arrived PORTLAND CAMP near CROMBEKE (PROVEN AREA) 7.30 p.m. Coy left 10.30 A.M. Marched to RENESCURE entrained 12.30 P.M. detrained 2 mile S. of PROVEN 5.05 p.m. Reached Camp 7.45 P.M. Left one lame mule behind at CAMPAGNE No men fell out on march.	fine Cloudy

WAR DIARY
INTELLIGENCE SUMMARY

Army Form C. 2118.

Place	Date	Hour	Summary of Events and Information	Remarks and references to Appendices
PORTLAND CAMP NEAR CROMBEKE X28.a.2.9.	19/10/17 20/10/17		General clean up. Saw Bde HQ re formation of Pioneers.	ree CRO
			HQ Pioneers reported (2 off + 96 O.R.) Officer Capt Helme. Sent Pioneer details with this Coy today. OC attended conference at CRE's PR BGN re minor operation	ree CRO
	21/10/17		Training in Camp	
	22/10/17		Route march OC Capt Savian & E Helme to Canal Bank re OC OC 209 Fd Co R.E. (Sappers) at work to take over 1 Dutch & 6 O.R. recce no advance party	Sur CRO
YSER CANAL BANK C.19.a.0.5 (28NW2)	23/10/17		Coy moved by tram to BOESINGHE. Transport No I Section to HOOL Farm at B.20.b.5.0. No I to work under Field Engineer WELSH FARM. No IV Section working with much area Commandment. Canal Bank. Other 2 sections to work B. Track (Capt Saviar of 1st Pioneers of 12 Sappers Capt Helme & 100 Pioneers dumped to accessible point was V Bank) re Stelchu & Creek. Lt Pence laying out assembly line to 170 It Inf Bde. 200 yds behind front line of shell holes. Lieut Weir & Richan to Pioneer & No I. Section widening trench. OC Capt Helme each with 100 Inf & 50 yds. Returning to entrain head at BARD. Capt Saviar & 3 pontoon & 4500 strengthened BARD DUMP C.13.C.0.2 & took them to MILITARY BRIDGE C.4.b.8585 (4A.M.)	ree CRO wet CRO
	25/10/17		Area Commandant only requires I section to put most of sappers on repairing track	

Army Form C. 2118.

WAR DIARY
or
INTELLIGENCE SUMMARY.
(Erase heading not required.)

Instructions regarding War Diaries and Intelligence Summaries are contained in F.S. Regs., Part II. and the Staff Manual respectively. Title pages will be prepared in manuscript.

Place	Date	Hour	Summary of Events and Information	Remarks and references to Appendices
CANAL DYSER C.19.H.O.ST. (28.N.W.2)	25/10/17		O.C. reconnoitred roped and 300 yd extension of Track B. Capt. Helme & Lt Stables each with 100 men attended track 200 yd. Sapper FILMORE killed at Bde.HQ. STRAY FARM. 1st Field Coyn. Saprs Pioneers repairing track, which is very roughly laid.	Fine CQB
	26/10/17		17th Bde attacked 5.40 A.M. Scot. to have taken first objective but unable hold same so retired on the right to original line. on left, held way to same.	
		5 pm	interview with Lieut Armine Toffer P.E. Pence in Sh/c of henry towage laid out tape line 800 yds from end of track to REQUETTE FARM (V.14.C.5.9) to assist relief of 170th Bde. by 171st Bde.	
			50 Pioneers 2d whm. Coy. pushed forward pickets & tape for extension of tape line to encounterato bun line. O.C. with 50 Jnfy. took 90 duckboards to FERDAN HOUSE (V.19.9.8.6) unable to proceed owing to heavy barrage. Rest of Sapprs & Pioneers on repair work. Sergt Denly wounded	Wet CQB
	27/10/17		Mr. Stedm. evening work with 150 Infy. laid 100 duckboards. Capt. Helm & Pioneers laid 36. dumped 20. Sappers worked Lt. Slead on repairs.	Fine CQB
	28/10/17		Party of Infy + Pioneer encamped Encluterage returned after unsuccessfully duckfoard along tapes. No 1. Sect not moved to Canal Bank from Holzline. No 2 Section Encluterage with them	Fine CQB

WAR DIARY
INTELLIGENCE SUMMARY
(Erase heading not required.)

Army Form C. 2118.

Instructions regarding War Diaries and Intelligence Summaries are contained in F. S. Regs., Part II. and the Staff Manual respectively. Title pages will be prepared in manuscript.

Place	Date	Hour	Summary of Events and Information	Remarks and references to Appendices
CANAL DYSER Sq a.o.s. 28 Nov 2	29/10/17		R. Aitcheson + 70 Pioneers laid 75 duck Pbd & repaired front line + 40 R.E. laid 20 " " " Dollries + 120 Inf. dumped 80 " " at EAGLE TRENCH U.24.C.2.0. while trying after dusk most of Inf. had also appeared. Returned without proceeding further.	Ins. C.B
	30/10/17		O.C. Lieut Johnson + 70 Inf. laid 53 duckboards Capt Nelson " 70 Pioneers " 53 " Lieut Stowe " 40 Sappers " 40 " } in extension of track – 40 sappers also laid 40 m repair of track	Ins. C.B
			2nd Lt Sutton reporting track by daylight. Sapper Gourlay slightly wounded. Major Bishop ROM (late 221st Field Co.) killed. Lieut South reported from home.	
	31/10/17		Lieut Stowe + 40 Sappers laid 38 duckboards. Lieut Hirdlu + 110 Inf. & carried 50 duckboards to near head of track. Capt. Nelson + 60 attached Inf. carried 53 duckboards. " Party of Inf's all parties much interfered with by shellfire, gas shells &c. 110 Sappers returned to camp on their own initiative but were later sent off to wreck near their carry on.	Ins. C.B

C.L. Dox MAJOR,
COMMANDING 502ND
WESSEX FIELD Co. R.E.

503RD. (WESSEX) FIELD CO. R.E.

TRAINING CARRIED OUT WHILST AT FLECHINELLE.

<u>Squad Drill</u> - With and without Arms.

<u>Section Drill</u> - With and without Arms.
           Practice March-Past.

<u>Rifle Exercises</u>.

<u>Musketry</u> - An Instructor provided for 3 days by 170th. Infantry Brigade.
    3 Sections fired 25 rounds course.
    2 Sections fired 10 rounds.
    3 Competitions on the range in addition included 64 men.

<u>Bayonet Fighting</u> - An Instructor, Sergt.Major W.Wells, provided by 170th. Infantry Brigade. - All Sappers instructed.

<u>Use of Prismatic Compass</u> - Lecture to N.C.O's, and several hours practice in use by day and by night. Marching and laying out tape, making traverse etc.

<u>Wire Entanglements</u> - 3 Sections spent several mornings with screw pickets and French wire making standard apron fence etc.

<u>Strong Points</u> - Each Section constructed one (one Section constructed two) by night.

<u>Gas Drill</u>. - A little Drill. Men were practised in wearing S.B.R. when firing, when pontooning, and on wire entanglements.

<u>Bridging</u>. - One day at Army Bridging School, AIRE, on Light INGLIS Bridge. One day pontooning and trestle bridging at COYECQUE.

<u>Knots & Lashings</u> - Several hours.

<u>Route Marches</u> - One of 12 miles, and several shorter.

<u>Explosives</u> - Several hundred shell holes blown with Stoke's shells and guncotton.

<u>Drivers</u> - Practiced for Driving Competition.

WORK DONE ON MANOEUVRE AREA.

9 dummy pill-boxes erected. 3000 yards trench taped out and dug by Infantry under R.E. supervision. Other work included above under "Strong Points" and "Explosives".

WORK DONE NEAR ENGUINEGATTE BY NO.1 SECTION IN 16 DAYS.

      30 Nissen Huts built.
      3 Hospital Huts built.

RECREATIONS.

3 Rugby games and matches played.
6 Association games and matches played.
4 Paper-chases run.
1 Cricket game played.
Rounders and Skittles.
Sports days etc.

C O N F I D E N T I A L.

WAR DIARY
OF
502ND.(WESSEX) FIELD CO.R.E.

From: 1st. November,1917   To: 30th. November,1917.

(Volume 10)

Major.
Commanding 502nd.(Wessex) Field Co.R.E.

WAR DIARY
INTELLIGENCE SUMMARY.
(Erase heading not required.)

502nd WESSEX FIELD COMPANY R.E.
No. 1154

Place	Date	Hour	Summary of Events and Information	Remarks and references to Appendices
CANAL D'YSER. C.19 A.O.5.	1/11/17	5.30 P.M.	Lieut Yeoman & Lieut Garth took 100 Inft with duckboards to head of track + laid 30 duckboards on road. Progress of night's work recently have much helped this work. It is reported very little shellfire this night.	Fine weather. C.A.D.
(FRANCE 28.N.W.2 1/10,000)	2/11/17	7.30PM	Moved taking Stuck each with about 25 Inft who proceeded to repair track. 2/Lt Ditcher took (about) reported stand of stretcher 800yds stuck bearing U.24 C.3.1. to U.24 G.6.2 U.29 C.2.5. Lieut Stuck's party came under heavy shellfire while on road near U.29 C.2.5. + suffered 14 casualties —	
			Sapper Laurence W. killed	
			" Boucher A.C. wounded admitted to hospital — died of wounds there 2/11/17	
			Sapper Stainer J. " — died of wounds there 2/11/17	
			" Tolley H.A. "	
			" Seymour A. "	
			" Pike R. "	
			" Clift G.A.J. "	
			" Elwin C. "	
			Cpl. Silvester A.H. wounded slightly remained with Unit	
			2/Cpl. Perring W.J. "	
			" Stratton A.E. "	
			Sapper Cummings A.E. "	
			" Johns R. "	
			" Barnsby C.H. "	
			Considerable difficulty encountered in getting Sapper Stainer back to A.D.S. owing to continuing shellfire. He + Cpl Haines + Sapper Howell + Robbins with field stretcher drove to about 1500yds + not + head of track. Lt Yeoman + 150 Inft carried duckboards to about 1500 + not + head of track. Enemy gas barrage Inft Spotsman slightly gassed. Cold nature + 80 pioneers to head of track + laid 75 duckboards. Previous Call Relieve + 80 pioneers to head of track + laid 75 duckboards and there. 2 casualties (wounded).	Fine weather. C.A.D.

Army Form C. 2118.

WAR DIARY
or
INTELLIGENCE SUMMARY.
(Erase heading not required.)

Instructions regarding War Diaries and Intelligence Summaries are contained in F. S. Regs., Part II. and the Staff Manual respectively. Title pages will be prepared in manuscript.

Place	Date	Hour	Summary of Events and Information	Remarks and references to Appendices
CANAL DYSER C.19.a.0.5 (FRANCE 28.N.W.2. 1.10.000)	3/4/17	10.a.m.	Sapper Lawrence W. buried in Cemetery C.19.a.0.5. O.C. C.S.M. & most of No. 4. Section present.	Foggy C.P.S.
		3 p.m.	O.C. with Pioneers carrying 40 duckboard to Eagle Trench laid alongside track with view to starting same. Interfered with by heavy barrage for 1½ hours on Eagle Trench but no casualties	
		5 p.m.	2nd Lieut. Pearce + 150 Inf. carried duckboards (50) to FERDAN HOUSE (V.19.a.7.5)	
	4/4/17	6 a.m.	Lieut. Fletcher + 20 Sappers repairing track by Eagle Trench	
		6 a.m.	Lieut. Fletcher + 35 Sappers doubling track near Eagle Trench. Capt. Relive + 60 Pioneers laid duckboards previously dumped at FERDAN HOUSE in extension of track to within about 60 yds of REQUETE FARM. Casualties 2 slightly wounded.	Fine C.P.S.
		4.0 p.m.	L' Pearce carried 50 duck bomb (8ft x 100 Inf.) to about U.29.a.6.9 & laid along cycle track to southern same U.29.a.6.0 thru Lieut. Garrat left. Reported to C.E. Infantry to join next employment day.	
	5/4/17	6 a.m.	L' Fletcher + 40 Sappers nailed 50 duckboards to bearers near STRAY FARM to EAGLE TRENCH doubling track. Also by Garrat with 70 from STRAY FARM to EAGLE TRENCH	Fine C.P.S.
		5.0 p.m.	2 Lt. Johnson with 70 Infantry carried 35 duckboards to about U.29.a.6.0. Started one food & comp for doubling track. O.C. went to horse lines. Generally stolen in good order. Copy of same attached. Sent C.R.E. handing over trucks.	
	6/4/17		Capt Nelson + 20 R.M. Inf. fixed 22 riffles, found 2d Lt. Pearce + 40 R.E. + 10 Inf. + 80 yds of track man-worked on Linea near MILITARY BRIDGE, & also rivets note in road, repaired track Received orders to proceed to HOCQUINGHEN (near AUDRUICQ) on the ST.O. by Train. Transport to move separately	Showery C.R.J.

WAR DIARY / INTELLIGENCE SUMMARY

Army Form C. 2118.

Place	Date	Hour	Summary of Events and Information	Remarks and references to Appendices
CANAL D'YSER C.19.a.0.5. (FRANCE 28NW 2. 1:10000)	7/10/17	9 a.m.	Lieut Pearce & 40 Sappers repairing "B" track between BARD CAUSEWAY & STRAY FARM. Lieut Stebin hauling over to Lt Thomas, advance officer of 9ord Div to. (17th Divn.)	
		12 noon	Attached Infantry under Capt Kebine left by lorry to report work of 170 & 173 Bde. They have done very valuable work while here - Lieut Carruthers O.C.	
		6.15 pm	O.C. Seany 172nd Bde & Returns to Mazet. Lt. Tromham & RE's leaving with 421st Coy. - 20 min advance billeting party for work done by this Coy here, see Haistins Div not attached. Casualties have been 2 killed 2 died of wounds. 9 evacuated wounded. Lt. Steel & 10 R wounded slightly - total 20 all ranks. Several N.C.O.'s & men have been evacuated sick, the hard work & long marching told on all ranks severely on the advance. Two half Coys left of the Coy (infantry att.) owing to being physically not strong enough for military work.	APPENDIX No. 1.
CANAL D'YSER C.19.a.0.5. FRANCE 28 NW 2. 1:10,000	8/10/17	1.00 6.00	3 sections under O.C. Lieut Stebin & Pearce (2nd Recon attached) paraded for march to BOESINGHE, entraining point. The Coy marched at the station until 6.30 p.m. train left at about 6.45 p.m. arrived at Vlamer- tinghe AUDRUICQ (Esquerdes 5-A 2.A.9.5.) detraining point.	
		6.00 a.m.	Transport under Capt Davies Lieuts Elliot & Stone took the route from HOOGE PROVEN, WATOU, HOUTKERQUE, HERZELE, HORMIOUDT to POMBROUGH. Arrival at POUISNOUCH 9.30 pm. Battalion here the night.	

Army Form C. 2118.

WAR DIARY
INTELLIGENCE SUMMARY.
(Erase heading not required.)

Instructions regarding War Diaries and Intelligence Summaries are contained in F. S. Regs., Part II. and the Staff Manual respectively. Title pages will be prepared in manuscript.

Place	Date	Hour	Summary of Events and Information	Remarks and references to Appendices
HOOGUINGHEM 3.F 23. 21. Sheet 13 Calais 1:100,000	9/11/17	7.30 a.m.	3 sections under Subalterns to Sketch & Trace, sound at HOOGUINGHEM after manuaby attempt daily one man, left sub. James (Sapper WRIGHT) left to report later.	
		7.30 p.m.	Transport arrived after an all day march two new Lewis Guns & spare supply rifles, into one exists about Battalion in sufficient ammunition for all	
"	10/11/17	10.00 a.m.	Visit from G.R.E. Employ and gases.	Memo 9/11
		2.15 p.m.	No 10 2 section under Subalterns left by lorries for NORTBECOURT	" 10/11
			(3.B 12.26 Hazebrouck S.A.) for work for 5th Army Mountly Corps. Transport of Rd. two sections to Patterson the 13th	See 4/11
"	11/11/17		Capt. D Awdas inspected all billets & Lonelins the Time - lines Awdas advised, had all working groms, no mile class sent up. All men in very comfortable circumstances	
"	12/11/17	6.00 A.M.	#8 section transport under Lee Col. Dredge, left for MERCKEGHEM HAZEBROUCK SA. 2 D 59 36.	
		7.30 A.M.	#10 2 sections transport under Col. Saunders left for NORTBECOURT (Clairmarais SA. 3. B 12.26)	

Army Form C. 2118.

WAR DIARY
or
INTELLIGENCE SUMMARY.
(Erase heading not required.)

Instructions regarding War Diaries and Intelligence Summaries are contained in F.S. Regs., Part II. and the Staff Manual respectively. Title pages will be prepared in manuscript.

Place	Date	Hour	Summary of Events and Information	Remarks and references to Appendices
HOCQUINGHEN	12/9/17	11.00 AH	Lieut. Fletcher, with 12 picture staffs for work at MERCK & HESDIN by Major Larg.? was a Sanity Staff detailed to meet & live	Lieut Larg Off
3.F. 28.21. Sheet 13 CALAIS 1-100,000.	13/9/17		Lt Laut accompanied G.O.C. 170ᵗʰ Brigade to Manœuvring Ground. RECCE'D WEST TRAINING AREA. No action to augh him and fit up Area.	Home app. Off Casualty 13/9/14
	14/9/17		Spent leave & work around camp.	
	15/9/17		Went sketching. Training Area. Major Duke wireless took him motoring and agreed with him as accept of work. Area Commander wants bullets	Some 15/9/17
	16/9/17		Lieut Laut gave instruction GOC 170ᵗʰ Brigade to Training Area. Survey a copy 1/10,000 of our line done by the Cox.	Home 16/9/17 Casualty 16/9/17
	17/9/17		Nothing to report	
	18/9/17		Lyon after received in the infantry of Pearson CRE. 13 men of each battalion under Capt HODGSON 3/6ᵗʰ O. Regt to be billeted at GUEMY (3.A. 31.65) to march to Hazebrouck 5-A) & no regd to training Area the intendant to be charge 27/9/17.	Labour entered Labour Off
			(GO Stand proceeded on Leave to United Kingdom 0K.) to 100 Later. Lieut Laut with 16 others and the pioneers at night in Training area. Pioneers passed most of DA.A.R.H.G. & two to-budled apparently relentlessly various pestifieres with woolly	Home Off Labour Off
	19/9/17			
	20/9/17			
	21/9/17		Nothing to record.	Recent 21/9/17

Army Form C. 2118.

WAR DIARY
INTELLIGENCE SUMMARY
(Erase heading not required.)

Instructions regarding War Diaries and Intelligence Summaries are contained in F.S. Regs., Part II. and the Staff Manual respectively. Title pages will be prepared in manuscript.

Place	Date	Hour	Summary of Events and Information	Remarks and references to Appendices
HOCQUINGHEN	22/11/17		Nothing to record. All horses 5 miles under cover (Billeted) yes	Mostly fine 9/.
3.F. 23.21 Sheet 13 CALAIS 1:100,000	23/11/17		Nothing to record. Captain Dawson proceeded on leave to the United Kingdom	Stormy wet & cold
	24/11/17		Work on "Regina" manoeuvre area completed. Inoculation Parade. 35 O.R.	Stormy wet
"	25/11/17		Nothing to record.	Stormy wind rain
"	26/11/17		Nothing to record.	Stormy wet rain
"	27/11/17		O.C. returned from leave. Inspected billets & stables.	Showery cold
"	28/11/17		O.C. visited stations at NORBECOURT. weather fine.	
"	29/11/17		O.C. inspected men working on a cage to be erected for 40 Prisoners whom P.O.W. to be employed on those at GEMY. (3 A 40.60 HAZEBROUCK STA) bo Pioneers (attached but) Also saw Capt. Hodgson O.C. Stan Kings. SERGT. J. A. ANNING (No. 508286) and Sapper P.E. PEARCE (308374) awarded Military Medals Detached duty for 1/5 K.O.R.L Rejoining	Fine Cold
	30/11/17		Work on P.O.W. Cage proceeding, also on Detachment erected at SANGEN (3.E.90.4.b. CALAIS 13.)	

WAR DIARY
or
INTELLIGENCE SUMMARY
(Erase heading not required.)

Army Form C. 2118.

Place	Date	Hour	Summary of Events and Information	Remarks and references to Appendices

General Monthly Summary.

For first week Coy. was working on Duckboard track between CANAL DE L'YSER and front line. Also on smaller jobs near to. Behind CANAL. Capt J. M. HOLME 2/Lt KORIR & 50 to 60 men (attached Infantry) of original 170th Pioneer Coy. billeted & worked with this Coy. They did excellent work (after 3 months in trenches). Capt Kelme commands the men & shows much determination coolness. The Officers, NCOs & men of this Coy. exceeded my expectations. Behaved splendidly under at times very dangerous circumstances. They could all be relied on to show coolness under fire & determination to finish the job in hand — Total casualties were 20.

Tarbuck Section also did exceedingly well carrying duckboards forward on attacks road often under shell fire.

The move from the "line" to "Rest area" was very arduous. The Sappers had all night journey & trains (one by one) (marching 16 miles with full pack & two blankets) the drivers & horses were the 2 days on the road 30 miles & 23 miles being distances covered. They arrived dead beat. No animals were sick. The weather was stormy. Wet.

For last three weeks work has been on R.E. Services. No 3 Section for Corps School MERCKEGHEM. No 1 & 2 Sections for 1th Army School of Musketry NORBECOURT 2nd Lieut SUTTON took No 6 C.R.E. 5? First at HOCQUINGHEM. Work is mainly construction of camps, erection of WINNER + TARRANT huts. Baths. Water Supply. Cookhouses &c. Health of Coy throughout generally good.

Geo? Major
COMMANDING 502ND
WESSEX FIELD Co. R.E.

APPENDIX NO. I

HANDING OVER NOTES.

Report of work being carried out by 500nd.(Wessex) Field Co.R.E. on 5.11.17 to be handed over to 93rd. Field Co.R.E. on 8.11.17.

R E A R.

Divisional Baths. Completed, save for one 6' length and 2 elbows 1" pipe required to make hot water circuit.   This has been indented for.

Horse Lines and Camp. B.20.b.5.9. Construction of earth and sandbag splinter-proof protection :
    to one stable – completed.
    to the other stable – 75% completed.
    to the huts – 25% completed.

F O R W A R D.

Drying Shed at SEAGULL FARM. C.5.b.6.9.
    Building – 90% completed.
    Splinter-proof protection – 50% completed.
    Stove to be fitted.

Battalion Headquarters (near DOUBLE COTTS). U.23.d.9.1.
Concrete wall cut through to make another entrance 3'6" x 3'
60% completed.

Directing Boards for "B" Track.
    30 painted (not fixed).
  For Front Line Posts
    15 to be painted and fixed, **as per list attached.**

Shelters at EAGLE TRENCH" U.24.c.9.1.
20 Sections Baby Elephant and 3000 sandbags have been carried to this place and used for construction of shelters in this trench.   Two Sappers have lived (relieved daily) in this trench to assist this work.

R.E.Dump, Broad Street. C.6.a.5.2.
Two men were found by this Company to take charge of this Dump.   The dump was very little used; not once by me, and only two or three times by the other Divisional Companies.

"B" TRACK.
1. This Company has carried out the following work :-
  (i) Extended Track from FERDAN HOUSE (V.19.a.8.6.) to REQUETE FARM (V.14.c.4.9.).
  (ii) Laid track firmly (generally on bearers) from EAGLE TRENCH (U.24.c.9.1.) to FERDAN HOUSE (V.19.a.8.6.).
 (iii) Doubled track for about 300 yards between U.30.c.3.4. and EAGLE TRENCH (U.24.c.9.1.).
  (iv) General repair and maintenance of track from BARD CAUSEWAY (C.15.c.5.9.) to REQUETE FARM (V.14.c.4.9.).

2. General Remarks.
1. **Duckboard** track is now in good order up to FERDAN HOUSE (V.19.a.8.6.), but needs constant repair where blown up etc.
2. Portions of track that are double when handed over shall be shown as doubled on tracing of track.
3. In two places, from C.4.b.1.7. to C.4.b.4.5. (160 yards), and from C.4.b.5.6. to U.30.c.3.4. (400 yards), track runs along roads (without duckboards); both these roads are very rough and constantly shelled.   The portion of track between them, from C.4.b.1.5. to C.4.b.5.6., is outside the Divisional Area and is part of a track belonging to the Division on the right.

"B" TRACK.
General Remarks (Cont'd).

It is strongly recommended that a fresh track 700 yards long be laid connecting in a straight line C.4.b.4.5. to U.29.c.3.4. A bridge over the STEENBEEK suitable for this track already exists.
(4) Duckboards forward of FERDAN HOUSE need laying on bearers.
(5) Track needs doubling over greater part of its length, but chiefly for 600 yards E. of EAGLE TRENCH (U.24.c.8.1.) as blocks most frequently occur here owing to reliefs of men in EAGLE TRENCH.
(6) Best times of day to work on track have been found to be :
  Forward of EAGLE TRENCH - night time, 9 p.m. to 3 a.m.
  In rear " " " - 6 a.m. to 12 noon.
(7) Spots most frequently shelled :
  (i) Road between C.4.b.1.9? and C.4.b.4.5.
  (ii) Road between C.4.b.8.5. and U.29.c.3.4.
  (iii) EAGLE TRENCH, U.24.c.8.1.
Otherwise shelling seems very haphazard and spasmodic.
(8) Organization of Parties :-
  (i) Large working parties are liable to be split up and go astray, and each Platoon should have a Sapper guide who knows the work to be done and who can direct the Platoon Commander in case it becomes separated from the rest of the party.
  (ii) A Section of Sappers should not be kept closed up; otherwise casualties caused by one shell may be heavy.
  (iii) It is found for long distances that every man cannot carry a duckboard, and that 2 duckboards for every 3 men, thus providing reliefs, is a fair task.
(9) Enemy Machine Guns firing on end of track have been heard on two or three occasions.
(10) Artillery and Infantry are apt to take duckboards left unguarded or not nailed down.

TRANSPORT.

(1) Tram system was not used at all.
(2) 2 G.S. Wagons and 4 limbered G.S. Wagons were obtained from Division. These and the Company's 3 Pontoon Wagons carried all stores that were required.
(3) Limbered G.S.Wagons can proceed as far as EAGLE TRENCH (U.24.c.8.1) and turn round there.
(4) Other Wagons can proceed as far as C.4.b.4.5.
(5) G.S. Wagons are very awkward owing to their poor lock, and the narrow roads.
(6) It is advisable for an Officer always to accompany transport as all sorts of difficulties arise, such as blocks, shell holes, shell fire, breakages to wagons, etc.
(7) 45 duckboards per wagon is a heavy enough load, and G.S. or Pontoon Wagons should have 4-horse or 6-mule teams.

DISTRIBUTION OF PERSONNEL.

Company Headquarters and three Sections at CANAL BANK (C.13.c.2.7.). Sappers at work forward of Canal, usually 2 Sections on repair of Track "B" by day and one Section on sundry smaller jobs - guides for carrying parties etc., work for Area Commandant.
One Section at Horse Lines (B.20.b.5.0.) on various jobs as ordered.
100 attached Infantry carrying duckboards or assisting Sappers repairing Track.

CONFIDENTIAL

WAR DIARY

OF

502ND.(WESSEX) FIELD CO.R.E.

From 1st. December,1917 to 31st. December,1917.

(Volume 11)

Major.
Commanding 502ND.(WESSEX) FIELD CO.R.E.

WAR DIARY
INTELLIGENCE SUMMARY.
(Erase heading not required.)

603rd WESSEX FIELD COMPANY R.E.
No. 1383

Place	Date	Hour	Summary of Events and Information	Remarks and references to Appendices
CALAIS 13.1.100.000 3 F.J.2.	1/12/17		O.C. to Bde re Horse standings & materials, & to Horse standings at GENY.	See CRS
	2/12/17		O.C. with Lieut. O.C. HEARD (A.C.T.O.) to CALAIS abt spiral pipe for portable Coy-bath plant. Lieut STREET & Section at work on horse standings + huts &c.	See CRS
	3/12/17 Sunday		O.C. visited Capt. HELME (late O.C. attached uft.) re his leaving Company attached uft. He said it was in consequence with his own wishes. He will be taken charge of his being known that he is now manning a Company. Promised that he to be prepared to move in never 7 be out. Received warning order to be prepared to move in never 7 be out.	See CRS
	4/12/17		O.C. visited Horse standings at GENY. Then to RE Headquarters in CR's absence on leave. WOLPHUS to act as C.R.E. in CR's absence on leave. Sections in attachment ordered to your unit.	See for CRS
	6/12/17		O.C. to HOCQUINGHEM re several matters. Lieut. FLETCHER + Section (No.3) returned from XIX Corps School of Instruction at MERCKEGHEM. He reports chief work done there during three weeks :- 14 Nissen huts roofed, 15 " " half erected, 4 other huts " " erected. Butts + firing points on a rifle range started. Several other suicide repairs + completion of work on huts + camps.	See CRS

Place	Date	Hour	Summary of Events and Information	Remarks and references to Appendices
CALAIS. 13.I–100,000 3.F.3.2.	5/12/17		Lieuts Trotman and Pearce with Sections 1 & 2 from V Army Musketry School at Northcourt. (NORTBECOURT) They report work done as follows, during three weeks:— Completion of two Hospital Marsh huts including "Jungle hosph" and covered passages to three other huts. Completion of several Nissen huts. Two Bath houses (1–12 Spray & 1–6 Spray) Erection of one "Tacha" hut to partial enclosing of two others. System of 4" water supply to camp, including Water tower, pumps and stand-pipes. Sub system of 2" water supply to NCO's Mess & Officers Mess. Painting & tarring of huts, completed & erected during period. Much small repair work & minor construction.	

Army Form C. 2118.

WAR DIARY
or
INTELLIGENCE SUMMARY.
(Erase heading not required.)

Place	Date	Hour	Summary of Events and Information	Remarks and references to Appendices
CALAIS 13.1-100.000 S.F.3.2	5/12/9		Lieut Shead return from leave having been detained by bad weather for two days at DOVER. Lieut Shead reports as follows re work done during the previous five weeks at HOCQUINGHEM. 170th Inf. Bde. training area fitted out with 40 ▲ imitation pill-boxes, 100 shell-holes, barrage lines etc. Previous compound constructed at GUEMY. Erection of one Tarrant hut 15'x60' at SANGHEM. Existing bath set and erection of 1-6 spray set at LIEQUEST. Assistance rendered to units in the Bde in Rifle ranges, Shell holes blown etc. a bayonet fighting course. Divisional training area near GUEMY fitted up to represent previous Bde. front at POELCAPELLE. Barrage huts and imitation buildings erected. Billeting area improved numbered. Bins hutment for horse standings at GUEMY, Cuft down.	WF

Army Form C. 2118.

WAR DIARY
or
INTELLIGENCE=SUMMARY.
(Erase heading not required.)

Instructions regarding War Diaries and Intelligence Summaries are contained in F. S. Regs., Part II. and the Staff Manual respectively. Title pages will be prepared in manuscript.

Place	Date	Hour	Summary of Events and Information	Remarks and references to Appendices
CALAIS 13.1.-60000 3. F. S. 2.	7/2/17 8/2/17	7.15 a.m.	Lieut Stead left HOCQUINGHEM for U.K. on 14 days leave. Transport & bicycles under Lieuts. Stead & Trotman left HOCQUINGHEM for PROVEN. A halt for the night was made at LEDERZEELE and the journey was completed on the following day.	Roads getting frozen. JWF
PROVEN AREA.	9/2/17	8.15 a.m.	under Lieut Hitchin Coy less transport and bicycles left HOCQUINGHEM for PROVEN. The journey was made in buses in company with the 170th Inf. Bde.	Showery JWF
		5 p.m.	Coy. arrived in camp (PARDOU camp.) at PROVEN.	
		6.30 p.m.	Transport & bicycles under LIEUTS. Stead Trotman arrived at PARDOU camp.	
	10/2/17	8 a.m.	LIEUT S. Pearce left with two other ranks for ELVERDINGHE to take over work 8 hours from 505 Fd. Coy R.E.	Frost JWF
		10.30 a.m.	Coy less transport and bicycles left for ELVERDIN GHE under Lieut Tucker, Lieut Hitchin.	
		1 P.M.	Transport under Lieuts Stead and Trotman left PARDOU Camp for ON DANK (Sheet 27 G) where transport lines were situated	

(A7092). Wt. W12899/M1293. 75 10.00. 1/17. D. D. & L., Ltd. Forms/C.2118/14.

Army Form C. 2118.

WAR DIARY
or
INTELLIGENCE SUMMARY

(Erase heading not required.)

Place	Date	Hour	Summary of Events and Information	Remarks and references to Appendices
HAZEBROUCK 5A-1-100000 23, 72 & 64.			Coy under Lieut. Fletcher arrived at ELVERDINGHE	
SHEET 28. B14 & 27. (ELVERDINGHE)	12/12/17 12.30 pm		Capt Davidson reported for duty from U.K. Transport under Lieuts Bland and Trotman arrived at ONDANK Farm Enns (A11 c29) (Sheet 28.)	Map 14/1/91
	13/12/17 8.30 am		Company paraded at 8.30 am for work in XII Corps area, also accompany transport of the same unit. West from C.R.E. XII Corps. O.C. rejoined unit. Transport used and OC so & Coy taking over a spec of line.	
	13/12/17		OC inspected work mainly Nissen Huts & stable rags for 50th Div R.A. and R.F.A; 18th Reserve Park 2/C & 5th Army Aux + H.Q. Co. Lieut Trotman taking over work, papers from 79th Fields whose we relieve	
	15/12/17		OC & Lt Pearce to MQ 79th Field Co. Thence with OC that Coy to "CORPS LINE" by CLARGES ST. Thence along line probed back by HUNTER STREET Area seemed very quiet compared to last time in line.	
	16/12/17		L/Cpl Cole left on leave OC to HQ 5th army RE in evening	

WAR DIARY or INTELLIGENCE SUMMARY

Army Form C. 2118.

Place	Date	Hour	Summary of Events and Information	Remarks and references to Appendices
ELVERDINGHE Sheet 28. B.14.b.2.7	15/12/17	(cont'd)	Reinforcement of N.C.R. received. Inspected no. 3 Officer of 12 to 24 months' shooting. He had several prismatics badly blurred & no 35 deg shooting cone. 2 Sections granted leave to visit POPERINGHE in evening. Other 2 Sections granted leave previous evening.	(A)
	16/12/17		C.R.E. XIV Corps troops inspected work & called on O.C. & same – Manned our first Tape no to CAPT. GRIFFITHS for O/C 79th Field Co.	(A)
	17/12/17		Visit from B.G.C. 170th Inf Bde. & working parties he is providing	cold fine (A)
		11.0 a.m.	Capt HQ. work & Elverdinghe moved to BOESINGHE. B.5.b.5.3 (Sheet 28) Received orders from HQ. as work to be started tomorrow.	
		6.0 p.m.		
BOESINGHE Sheet 28 B.5.b.5.3	18/12/17 5-30 a.m.		Capt Davison went to BOESINGHE DUMP to meet 2 Corps 2/4 L.N.L. who are to work on HUNTER ST. @ RAILWAY ST. (Duckboard track) Corps did not arrive	windy cold (A)
		9-0 a.m.	O.C. & Johnson met Officer Nicols & 2 Corps 2/5 L.N.L. who are to work on drainage scheme. O.C. investigated ? crop at R.E. workshop re pumps	
		9-30 a.m.	D & Pearce reconnoitring wiring required on CORPS Line –	30 BES. 1/17 PCE. OD
		3-30 p.m.	1 Coy 2/4 L.N.L.R. reported to Lieut Pearce & started wiring on "Corps Line".	
	19/12/17		O.C. conferred OC 505 Coy. re work on "Alphabet Subways" & Q.H.Q 172 MI Coy which are to be transferred to this Unit temporarily from 2 Corps. O.C. reconnoitred Boeche pumps & nr. LANO @ MARCH station. Various Serial numbers typed & read metal, also much concrete various reinforcement conduits etc. concrete work – (reported same v. cold & W.E.R.E.) then met DMG O.C (Capt watch aching) who pointed out OF round My who D.2 M.G dug-outs to be made by me with Dc some starting this evening. Camouflage from Burine carried up during the day	v. cold (A)

Army Form C. 2118.

WAR DIARY
or
INTELLIGENCE SUMMARY.
(Erase heading not required.)

Place	Date	Hour	Summary of Events and Information	Remarks and references to Appendices
BOESINGHE Shee/28 1/2 B.15.b.5.3	20/11/17		"Atacks" Infantry 172 noTde arms Accompanied, & Le Mans Crossing concentrating other officers & 25 Inniskillen + Brown O.C. with firepickets Leaving to M.G. Dugouts. Three relief against 2.30 pm 6.30 pm. 6 Gappers going up at 8am. A.C.C.G. effective. Continue "taping"— Up Working Parties TRG Officio & from many he laid APPENDIX "A" O.C. — Cyders w with to BROEMBEEK we working field to R.O.Q. Pill boxes (Protecting Entrance to Boel Pill boxes) also 3 cold M.G. Dugouts to be camouflage progress —	Fine Cold CWG Cold CWG full Cold CWG
	21/11/17		O.C. PLANERTINGHE to see CORPS Camouflage depot – & was given on a two useful runs it camouflying. Capt. Davison to SAN SIXTE Corps HQ to send money to buy men as our funds suddenly (?) in future some during the Bombers standing in camp, rebuilding allowed to bury – 15 Myrds been cold nightly Lt. Pearce. FM E. & W. Hood (AIF Inf) & L.N.L. Regt (attached to 21st South Lanc Regt.) with wiring party rebelled with by barrage of Bosch Lewis I- Lt. Hood being hit by M.S. bullet in shoulder evacuated Lt. Pearce carried on 1. Our troops also intuitioned with Cpl. SANDERS showing courage rising G & M. Baker took up 1 Coy Infy to fill gap Stopped with Lewis gun Guncade for M.G. Dugouts also interfering with fast relief of worken on M.G. Dugouts stopped by Bosh barrage, returned to Camp.	Finer Cold C.W.B.

WAR DIARY or INTELLIGENCE SUMMARY

Army Form C. 2118.

Place	Date	Hour	Summary of Events and Information	Remarks and references to Appendices
BOESINGHE Sheet 28 B.5.b.5.7.	27/12/17		O.C. & Lt TROTMAN with Sapper & working party to M.G. dug outs which require slabs for excavation. Shoring up - also inspecting connecting & laying which is good & drainage work done in GRUYTERZALE FARM area. INSTEAD reported from horse lines & at wiring party to work.	Fine cold
	28/12/17		O.C. inspected work on M.G. dugouts. Work of excavation has been impeded by frost. Playing water. Trehemi. Half done. Pits & bonk slabs cut in by Section to POPERINGHE to get purchases for same. (unfin) R. STREET returned from leave. CRE has returned.	Thawing Cold
	29/12/17		No parties for work today. A few men only at work. O.C. being over at the Coy 421 Corps. O.C. held shoot during Chings. Coy (one attached) Infantry. Sent a few out of every one including attached Infantry. wiring in front of CORPS LINE. Also to do M.G. wiring. O.C. received to "do all S.N.N.L.D wiring" by Corps. One Section sent to RIDGE WOOD when to attach. Major's Coy were Section to LANGEMARCK STATION when in Stead + 2 Sections are working. O.C. for working reinforcement. M.G. Dugouts. Boche round iron re-inforcing - lewis gun service sent through into one-man turrets Bridge screw bars. Also sorting + tying into Two - man turrets to do anything for Trichet.	Officers visited Coy that am in the Coy Chts APPENDIX B
	30/12/17		Snow on ground & sheet of wire. 1 Coy or damage. Lt J. Donnan out with 1 Coy carrying + 1 Coy filling sandbags with concrete at site. 1b Steel Pickets each with 1 Coy. carrying wire near work.	Snow showers Cold
	29/12/17		O.C. & Lt Johnman visited 501 + 504 Heavers & inf. Coy's in Canal Bank 504 in own old bullet line - was quarterly 172 Ack erect Section in co'pisine -	Cold Cld
	25/12/17		O.C. to C.R.E. at various matters. Received O.R.E's movement orders to be released by 79th N.Z. Co. Wiring parties during am	Dull Cld

ARMENTIERES — The Coy to be relieved by 79th N.Z. Co.

WAR DIARY
INTELLIGENCE SUMMARY.
(Erase heading not required.)

Army Form C. 2118.

Place	Date	Hour	Summary of Events and Information	Remarks and references to Appendices
BOESINGHE B.28 B5.b.5.3	28/12/17	5.0 p.m.	2 Lieut Read leaving for Sub Army (or 2nd Army) School, FLIXECOURT. Recd 170 ½ Bell phones and Cable in parts. 2 A 30th, 31st & forming from 153 yrds & 172 yrds D.E. Party for consolidating Corps Line to work from 172 yrds D.E. did not report.	Cold R.A.F.
	30/12/17		OC with 2 Lieut Pearce wiring on CORPS LINE – 2 Lieut Inman on drainage & revetting. Bivouacs of Christmas greetings from Mayor of BATH. Received telegram of Christmas greetings from Mayor of BATH.	Cold Clo.
	31/12/17		Handed over papers &c to 79th Field Co. R.E. 2 Lieut Pearce finishing wire. Visit from C.R.E. by handing over & reporting in ARMENTIERES SECTOR. Sent chq for £9 to Somerset Voluntary Help Organisation Christmas no Gift in testimony of our appreciation of the gifts they have sent us. Every man contributed. Coy 6 hours at full establishment on all ranks.	Cld. Clo.

[signature]
COMMANDING 500ND
WESSEX FIELD Co R.E.

Appendix 'A'.

Return of Working Parties employed by 502(2/1)(WESSEX) FIELD Co.R.E. on 22-12-17.

Party.	Locality.	Nature of Work.
1 Coy. 2/5 L.N.L.R. (B. Party)	GRUITERZALE FARM. (U.16.b.6.7.)	Drainage.
1 Coy. 2/5 L.N.L.R. (A. Party)	CANNES FARM. (U.22.a.3.8.)	Drainage.
1 Coy. 2/4 L.N.L.R. (L. Party)	CORPS LINE	Wiring.
2 Coys. 2/4 L.N.L.R. (F. Party)	LANGEMARCK STATION to M.G. Dugouts, BROEMBEEK.	Filling and carrying sandbags. Felling material for concrete.
60 men Attached Infantry (173rd Brigade)	M.G. Dugouts. (U.17.b.2.7.) (U.17.c.8.7.)	Excavating.
15 men — ditto —	RAILWAY STREET.	Repair and maintenance.
15 men — ditto —	HUNTER STREET.	Repair and maintenance.

22/12/19.

Ch. H. M. Major
Commanding 502 (2/1) Field Coy. R.E.

COPY.

Appendix B

To the Officers, N.C.O's and Men of the 502nd. Wessex Field Co.R.E.

Christmas, 1917.

At the approach of Christmas my thoughts, never very long absent from my old Company, are more than usually with it.

At this, in years past, festive season, you are engaged in the strenuous work of active service, nevertheless it is my hope that it may be possible for you to obtain at any rate some small relaxation, and even enjoyment.   My best wishes are with you.

The Company has fulfilled my highest hopes by its action in the field, and the honours already received by Officers and Men will I am confident be followed by many other distinctions when opportunity presents itself.

May God protect you all.

              (sd)   W. JANE,   Major.

CONFIDENTIAL

WAR DIARY OF

502ND.(WESSEX) FIELD CO.R.E.

From 1st. January,1918 To 31st. January,1918.

(Volume 12)

C.H.M. Major.
Commanding 502nd.(Wessex) Field Co.R.E.

WAR DIARY
INTELLIGENCE SUMMARY.
(Erase heading not required.)

Army Form C. 2118.

Place	Date	Hour	Summary of Events and Information	Remarks and references to Appendices
BOESINGHE B5b 5.3 Sheet 28.	1/11/18	6.30 a.m.	Part of Transport left Camp for Horseline. 7.30 a.m. Sappers left. 4" Street 4 O.R. halted over to officer of right Sec. No complaint by him as to cleanliness of hut until subsequently when complaint sent to C.R.E.S. until subsequently when complaint sent to C.R.E. Sappers stopped at operation Horse-lines (DE WIPPE X ROADS) for ½ hr. also at INTERNATIONAL CORNER where 14 + 15 Canteen visited by all + cafe + tea bought. Reached PORTLAND CAMP 1.0.6 m. Found Camp occupied + were told to go to PUTNEY CAMP. Spent 2 hours on road trying to find this. When found, it was occupied also. Found some Hut to spent night in there. O.C. Lt. TROTMAN (Acting W.O) in a farm + meeting with 92nd Field Co. at PUTNEY. No sign of 170th Bde Group on road. Transport with Capt DAWSON LIEUTs PEARCE FLETCHER (just arrived from leave) + HEARD (Act O) left DE WIPPE X ROADS 10 a.m. + proceeded with 42 Coy. after much difficulty found billets in GODE AREA (THOLGODEWAERS-VELDE) at 9.30 p.m. Almost all the party spent the whole night getting wagons out of ditches. Finished this 6.30 a.m. Owing to Lorry sends Trestle wagon ditched twice. Pontoon Wagons 2 trestle carts each ditched once. 4.2.1 in worse plight + crew man's leg broken, sent for ambulance, reported it to 4.2.1 + an officer sent by him for 3 hours no officers from 4.2 arrived. Road were so bad wagons completely out of control slipping sideways into ditches, + animals had to be double traced up every incline, too Carts taking 12 mules each. Marching was also very bad, road rough hard + slippery. No cavalry this + march discipline fair.	C.R.E.S. operation APPENDIX A Fine very cold Ctd.

WAR DIARY or INTELLIGENCE SUMMARY

Army Form C. 2118.

Place	Date	Hour	Summary of Events and Information	Remarks and references to Appendices
PROVEN AREA 19/X.26.c.4.b	2/1/18		Sappers left Camp 8.30 a.m. Entrained at BAILLEUL 12.30 p.m. Reached LA HAYE FARM 3.30 p.m. Weather still cold to start with & very very bad at PROVEN. March described the poor. Men had a poor night & no hot pot to break fast. Transport arrived 3.0 p.m. and marched by 3km outside fair journey, one wagon ditched - finding Mule lines (this Coy) & OD lines) of LA HAYE empty, but billets for men. Showery for night occupied. Searched for new hut accommodation - no casualties.	Cold
LA HAYE B.26.B.2.6.	3/1/18		OC to ARMENTIERES. took over papers from OC 11th Australian & OC who has been in Ludo. 14 huts having perhaps 38½ sub RE. OC noticed that which are in JUTE FACTORY & one very roomy & two others. Men went up the line with Lieut. FLETCHER & PEARCE. Inspected works in hand. There appear to be 2 no RE S/100 in area. Sappers marched in new huts in silence as punishment for poor march discipline yesterday. All ranks very pleased with billets to have finished the move which has been a bad one & uncomfortable one. During fatigue at BOESINGHE Canton Dingley 450 finds as the men evacuated on coming into at BOESINGHE. Coy now 2 over Strength.	Cold fine Cold
ARMENTIERES Sht/36 B.29.b.5.2	4/1/18		Men at work - 2 Pearce on demolition of troops ERQUINGHEM "B" & PONT DE NIEPPE (Capt DAVISON swinging bridge (right) CE. & F AB STREET C. FLETCHER in line on Enquiry into the Prisonburg Branch Spain R. C.T.S. PG. OC arranged move to line near (ERQUINGHEM LAUNDRY) with 17th Bde CRE. Conference at Divn Engr Office. New network & district when & state of which they are much.	Cold Cold
	5/1/18		When ready to move learn that no room as expected by Bde. at ERQUINGHEM LAUNDRY. So must stay where we are - OC to cu CRE at STEENWERCK. re billeb reports. Capt DAVISON seeing APM ARMENTIERES re spiations in the town & struct orders a footing & Kindred offences APM issuing very strict orders (a looting & kindred offences) OC awarded MC (New Years Honours)	Cold Cold

WAR DIARY
INTELLIGENCE SUMMARY
(Erase heading not required.)

Army Form C. 2118.

Place	Date	Hour	Summary of Events and Information	Remarks and references to Appendices
ARMENTIERES 36/B 29.b.5.2	6/1/18	A.M.	OC with LIEUT PEARCE inspecting Emergency Routes which have been inspected - No 2 section repairing same.	
		2 P.M.	CRE's Conference at this Coy. HQ. Much new work required to maintain "5.9" proof accommodation for another Bn on the Divl Front. IN this Corps work in hand will be attacked first.	APPENDIX B
		10 P.M.	Practically no stores available yet. 38th Dud harry shawed all tempor Wire Sections of this Coy to work forward of R. LAIES for B.G.C. 170 I.Bde. other 2 sections refining R. LAIES. CRE'S Corp of Inf. to be permanently attached to this Coy. 1 Bath available for 170 Bde for work near R. LAIES. [strikethrough] Telegraphed Engr requisition. 3000 coils Barb wire required by 13 Bde. delivered	
		4 P.M.	OC attended 170 & 18 Bde. Conference. Work of Divl Coy - 13 Bde awaiting CRE's Bde Majors for details as to drawing R.E. Stores & Coys to be allotted for their carrying parties to this Coy. instructions. Received CRE's instruction No 3 re Bridges. Five officers in care of this Coy.	See CO's OR See CO's OR
	7/1/18		OC reconnoitred three jobs to be made shell proof. Called on A.P.14. M. PICOUT, Interpreter attached to us, & joins Officers Mess.	
	8/1/18		OC with Lieut PEARCE reconnoitred shell proof works to be constructed - very awkward snow jobs. also to Bde MQ.	[illegible] Cpl [illegible] Cpl
	9/1/18		OC attended Confce (C.R.E'S) at 505 b1441 (PONT DE NIEPPE) Sketch of pillbox shelters approved. also plans for dealing with LA ROLANDERIE + other works.	[illegible] Cpl.
	10/1/18		OC with Lieut STREET inspected Nos 1 & Sections work - Subway of PARK ROUTE L.20.a.c. Started R.Q.P. Coy HQ Site + Firestepping of PARK ROUTE, L.20.a.c. To Bde HQ with Capt DAVIDSON a mustard gas instructional general discussion with 12.E. re work Two forts in GALLOWGATE to be built by us also ROUEN BERTHA (I 20.d) BG wants new Bn. HQ in line.	[illegible] Cpl.

WAR DIARY

INTELLIGENCE SUMMARY

(Erase heading not required.)

Army Form C. 2118.

Instructions regarding War Diaries and Intelligence Summaries are contained in F. S. Regs., Part II. and the Staff Manual respectively. Title pages will be prepared in manuscript.

Place	Date	Hour	Summary of Events and Information	Remarks and references to Appendices
ARMENTIERES 36.B.29.652	11/4/18		OC with Lieut FLETCHER inspecting his job, & chose site for new B"HB. also visited SANDBAG CORNER (II d 5 in) + RUE FLEURIE FARM, saw OC Bn in RUE FLEURY SWITCH reviewing is erecting said wire, + proposed concrete Coy HQ at LA VESEE. also Bde Recce HQ at LA VESEE & visited we are working at. - Submitted to B.G.Q. 170th Bde scheme for Emp + Bn obtaining R.E. stores approved. Shored R.E. work for proposed Bn (with HQ in DECLAROUE FARM (I 14 a) supp mes 2 officers & 100 OR 2/5-K.O.R.L.R 2 officers & 100 OR "D"175/4/2/4 L.N.L.R Cpl called — Saw materials (only 4 lb shot on wheels) which we carry trench. He saw with - OC. Capt D review new Town Major if 60 ready for Major Lewin N.C.O. to enter premises in search of R.E. materials Lieut Duigenan 2/5- K.O.R.L.R. force OC fixed at Adv. HO Attached Inf "Officers au II Lieut Bilsborrow 2/4 L.N.L.R. Chief	showing
	12/4/18		OC car taking an ARMENTIERES found E very few found plenty in barber's saw found sofa rugs used. INGLES Bridge ready by 3rd Coy. still standing orders to move to PONT DE NIEPPE received. OC rode - Area Commandant force ERQUINGHEM sent Truth refill re Hammate at ERQUINGHEM. Capt DAWSON C.S.O. very may these days at R.E. omits into. I was very daily available about from Bde Transport	
	13/4/18			

Army Form C. 2118.

WAR DIARY
INTELLIGENCE SUMMARY.
(Erase heading not required.)

Instructions regarding War Diaries and Intelligence Summaries are contained in F. S. Regs., Part II. and the Staff Manual respectively. Title pages will be prepared in manuscript.

Place	Date	Hour	Summary of Events and Information	Remarks and references to Appendices
PONT DE NIEPPE	14/1/18		ORx Moved to this place today, billeted in empty houses; rained hard overnight & houses proved leaky	
36.D.23.a.8.5.45	15/1/18		O.C. took party to ARMENTIERES to salve old iron, then visited jobs behind. Subsidiary Line. Sections at work. A/Cpl W.F. WITHERS Y/c & 3 wagons wounded slightly in CHAPELLE D'ARMENTIERES, also 2 animals. He showed considerable pluck & devotion passing 6 times through zone of fire bringing up transport, & was wounded on last journey. 4 or 5 men of platoon on obstructions Coy. Distance from this billet to line is 4 to 5 miles & no men & horses in view of this arranged to move these sections forward; today Lieut FLETCHER & STREET with No 3 & 4 Sections moved to LA ROLANDERIE FARM, A.H.C.5.3. Men in huts, for present at any rate.	
	16/4/18		O.C. to Secure Support Subsidiary Line inspecting works, remains required, seeing Coy. Qm. stores & channing trenches. To LA ROLANDERIE & to No 2 Sections work intended billet. Received attached letter from Service Col. Help Adv.4 C.	O. Wet Ch'd APPENDIX C.
	17/1/18		Lt PEARCE & Section move to farm at H.5.C.2.7. where he is working. Found the place very wet, but made it all right. O.C. to C.R.E. STEENWERCK re	

WAR DIARY
INTELLIGENCE SUMMARY
(Erase heading not required.)

Army Form C. 2118.

Place	Date	Hour	Summary of Events and Information	Remarks and references to Appendices
PONT DE NIEPPE 36 B.23.a 85 45	17/4/18 (Cont⁴)		method of construction, reinforcement, also a shortage of materials & additional working party of 1½ Coys to be found by Res've Bde. 2nd R.W.K. to Bde in reserve to inspect & send for help in repairs of posts, & drainage of trenches. Owing to post following by heavy rains sides of all trenches crumbling on to duckboards, & low lying trenches full of water - Bns in line have done no work in drainage under such conditions, or clearing trenches, or water by Bde, although attention often drawn to necessity of this by Bn toys officers. Garrison of EVELYN POST recently captured & complete by Boche, so Bde are anxious at wiring of posts & covers of posts. 2nd L.N.L. Regt report a lot of wiring done by them, but probably this is party "eye wash" - B-G. Gregsberg ill with lumbago - He's afraid of trench feet, so relays fatiguing parties every three days.	Strong artillery duel
	18/4/18		OC + 2/W FLETCHER-STREET allowed Conf'ce at Bn HQ in line & arranged for parties with R.E. Assistance to repair ADA POST, WILLOWAYS, & COWGATE AVE. OC trench by LA ROLANDERIE & Bde HQ sectories at LA R gradually making themselves comfortable.	free etc

WAR DIARY
INTELLIGENCE SUMMARY
(Erase heading not required.)

Army Form C. 2118.

Place	Date	Hour	Summary of Events and Information	Remarks and references to Appendices
PONT DE NIEPPE 36.D.23.a.6.5.	19/1/18		Capt. DAVISON left for 3 weeks course at BLANDECQUE & O.C. 1st Coy. in command during his days. Has done good work lately in organizing transport, materials, hauling parks etc. O.C. visited all works in hand. Bde H.Q. Dined with G.O.C. Div?	Snowing hard
	20/1/18		Lieut TROTMAN returned from leave. O.C. 1st Coy 1st. T to Sand-hopper & dumps & T'd jobs. O.C. to LA ROLANDERIE where excavation being filled & to ERQUINGHEM dump. Materials very short owing to floods having covered all gravel & surrounded so newly arrived sandbags. also owing to the restrictions preventing motor lorries bringing stores. All Emergency Routes supplied. OC inspected box in line which we have put in over - GALLONSGATE trench neglected at present for lack of proper efficiency of other work - Work on Bde HQrs very slow for lack of labour. Kept moving parties arranged But? Material about Huns mounting of trenches Inc? mounting of to ARMENTIÈRES	absent
	22/1/18		Cont'd A.P.T. to ERQUINGHEM or tilting up tramps for "Foot Drill". OC with ORE CAPT.ALASTON (G.H.Q.2) along tram cut electrifying positions for Subway - Line with tram cross cut visit a "Surprise" line of defense.	Interview Etc

WAR DIARY / INTELLIGENCE SUMMARY

Army Form C. 2118.

Place	Date	Hour	Summary of Events and Information	Remarks and references to Appendices
PONT DE NIEPPE 36.B.23.a 65°45′	22/1/18	(cont'd)	by cutting firesteps & hiding up on sausage for 2 Coys front floorboards laying 1 ft earth off bank onto duckboard. Otherwise trench in good order. It is remarkably hidden along whole length from direct observation, but F.O. of Bn. is poor. OC attached Coys of Bn. H.Q. (we attached) Bn. main centre so to get moremen to work were able to arrange for 2 Coys nightly on telegraphs wire across & without opening fire.	APPENDIX D
	23/1/18		OC working with 5 Bde Bombing Div. HQ. re working parties — Others Staff Officers working on trains with a/cmdg their own men & some form working parties. Lieut. STREET & TROTMAN sick so far 2 Coys with individual charges which is attracting many men. Trying to dred milk powder @ £4 & 70. on to aircover'd. Suits & rain water in all wells. A good deal of sickness generally. Have to take care of sick O.C.Bs. who are not available to live. Starting a sick bay & a dry loft floor —	
	24/1/18		OC attend Coles (rifles) at RUE SADI CARNOT (cnr rd billets)	

WAR DIARY

INTELLIGENCE SUMMARY.

(Erase heading not required.)

Army Form C. 2118.

Instructions regarding War Diaries and Intelligence Summaries are contained in F. S. Regs., Part II. and the Staff Manual respectively. Title pages will be prepared in manuscript.

Place	Date	Hour	Summary of Events and Information	Remarks and references to Appendices
PONT DE NIEPPE 36B 23 a.85.45	24/1/18		Division taking in hand the detailing of Working Parties & work in the rear. Discussed this, also construction of reinforcement in M.G. dug outs etc.	
			O.C. twice to Bde. required the second drive by B'res for general talk.	
			Told him I am concentrating work in 2 shifts on Bn. Batt'n H.Q. in Subsid'y Line now Centre Coy. H.Q. second shift on Line - Right Coy. H.Q. Subsid'y Line + M.G. Dugout. COWGATE AVENUE. Approved	Fair Cold
			by him. He wants a new Emergency Route - "M.3".	
	25/1/18		O.C. to Line. M.G. Dugouts nearly excavated. Deep dug outs Subs'y Line near COWGATE AVENUE full of water to top - are installing PELAPONE 2½ H.P. pumping plant. Jobs at LA ROLANDERIE + SANDBAG CORNER (Bde Batt'n H.Q.) progressing satisfactorily	Fine Cold
ERQUINGHEM 26/1/18 H.8.6.9.2.			Coy. H.Q. moved to this billet also No.7 Section- very good billet. O.C. to SANDBAG CORNER + CROSS CUT showing Sergt. Stevens positions to be made defensible.	Fine Cold
	27/1/18		C.R.E.'s Conf. at H.21st H.Q. re work - All cement work except Bde Battle H.Q. to be stopped. No new trench work to be revetted but	

WAR DIARY
INTELLIGENCE SUMMARY
(Erase heading not required.)

Army Form C. 2118.

Place	Date	Hour	Summary of Events and Information	Remarks and references to Appendices
ERQUINGHEM Sh.36.S.6.9.2.	27/4/16	(Contd)	Trenches made 10/4 breed at tops 3/4 at bottom, sides with food slope & berms. O.C. to live & to Bde. where it was agreed to bring one Section (No.3) out of line owing to no concreting to be done. No 4. Section to be with Bde. for trench repairs.	
	28/4/16		Lieut. TROTMAN to Hospital Sick. Has been mainly off duty for 3 or 4 days with biliousness. O.C. the same with heavy cold & many N.C.O.'s with colds & rainheat. 12 men of the 100 attached Inf.y have gone to Hospital in as many days, and their sick parade still musters 6-12 daily. Only 3 Officers of this Coy now on parade, 2 men on Courses one dean, one sick. Have at last obtained Service of "Detenues" for furnishing fuel & rations. It was rather badly needed.	face Ord. face Ord. since Ord.
	29/4/16		Lieut FLETCHER & No 3 Section moved to this billet. O.P.S. called re work on cross cut wanting T. trenches organ. front of CROSS CUT. Also requiring Section's Remainderent at ARMENTIÈRES at east of R. Railway Bridge. ERQUINGHEM Bridge for possible use for orguila.	

WAR DIARY
INTELLIGENCE SUMMARY
(Erase heading not required.)

Army Form C. 2118.

Place	Date	Hour	Summary of Events and Information	Remarks and references to Appendices
ERQUINGHEM H.8.b.9.2.	28/1/18 (Cont')		C.R.E. Staffs Corps Comds wish another Bosch break out defences worked on & on behind our lines so as to make probable a big preliminary bombardment in case we suffer for use there. Sent us notice of his intention to CRE authorises the finishing of shellproof cover to me dug out B7.HR (Subsidiary) to Centre Coy H.Q. (Steenwerck perkin). CC to SANDBAG	five Coys
	29/1/18		CORNER + LA ROLANDERIE O.C. met C.R.E - D.A.Q.M.G. at JESUS FARM (B.26.d) + fixed site of new Baths to be erected there; thence to CROIX DUDAC where D.D.R. cood 2 dangerous points. In p.m. inspected old explosive magazine ARRIENTIERES. LA ROLANDERIE where Lieut PEARING %c in absence of Lieut PEARCE. A very westward job, pulling reinforced steels. 18" walls + 2" roof, inside CO 4 2/Prof Bynis. To C.R.E. re cross cut which was not going well. Corps Comm.r. recommends new series of strong points along cross cut	five Coys

Army Form C. 2118.

WAR DIARY
INTELLIGENCE SUMMARY.
(Erase heading not required.)

Instructions regarding War Diaries and Intelligence Summaries are contained in F. S. Regs., Part II. and the Staff Manual respectively. Title pages will be prepared in manuscript.

Place	Date	Hour	Summary of Events and Information	Remarks and references to Appendices
BROUNGHEM R.H. & H.Q. 2	31/1/18		OC to O.Z.OI.COT + SANDBAG CORNER. CO. XV Corps inspected latter. Asked how many rooms to be built. The cellars are so large 5 rooms could be made. OC Signals also there & call cinerium. returns. Too ty weather to necessitate postponement of concreting + stopping job at Bn HQ in line. Leave allotment increased to 4 n.c.'s per week from this Coy. Sections + cub cooking lots to go to ovens & become O.C. to every list with a view to giving N.C.O.'s married men sick men, or wayfoot Sappers earlier chance. Forage allowance reduced by 2 lbs per animal from 27/1/18. 10/5/1 Elf	

Ch.M.X MAJOR,
COMMANDING 500ᵗʰ
WESSEX FIELD Co. R.E.

APPENDIX A

SECRET.   Copy No. 2

57th DIVISION.

C.R.E's. OPERATION ORDER No. 14.

Map reference:-
HAZEBROUCK 5a, 1/100,000.   Headquarters, R.E.,
SHEET 20 S.W., 20 S.E., 28 N.E., 1/20,000.   29th December, 1917.

1. The 57th Divisional Engineers will be relieved by the 18th Divisional Engineers in the Forward Area as follows:-

   (a) The 421 Field Company R.E. will be replaced at CANAL BANK (B.6.c.8.2.) by the 80th Field Company R.E., on January 1st, 1918. The work being done in Line by the 421 Field Coy. R.E. will be taken over by the 92nd Field Company R.E. Advance Parties from this Company reporting to 421 Field Company R.E. on December 30th, 1917.

   (b) The 502 Field Company R.E. will be relieved by the 79th Field Company R.E. on January 1st, 1918.

   (c) The 505 Field Company R.E. will be replaced at HAMPTON CAMP (B.11.a.2.3.) by the 92nd Field Company R.E. on January 2nd, 1918. The work being done by the 505 Field Coy. R.E. will be taken over by the 80th Field Coy. R.E.

2. (a) The R.E. Personnel at BOESINGHE DUMP will be replaced by 18th Divisional R.E. on January 1st, 1918.

   (b) The 20 Other Ranks at BOESINGHE DUMP will rejoin their respective Units on night of December 30th, 1917.

3. (a) R.S.M. Cook, R.E., will be relieved at ONDANK R.E. DUMP on January 2nd, 1918.

   (b) The R.E. Personnel at ONDANK DUMP of 57th Divisional R.E. will rejoin their Units the day prior to the move of their respective Companies.

   (c) The 2 O.R. at ONDANK DUMP will rejoin their respective Units on night of December 30th, 1917.

4. (a) Movements in connection with the Relief will be carried out in accordance with attached March Table.

   (b) The attached Infantry will move with the Field Companies.

5. On Relief the 57th Divisional R.E. will be transferred to the 1st Anzac Corps.

6. Completion of Moves will be notified to this Office daily.

7. All Plans, Papers, etc., relating to the Sector will be handed over to the incoming Companies and receipts obtained.

8. C.R.E's Office will close at ELVERDINGHE CHATEAU 10 a.m. on January 3rd, 1918, and reopen at a place which will be notified later.

9. ACKNOWLEDGE.

Issued at 3 p.m.   Lieut.-Colonel,
                               C.R.E., 57th Division.

DISTRIBUTION:-

Copy No. 1 - O.C. 421 Field Company R.E.
       2 - O.C. 502   - do -
       3 - O.C. 505   - do -
       4 - C.R.E., 18th Division.
       5 - "G" 57th Div.
       6 - "A" & "Q" 57th Div.
       7 - 170th Infantry Brigade.
       8 - 171st   - do -
       9 - 172nd   - do -
      10 - 57th Divl. Sig. Coy.R.E.
      11 - 57th Div. Train.
      12 - R.S.M. Cook, R.E.
      13 - War Diary.
      14 -   -do-
      15 - File.
      16 - Spare.

MARCH TABLE ISSUED WITH C.R.E'S OPERATION ORDER NO. 14.

1. Serial No.	2. Date.	3. Unit.	4. From.	5. To.	6. Bus, Train, or Road.	7. Route.	8. Remarks.
1.	1st Jany. 1918.	421 Fld. Coy. with attached Infantry.	CANAL BANK.	GODE AREA.	Road.	To join the surplus transport of 170th Inf. Brigade and march with them under orders of G.O.C. 170th Inf. Brigade.	Billets in GODE AREA will be allotted by Staff Captain 170th Inf. Bde. 1 3 cwt lorry will report to carry surplus kit of attached Infty. Reach POPERINGHE Switch Rd. at 10.15 a.m.
2.	1st Jany. 1918.	502 Fld. Coy. Personnel.	BOESINGHE AREA.	PROOSDY AREA.	Road.	F.11.o. & d.	Clear INTERNATIONAL CORNER at 10.45 a.m.
3.	1st Jany. 1918.	502 Fld. Coy. Transport.	- do -	GODE AREA.	Road.	POPERINGHE SWITCH ROAD, ABEELE.	To join 170th Brigade surplus Transport at POPERINGHE Switch Rd, at 10.15 a.m.
4.	2nd Jany. 1918.	421 Fld. Coy. & Attd. Infantry.	GODE AREA.	LA HAYS AREA.	Road.	Via BAILLEUL.	Motor lorry to return to Unit on arrival at LA HAYS.
5.	2nd Jany. 1918.	502 Fld. Coy. Personnel.	PROOSDY AREA.	BAILLEUL WEST by train thence to LA HAYS by road.	Road, Rail, Road.		Entrain at PROVEN under Brigade arrangements. (Sufficient Camp kettles to be taken by Unit.)
6.	2nd Jany. 1918.	502 Fld. Coy. Transport.	GODE AREA.	LA HAYS.	Road.	BAILLEUL.	Move with 421 Fld. Coy. and surplus Transport 170 Bde.

1.

- 2 -

1. Serial No.	2. Date.	3. Unit.	4. From.	5. To.	6. Bus, Train or Road.	7. Route.	8. Remarks.
7.	2nd Jany. 1918.	505 Fld.Coy.& Attd.Infantry.	BOESINGHE AREA.	WESTOUTRE.	Road.	VLAMERTINGHE, OUDERDOM & RENINGHELST.	Billets to be obtained from Town Major. To arrive WESTOUTRE between 3 & 4 p.m. 13 cwt. motor lorry will report to carry surplus kit of attd.Infty. on Jany. 2nd & 3rd.
8.	3rd Jany. 1918.	505 Fld.Coy.& Attd.Infantry.	WESTOUTRE.	LA HAYS AREA.	Road.	LOKRE & RAILWAY.	
9.	3rd Jany. 1918.	421 Fld.Coy.with Attd.Infantry.	LA HAYS AREA.	To billets of 3rd Aust.Div. Fld.Coy. AFLENTIERES.	Road.	Any.	Application to be made to train Coy at STEENWERCK for G.S. wagons required to carry surplus kit of Attached Infantry with 505 and 421 Coys.
10.	3rd Jany. 1918.	502 Field Coy.	LA HAYS AREA.	- do -	Road.	Any.	
11.	4th Jany. 1918.	505 Field Coy. with /ttd. Infantry.	LA HAYS.	To billets of 3rd Aust.Div. R.E.	Road.	Any.	Orders with regard to Reliefs of Aust. Field Coys. will be issued later.

SECRET.   Copy No...... 2 ......

57th DIVISION.

C.R.E's. OPERATION ORDER No. 15.

Map reference:-
HAZEBROUCK 5a, 1/100,000.   Headquarters, R.E.,
SHEET 20 S.W., 20 S.E., 28 N.W., 1/20,000.   30th December, 1917.

1. On arrival in the 1st Anzac Corps Area, 57th Division will relieve 3rd Australian Division in Line.

2. The 57th Divisional Engineers will relieve the 3rd Australian Divisional Engineers.

   (a) The 421 Field Company R.E. relieving the 9th Australian Field Coy. R.E. on January 2nd, 1918.

   (b) The 502 Field Company R.E. relieving the 11th Australian Field Coy. R.E. on January 3rd, 1918.

3. Officers Commanding concerned will arrange details of take-over direct and will occupy billets vacated by outgoing Companies.

   All documents, plans, etc., relating to their Sector will be taken over.

4. Advance Parties consisting of 1 Officer, 2 N.C.O's. and 2 Sappers from the 421 and 502 Field Companies will proceed on January 1st, 1918, by cycles, reporting same day to 9th and 11th Australian Field Companies respectively.

5. The March Table issued with C.R.E's Operation Order No. 14, of 28th December, 1917, will be modified as attached.

6. MOVEMENTS BY TRAIN.

   (a) Two personnel and 1 transport train will be allotted to 170th Infantry Brigade on 2nd January.   Time Tables will be issued in due course.

   (b) Troops and Transport must be clear of trains within 30 minutes of arrival at destination.

7. MOVEMENT BY ROAD.

   (a) Transport moving by road of Brigade Groups going by train will march under orders of O.C. Affiliated Company of Divisional Train.

   (b) An Officer will be detailed to proceed in advance in sufficient time to arrange billets and horse lines.

8. The following minimum distances will be maintained between Units on the march :-

Between Companies	100 yards.
,, Unit & its Transport...	100 ,,
,, Battalions	500 ,,
,, Transport of Units when Brigaded	100 ,,

   In addition, vehicles of all kinds, whether mechanical or horse must leave gaps of 25 yards between each section of 6 vehicles, and 50 yards between columns to enable traffic to pass.

9. Columns of troops and transport will not be allowed to halt in the following sections of road :-
   (A) Roads in BAILLEUL.
   (B) BAILLEUL - LOCRE - ECHERPENBERG - LA GLYTTE - DICKSBUSCH - CAFE BELGE ROAD.
   (C) Roads through POPERINGHE.
   (D) POPERINGHE Switch Road.

10. ACKNOWLEDGE.

                                                        Alex Scott Campbell.
                                                           Lieut.-Colonel,
                                      C.R.E., 57th Division.

Issued at 8 a.m.

D I S T R I B U T I O N :-

Copy No. 1. - O.C. 421 Field Coy. R.E.
        2. - O.C. 502   - do -
        3. - O.C. 505   - do -
        4. - C.R.E., 18th Division. MO.RE.
        5. - "G" 57th Division.
        6. - "A" and "Q" 57th Division.
        7. - 170 Brigade.
        8. - 171 - do -
        9. - 172 - do -
       10. - 57th Divl. Signal Coy. R.E.
       11. - 57th Divl. Train.
       12. - R.S.M., Cook, R.E.
       13. - War Diary.
       14. -   - do -
       15. - File.
       16. - Spare.
       17. - C.R.E., 3rd Australian Division.

MARCH TABLE issued with C.R.E's. OPERATION ORDER No. 15.

1. Serial No.	2. Date.	3. Unit.	4. From.	5. To.	6. Bus, train or road.	7. Route.	8. Remarks.
4.	2nd Jany 1918.	421 Fld.Co.R.E. with Attd.Infty.	GODE AREA.	Billets in ARMENTIERES, Rue Sadi CARNOT, C.25.c.30.30. Transport LA HAYS, B.28.b.05.65.	Road.	BAILLEUL, NIEPPE.	To relieve 9th Australian Field Company R.E., in Left Sector. Motor lorry to return to D.S.C. at once.
5.	2nd Jany 1918.	502 Fld.Co.R.E. Personnel.	PROOSDY AREA.	To LA HAYS FARM, B.28.d.7.9.	Road, Rail, Road.	BAILLEUL, Pont de NIEPPE, les 3 Tilleuls.	Company to billet in LA HAYS FARM for the night.
6.	2nd Jany 1918.	502 Fld.Co.R.E. Transport.	GODE.	LA HAYS FARM AREA.	Road.	BAILLEUL, Pont de NIEPPE.	Horse Lines at B.28.b.3.7.
7.	2nd Jany 1918.	505 Fld.Co.R.E. & Attd.Infantry.	BOESINGHE AREA.	WESTOUTRE AREA.	Road.	RENINGHELST LA CLYTTE.	Billets will be at LA CLYTTE Sheet 28, M.12.d.3.4.
8.	3rd Jany 1918.	505 Fld.Co.R.E. & Attd.Infantry.	LA CLYTTE.	ARMENTIERES. to Billets.	Road.	LOCRE, BAILLEUL, NIEPPE.	Billets for Company and attached Infantry in BLUE BLIND Factory, ARMENTIERES, B.30.a.7.0. Horse Lines will be notified later. Motor lorry to return to D.S.C.
10.	3rd Jany 1918.	502 Fld.Co.R.E.	LA HAYS FARM, ARMENTIERES. Billets of 11th Aust. Field Co.R.E.		Road.	Any.	Billets in Jute Factory, ARMENTIERES, C.29.b.5.2. Horse Lines to remain at B.28.b.3.7.

503ND.(WESSEX) FIELD CO.R.E.

WORK IN HAND.

APPENDIX B

Job.	Nature of Work.	Locality.	Started.	Factor of Completion.	Sect.	Remarks.
1.	Bridge	ERQUINGHEM	Taken over.	100%	2	To be prepared for demolition. Stores for alternative method not complete.
	Pontoon Bridge.	R. LYS.	"		2	More stores required to complete.
	Pontoon Bridge.	R. LYS.	"		2	More stores required to complete.
	Bridge.	ARMENTIERES.	"		2	
	Culvert.	ERQUINGHEM.	"			
	Barrel Raft Bridge.	R. LYS.				
2.	ERQUINGHEM CHURCH.	ERQUINGHEM.	"		2	
3.	Bde. Battle H.Q.	LA ROLANDERIE FARM, H.11.c.			2	To be made 5.9 proof.
4.	Do.	BRASSERIE I.1.d.5.4.			1	do.
5.	Do.	Farm H.5.c.2.3.			2	Concrete (5.9 proof) shelters to be made.
6.	Rebuilding 3 dug-outs.	I.13.c.8.7.			2	To be made 5.9 proof.
7.	Strengthening Cellar.	Farm I.13.c.6.3.			2	To be made 5.9 proof.
8	Making concrete shelters.	RUE FLEURIE FARM. I.7.d.55.20.			1	do.
9.	Battn. H.Q.	DESOLANQUE FARM.		95%	3	To be strengthened.
10.	6" T.M. Emplacement.	LEITH WALK.	Taken over.		4	
11.	M.G. Dug-outs.	Subsidiary Line. I.14.d.7.9.			3	Priority. To be made 5.9 proof.
12.	Do.	BREASTWORK AVE. I.15.a.1.6.			4	To be made 5.9 proof.
13.	Do.	COWGATE AVE. I.9.c.5.0.			4	Priority. To be made 5.9 proof.
14.	Do.	Subsidiary Line. I.20.a.3.6.			3	To be made 5.9 proof.
15.	Coy. H.Q.	Orchard. I.15.c.7.6.	Taken over.		4	To be made 5.9 proof.
16	Left. Coy. H.Q.	Subsidiary Line. I.9.c.2.4.	"		4	do.

Job.	Nature of Work.	Locality.	Started.	Factor of completion.	Sect.	Remarks.
17.	Right Coy.H.Q.	Subsidiary Line.I.30.a.4.7.	Taken over.		3.	To be made 5.9 proof.
18.	R. A. P.	Subsidiary Line. I.14.b.7.8.	"		4	do.
19.	Coy.Cookhouse.	STURT AVE. I.30.b.9.5.	"		3.	To be made Rx splinter-proof.
20.	Do.	QUEEN ST. I.15.c.8.7.	"		3.	do.
21.	Screening.	ERQUINGHEM - ARMENTIERES Road.	"	70%	1.	
22.	Drainage.	Forward of River LAIES.	"		3 & 4.	
23.	Supervision of wiring.	Forward of River LAIES.	"		3 & 4.	Section Officers to keep in daily touch with Battn. & Coy.Condrs. & see & note on map what has actually been done.
24.	Roads.	Forward of River LAIES.	"		3 & 4.	Supervision & repair.
25.	Repair of Trenches.	GALLOWGATE TRENCH.			3.	Opening up old trench.
26	Do.	PARK ROW AVE.			3.	Cutting fire-steps.
27.	Do.	PARADISE ALLEY.			4.	Clearing trench.

B.M. 207.
23:1:1918.
HEADQUARTERS
170th INFANTRY BRIGADE

PROCEEDINGS OF A CONFERENCE HELD AT
BDE. H.Q. 22nd Jany. 1918.

APPENDIX "D"

Present — A/Bde. Major.
Lieut. Col. C.J. Gasson, M.C.
  "   "   C.L. Harford.
Major C. Fox, M.C.

The following points regarding the urgency and priority of work in the forward system were discussed and conclusions arrived at. The policy as outlined below will be adopted forthwith.

1. The work at present in hand on ADA POST is to be completed under the supervision of the R.E. Parties for this work will be found from the garrison of the subsidiary line.

2. (a) Owing to the limited number of men available and the large amount of work required to put WILLOW LANE in a decent state of repair, it was decided, at any rate for the present, to abandon the idea of draining this C.T., and instead an overland duckboard track is to be laid at once from the support line to ANNIE POST. This means of communication will be the only one used in future between the Support Line and ANNIE POST, until such time as WILLOW LANE is drained.

(b) The work in connection with the draining of the support line from WELLINGTON AVENUE to AGNES POST was to be commenced at once under R.E. supervision, parties being provided by the subsidiary line garrison, assisted by the garrison of AGNES POST whenever possible.

3. The draining of PARADISE ALLEY has already been taken in hand by the R.E. This is to be continued, parties for this purpose being found from the garrison of the subsidiary line assisted by the garrison of the posts in PARADISE ALLEY.

4. The wiring of ESME II to be completed, a triple apron to be put up in front of and on the flanks of this post, and also a belt of wire in rear of it. This to be done by the garrison of the post.

5. AUDREY II is at present in a very bad state of repair and needs almost complete reconstruction. This work will be undertaken by the R.E. Parties being provided by the Subsidiary Line garrison assisted by the garrison of the post itself. This is a most urgent matter and the work is to be commenced at once.

6. It was suggested that a belt of wire should be put up extending from EUNICE to EILEEN and from EILEEN to the wire in front of ESME II and thence a diagonal belt across the front to CYNTHIA. This work is to be commenced as soon as possible and steadily kept up by the garrison of subsidiary line.

7. The wire in front of the Second Support Line from COWGATE AVE: to LEITH WALK is very weak and requires a large amount of work on it to put the S.S.L. between these two C.Ts. in a state of defence. It was decided to construct 3 new aprons in front of this line. Work to be commenced as soon as possible and to be carried out by the Subsidiary Line garrison assisted whenever possible by garrison of posts in the S.S.L. in the area affected.

8. The wiring of the front and support line posts is almost complete. Work on wiring these posts is to be continued and completed by the respective garrisons. This should be finished shortly.

9. The drainage...

9. The drainage of CAROLINE I to be completed, and the new breastwork from COWGATE AVENUE to this post to be carried on with and a duckboard track laid.

10. On nights of relief the entire personnel of the battalion relieved less L.G.Sections will in future be available for work on the forward system, half under the R.E., and half for work under the Bn. Comdr. in the line. See Administrative Instruction No.... issued herewith.

B.H. Hamilton
Captain,
A/Brigade Major,
170th Infantry Brigade.

Copies to:-
    O.C.2/4th L.N.L.Regt.
        4/5th L.N.L.Regt.
        2nd Fld. Coy., R.E.
        2/5th King's Own (R.L.) Regt. (For information).
        2/5th L.N.L. Regt. -do-
    Staff Captain.

CONFIDENTIAL.

WAR DIARY

OF

502nd. (WESSEX) FIELD COMPANY R.E.

From February 1st. 1918   To- February 28th.1918.

(Volume 13.)

WAR DIARY
INTELLIGENCE SUMMARY
(Erase heading not required.)

Army Form C. 2118.

Instructions regarding War Diaries and Intelligence Summaries are contained in F. S. Regs., Part II. and the Staff Manual respectively. Title pages will be prepared in manuscript.

Place	Date	Hour	Summary of Events and Information	Remarks and references to Appendices
ERQUINGHEM 36 H 8 b 9.2	1/2/18		O.C. to SANDBAG CORNER & LA ROLANDERIE where work going well — hour DUIGENAN & BLISBOROW on drainage daily with 40 men from Bde. do. fed with own men. Newspapers in English, apparently stolen from Boche planes seen who titled, apparently last night, picked up by no - pany (a subsequent days) GAZETTE DES ARDENNES & CONTINENTAL TIMES " "	good 263
	4/2/18		O.C. to line crossed with a Co. 4/5 L.N.R. wire so wired by work of informed by two officers who do N. Sector trenches R.E. help over several difficult points. Sniping much the last thing but CONGAVE Saved after much difficulty with 6/2 p. inf. 1/5 L.N.R. wiring. Dew off difficult very uneventfully 1/3 M. Picart. — Interpreter left us on leave to CALAIS	
	6/2/18		O.C. to SANDBAG CORNER. C.R.E.'s Conference at 50s but Btdes held. Subject New Programme all this Brigade to line — Establishment of Bde. to us allowed to 3 battalions each. Broke arriving from 55th Div. (our first time) to make our fathers	

WAR DIARY

INTELLIGENCE SUMMARY

(Erase heading not required.)

Army Form C. 2118.

Place	Date	Hour	Summary of Events and Information	Remarks and references to Appendices
ERQUINGHEM H8 b 9.2	3/4/15		up to strength. So reduce total to 3 tooff to 2/5 South Lancs + 2/5 KLR being typhoid, + 2/5 LNLR received in Div.	
			Private Balfour (Lancs wounded) - Field Coys stand they are to have 100 attached Sap.rs temporarily. also 150 attached working parties. Later to billet with them, but Batlook to terminate. (clothing boy etc)	
		4/4/15	Church service held. A/S. L.N.L Band present.	SWL Cto sent'd
	5/4/15		Lieut TROTMAN arrived from Hospital. OC to works + Bde let Q Lieut STEAD returned from Course at FLIXECOURT. reports on engineering hours prs of open warfare. OC 1st KAROL N PERIE OC XV Corps apparently thinks MICH:D.S inclu in plans	
			(see above) + (a previous). It was adopted only after much criticism. OC saw GOC 170 Bde re attached	
			Brtish- 38 OR 2/5 KORLR leaving for this Unit + 33 OR 1/5 LNLR to take their place - 14 OR 2/4 LNLR bring this Corps attached Inf.y to 100 - 10 ftcen 1 HVT BRAMWELL + 50 OR 2/5 LNLR also attached	SWL C/D

WAR DIARY
INTELLIGENCE SUMMARY

(Erase heading not required.)

Army Form C. 2118.

Place	Date	Hour	Summary of Events and Information	Remarks and references to Appendices
ERQUINGHEM 36 H 8 b 9.2	6/2/18		O.C. with C.R.E. & Lieut Guppisberg who are fixing sites for small defensive posts on RUE FLEURIE SWITCH, near RUE ALLÉE, also Nr.9 post to fire over level crossing CHAPELLE D'ARMENTIÈRES.	fine cold
	7/2/18		Lieut STEAD acting 2/c of No.2 Section at LA ROLANDERIE, work going well. Lieut FLETCHER building baths at JESUS FARM. O.C. to LA ROL'IE & Bde HQ. II Lieuts. TASKER & PICKUP 2/5 L.N.L.R. (Pioneer Bn) with 2 Sergeants reported for instruction in R.E. work. Are going round jobs with my officers. Sergt RICHARDS, Cpl BONIFACE & 4 Sappers reported to 2/5 L.N.L.R. to help instruct them.	showery cold
	8/2/18		O.C. to R.E. school BLENDECQUES for 3 weeks course. Return of Capt Darrand to work.	wet coldish
	9/2/18		O.C. 151 Fields Coy R.E. (Major McLAUGHLIN) came down for short visit in relief of the Coy. by the 151. Capt Darrand until Major McLaughlin's own officer arrived of 25/6/8/? and to bring down accidents. Capt Darrand until O.C. 92nd Canadian 151 Fields Coy, arrived all the Journeys.	wet coldish met
	10/2/18		Job on NEZ MACQUART sector Company landing new work. Pill boxes, pumps & tunnels.	

WAR DIARY
INTELLIGENCE SUMMARY.
(Erase heading not required.)

Army Form C. 2118.

Place	Date	Hour	Summary of Events and Information	Remarks and references to Appendices
ERQUINGHEM 36 H.Q. S.9.2.	9/2/18		Worked. Work on huts started today in change of SALOP & RUE DU BOIS AVS.	
			C.R.E's Instructions orders to 16 records asking the name of this Coy. to ARMENTIÈRES, received	
			The next we the CRE XI Corps Troops, at a date to be notified later.	
	11/2/18 6.25pm		Capt Davies Adams by B.G.C 170th Brigade that Bde H.Q. were as far as that	
			it was necessary to save to large gun buildings adjoining the huts Coy. timber and	
			a further 15 mounts with saws picks, saws a gun cotton, but as amount	
			exists were not known. All Brigade officers had to have	
	9.30am		Capt. D asked a Lieut Hebdew with O.C. 151 Fields Coy. R.E. writes all to XI	
			Corps arch, hearing those by 151 Coy. Depot a clerk communications officer	
			but 3 hours of timber (the Corps Lewis) taken to the hopkeepers. The first of two of	
			The section is furthermore complete, a probably ask hours work will be needed.	
			taken by Welch Pioneers.	
			Lieut Green CRE XI Corps Troops, Capt Davies, Lorien Chris not get seen.	
			Lieut J. Stern to LAGORGUE, XI Corps Art. to where Lieut heupha, 151 Fields Coy	
			Lieut H. Gat-as to ARMENTIÈRES to take over from 151 Fields Coy.	
	13/2/18		Company moved into ARMENTIÈRES in accordance with attached HQ ORDERS fast.	

Army Form C. 2118.

WAR DIARY
—or—
INTELLIGENCE SUMMARY.
(Erase heading not required.)

Instructions regarding War Diaries and Intelligence Summaries are contained in F. S. Regs., Part II. and the Staff Manual respectively. Title pages will be prepared in manuscript.

Place	Date	Hour	Summary of Events and Information	Remarks and references to Appendices
ARMENTIERES 36.B.30.d.00.30	14/2/18		Capt D. Watts with 7 officers 9 other NCOs covering the works. Met CRE XI Corps Lieut Troops in worse to experience in that the 19th (Western) Pioneers would take over all trench work. One went to front covering 9 two M.G. shelter frontis Junior officers already plotted, all senior officers conversant with the work.	10 Jan 91
	15/2/18		Sections started work No 1 near shelter (H.12.a.00.50), No 2 near Corps CH.5.d.85.90), No 3 shelter at H.12.d.60.00, remainder of O defence support line. No 3 shelter, 7 O.R. shelter at H.12.d.60.00, remainder of O defence support line and walls.	L.i.a 95 7/2 Jan 91 Windigo fort 10 Jan 91
	16/2/18		Lieut Staub left for 1st Army Heavy Bridging course at A.I.P.E. Clerks reported to Section 2nd/Lt Martin. OC worked all month CRE XI Corps Troops, visited No 3 Sec (M.G. photo No 13–14) 9 appointment to work busy elsewhere.	Italy 23 Jan 91
	17/2/18		Lieut TASKER & PICKUP (2/5 L.N.L.) Pioneer Batt joined the 10 officers this must and returned to the Batt with their two arguants. Lieut SPENCER & ROBINSON, a two sergeant, a Cpl of the 2/4 M.T. Pioneer Batt reported for a few days as are multi-unit. They are making of camouflage as they are going to secrete another two officers and fill here to learn. Old Alpha Infantry Officers work the 2 Pioneer Officers started the work.	

Army Form C. 2118.

WAR DIARY
INTELLIGENCE SUMMARY.
(Erase heading not required.)

Place	Date	Hour	Summary of Events and Information	Remarks and references to Appendices
ARMENTIERES 36.B.30.d.00.30			under as the shells can now accommodate in comfort about 200 and are too many.	
			C.E. 1st Army wants work opening of road east of HOUPLINES (M.C. shelters 21-22) pushed on inclusive of the clearing of moat + glacis of ditches, i.e. until shells could open gliacie to enable to destroy the dug-out next to M.C. shelter 19.20	
	18/2/18		M.G. shelter 13.on. (Houplines) found to require concrete next to M.C. shelter 19.20 (No.3 section) We ought for several reasons engineering material & a balcony, but all this has to be made up. Other work still open to doubt, but until this seems to be working as has for place to start concrete work on this last railway embankment we could advance the	Hoplay 9 very clear p.g.W.F.1
	19/2/18		a right over to a favourable few look out to get the nearest of the concrete of necessary the shingle, the only undetected dub of these, could somewhere up to prevent damage to the ground two inches. Lieut. FLETCHER, wind 100 & 34H enters & LIEUT. BILLS 80.P.O. runs to-day No attached anything to disturbed concrete work as to 2-3 job, namely the right to leave an 8 hour off. Weather very favorable, only sowers. We were concrete to	Mainly response to M.J.W.J
	20/2/18	5.p.m	the carried about 500 & 80.p. Granville trench, but enough of this I hope to do the job is to learn. All the new has a sub-floor & needs starting in 35 hours. Granville concrete commenced at M.C. 19.20, practically in 35 hours. As today we very clear	

Army Form C. 2118.

WAR DIARY
INTELLIGENCE SUMMARY
(Erase heading not required.)

Instructions regarding War Diaries and Intelligence Summaries are contained in F.S. Regs., Part II. and the Staff Manual respectively. Title pages will be prepared in manuscript.

Place	Date	Hour	Summary of Events and Information	Remarks and references to Appendices
ARMENTIERES 36.B.30 & 00.30	20/2/18		AA. and Lewis AA plant 3 Lewis guns shoots to enemy aeroplanes. The 9th Essex drove in the outpost line.	True 9 elev.
	21/2/18		Nos 39H pigeons taking day off. No 2 section pigeons supposed have experimented & ready to start second line wire 9/OC wanted cattle.	p/w B/ there wpn 8/
	22/2/18		CRE VII Corps two so noted Coy H.Q. reference move were to be done two more fell. Lave to be made at H18 & 35.25 & H12 B 90.20 respectively (4 reasons) found Off 46.2 q.b. taking down camouflage ele. To section doing of Rd & stores CRE VII Corps wishes Co request south of 9/OC Reserve Ines wanted Reserve east the one at H 12 & 90.20 pushed into wood & to mouth of tramway. He hears 20 to 6 Job Records w/4 Bf. of Worcesters & wooden hang day off.	wet wpn 8/ nature to raw rang
	23/2/18		Visit of CRE 57 Div to C.R. HQ offices recommendations for reserve & Reserve Labyrinth's wants his three.	True wpn 8/
	24/2/18		Henceforward & reason line, 114 Inf Bde furnishes a working party, to construct dugouts & shelters starting returned 3 Lewis guns absent on ground, 9 left, already to be Localised and positions, which nearly for use.	
	25/2/18			

Army Form C. 2118.

WAR DIARY
INTELLIGENCE SUMMARY
(Erase heading not required.)

Place	Date	Hour	Summary of Events and Information	Remarks and references to Appendices
ARMENTIERES 36.B.20.c.00.30	29/2/18		Schools. Leaving of LIEUT TROTMAN & Lieut PERRINS for new military course at Eure	appx B]
			A/PE returning March 6.	
	26/2/18		Received order not to store up any extra material to be taken by us in any case in which chambers all round ready, as the 2/2nd & a Section of 502nd at the disposal of a/s Brigade to put on rails flares on the western front to effect work at RIVER LINES. a/Lieut King & Capt. Stretton.	appx B]
	27/2/18		Lieut Col GOC & CRE 38th Division, to 10th of Feb, that guests assigned meets the requirement of Feb. 20 and they are now in flight but up to 10.5 hrs no accurate information received around today start.	appx B]
	28/2/18		C/OC on orders with CRE II Corps Lieut FLETCHER allocated armoured prisoner a succession in getting to Grove Court. (No 4937.)	

O.D. Dansey Capt
502ND WESSEX FIELD Co. R.E.

502ND.(WESSEX) FIELD CO.R.E.

MOVE ORDERS.

1. The 502nd. Field Co.R.E. will be relieved by the 151st. Field Co.R.E. on 13.2.18.

2. The 502nd. Field Co.R.E. will relieve the 151st. Field Co.R.E. on 13.2.18 at B.30.d.0.3.

3. All moves to be complete by 12 noon on the 13th.

4. Section Limbers will report to Sections at LA ROLANDERIE, THE FARM and Coy.H.Q. not later than 12 noon on the 12th.

5. Section Officers will arrange their own moves, in accordance with attached march table, and will arrange for the ordering of their Section animals etc. direct with their mounted N.C.O's.

6. A pontoon wagon will be available for kits etc. of Nos. 2 & 4 Sections, and will report to O. i/c No.2 Section at 8.30 a.m. on 13.2.18. It will move into ARMENTIERES with No.4 Section. Officers concerned will make their own arrangements re loading and unloading of same.

7. 1 pontoon wagon will be available for Nos. 1 & 3 Sections kits etc. and will report to O. i/c No.3 Section at 9 a.m. 13.2.18. It will move into ARMENTIERES with No.3 Section, Officers concerned making their own arrangements re loading and unloading of same.
   1 pontoon wagon will be available for H.Q. and Attached Infantry kits, and will report to C.S.M. at 9 a.m.

8. Lieut. J.Stead will report to Lieut. Morgan, 151st. Field Co.R.E., at XV. Corps Park, LA GORGUE, at 10 a.m. 12.2.18, and will take over work there.

9. Lieut. H.Trotman will proceed to 151st. Field Co.R.E. at B.30.d.0.3. with 1 N.C.O. on 12.2.18, and will act as Advance Officer.

10. Each Section Commander will detail 1 N.C.O. to report to Lieut. Trotman at B.30.d.0.3. at 9.30 a.m. 13.2.18. These N.C.O's will guide their respective Sections to Section Billets on arrival.
    In the case of Attached Infantry, 2 N.C.O's will be detailed as above.

11. Each Section Commander will render a certificate to O.C. by 6 p.m. that the billets vacated by him earlier in the day were clean etc. In cases where a relief takes place, a certificate signed by incoming unit will be attached.

12. Mounted Section will load up pontoon wagons on 12.2.18 by 10 a.m. and proceed to 151st. Field Co.R.E. Transport Lines at B.29.a.5.1. on arrival of 151st. Field Co.R.E. pontoons at our lines. This will be at about 11 a.m. Guard of 1 man for our pontoon stores will be found by mounted section, wagons off loaded at new lines, and returning to present lines.
    1 G.S. wagon will also report to C.Q.M.S.Stores at 10 a.m. on 12.2.18. This wagon, loaded with Q.M.Stores, will proceed to B.30.d.0.3. at 12 noon with an off loading party of 4 men to be provided by No.2 Section, and Sapper Best Sapper Best will remain at B.30.d.0.3. in charge of this stuff.

13. 1 G.S. wagon will remain with Mounted Section on 13.2.18, to move Mounted Section kit etc., and move of the Transport Lines will be complete by 12 noon 13.2.18.
    Sergt. Sloman will get into touch with Mounted Sergeant of 151st. Field Co.R.E. (B.29.a.5.1.) to arrange regulation of traffic along narrow road leading to "B" Bridge.

14. H.Q. G.S. wagon and Mess Cart will report to C.S.M. at Coy.H.Q. at 8.30 a.m. 13.2.18.

MOVE ORDERS - Sheet 2.

15. Nos. 1 & 3 Sections will detail 3 men each to report to C.S.M. at 8.90 a.m. 13.2.18.

16. Lieut. J.H.Fletcher, M.C., will act as Rear Guard Officer.

17. Transport must not be kept hanging about the streets of ARMENTIERES. Arrangements for off-loading must be made so that animals and surplus transport are returned to Horse Lines with as little delay as possible.

MARCH TABLE.

No.	Date.	Unit.	From.	To.	To arrive at.
1.	13th.Feb.	H.Q.Section & No.1 Sect.	RUE DORMOIRE	ARMENTIERES	11.00 a.m.
2.	" "	No.2 Section	THE FARM	"	11.15 a.m.
3.	" "	No.4 "	LA ROLANDERIE	"	11.30 a.m.
4.	" "	Attached Infantry.	RUE DORMOIRE	"	11.45 a.m.
5.	" "	No.3 Section	"	"	12.00 noon.

11.2.18.

Captain,
A/O.C. 502nd.(Wessex) Field Co.R.E.

Vol 14

— Confidential —

War Diary of

502 (Wessex) Field Coy. R.E.

From:- 1/3/18   To:- 31/3/18.

(Volume 14)

    C.W...
    MAJOR,
    COMMANDING 502ND
    WESSEX FIELD Co. R.E.

WAR DIARY or INTELLIGENCE SUMMARY

Army Form C. 2118.

Instructions regarding War Diaries and Intelligence Summaries are contained in F. S. Regs., Part II. and the Staff Manual respectively. Title pages will be prepared in manuscript.

(Erase heading not required.)

Place	Date	Hour	Summary of Events and Information	Remarks and references to Appendices
ARMENTIERES Sheet 36 B.30.d.00.30	1/3/18		OC returned from Leave. RE stores at BLENDECQUES. Capt Daniels attended works.	
	2/3/18		OC with Capt Daniels around works. Everything satisfactory. RE consolidated, together with 20 sappers & attached infantry.	
	3/3/18		No 1 & 2 sections days off. Capt Daniels around works. 2 estab the 6 H.G. abattis (H.12.S.90.20) done with OC 4/6 Battalion 38th Division.	
	4/3/18		Lieut Lines reported from 1st Army Bridging School. Lieut Toulmin Lyle as ordered to Leave D section to CAHIERS. No 3 & 4 sections day off. Every ability shown whenever in emergency fields. Reveille, but no work been up.	
	5/3/18		Visit of CPE XI Corps to Cap HQ. No 1 to 5 went to survey of the transference of operations. If the case of Major spoke to CPE 30th Division. The Company will continue to work under CPE Corps, but CPE 30th Division will be responsible for the latest movements. OC found out of the new programme appear satisfactory.	
	6/3/18		Capt Daniels moves around with HQ of HG abattis spent on arrangement for Leave. Lieut Lyle left OC left for leave to U.K. Lieut as inspectors from leave at AIRE.	
			To 1st Army Bridging School at AIRE.	

WAR DIARY or INTELLIGENCE SUMMARY

Army Form C. 2118.

Place	Date	Hour	Summary of Events and Information	Remarks and references to Appendices
ARMENTIÈRES Sheet 36 B.30 & 00.30	7/3/18		CRE 38th Divn. with Capt. Daniels & Lieut. Fletcher reconnoitred front line area of Corps Defence System and notes respecting his work. CRE forwarded to be arranged to on wire, and arrangements to make for R.E. sections with 3a Brigades up to to-day to discuss points with the enemy	stores Cos mortality vides C
	8/3/18		Every ability necessary, essentially. Detail the S.6. help necessary for a speedy discovery; the only enemy things go to casualties. Remembering by facts incurred must not interfere with to fronts work.	Vides C mortality vides C
	9/3/18		During posters E. of L'ARMÉE & at CROIX PRINCE HOUSE shelling of this S.6. no casualties. The huts so heavy overhead that they can not be resumed.	vide C
	10/3/18		Received intimation of death arrival of enemy bullets from 38th Divn. & to take steps for interview. S.66 was detailed by area to the different orders a new practices for great evacuation of Billets. Late reserve estimation 114 late to clean to North of river, as brigade was expected to attack. Did not do this but moved transport arising to be by groups to slaughter together mortality. Lieut. Bennett reported to Div. HqGroup & CRE to Batt. HQ & CRE IV Corps, Capt. Daniels attended March with GOC 38th Divn. He decided to move site of Hos. Mol. 50+ yards toward enemy, work stopped as thought he was dry.	three vide C
	11/3/18		And dug trench from KANDAHAR via Mill (A.55y) Wt. W.900/M.1672 350,000 4/17 Sch 52a. Forms C/2118/14	—

WAR DIARY / INTELLIGENCE SUMMARY

Army Form C. 2118.

Place	Date	Hour	Summary of Events and Information	Remarks and references to Appendices
ARMENTIERES Sheet 36 B30 d 00.30	12/3/18		(1) Having duties for some recruits from CRE 51st Div. Lieut D. Davies with Lieut Pearce inspected the 87th Field Coy RE at H2 S.6.10.90 with a view of having arrangements for the taking over of works in the following day.	
	13/3/18		Capt. Davies with Lieut Pearce to 87th Field Coy. Found that the Coy billets were not large and Coy grazed during the night, and that 17 mules & 1 horse were Lieut. Pearce went through the equipment, stores wagons and Cees of Jun. Cy Davies inspected lines & mules & came up with the 87th Field Coy, mules & saddlery today. Slept their billets today.	Lieut D Davies
	14/3/18		OC 87th Field Coy RE met Capt. D. Davies, mounted, mounted awards, being drawn by the Coy. Met CO 38th D.M.G. Bn No. 9 Rendezvous mentor of HQ Staff Lieut S. Stack transferred to special Ser. RE. left to join Lieut. was sent June 10/3/1915.	Lieut 13th Cy
	15/3/18		No. 508.361 Cpl T.H. Owens was billeted about 9 am whilst cycling down the road in front of GUNNER'S FARM, by a piece of shell which the lance A. Owens was by himself, casualty and not known until the afternoon, when a search party who went out to trace him in today he has been left at St Isle's billeting since we've been in the area.	Lieut J. H. Cy

Army Form C. 2118.

WAR DIARY
INTELLIGENCE SUMMARY.
(Erase heading not required.)

Instructions regarding War Diaries and Intelligence Summaries are contained in F. S. Regs., Part II. and the Staff Manual respectively. Title pages will be prepared in manuscript.

Place	Date	Hour	Summary of Events and Information	Remarks and references to Appendices
ARMENTIERES				
Sheet 36	16/3/18		No 1 section offerends to allot funds of Cpl Owen. Received orders	See above
B30d00.30			that move into dugouts indefinitely. Insufficient gas masks, came up	see Jun 81
			and further arrangements with our officer.	
	17/3/18		Capt Danvers to Nivelle to see CRE 57th Div. Nothing done to mount	see Jun 81
	18/3/18		Capt Danvers with CRE IV C.T. & G.SO.2 38th Div. in locations of Div. O.P's &c	
			No construction of concrete, after finishing M.G.E.s. Evacuation camouflaging No.5. Rain	
			jobs completed, although labor very seriously held up by gas. application for	see Jun 81
			lives made for 2 Guns to be removed until further permits.	
	19/3/18		Received orders to move no. 51 to relieve 87th Field Coy. Lieut. Fletcher coming	
			for making arrangements. Capt Danvers went up to	see Jun 81
			Lieut Fletcher to 87th Field Coy, billets H.13 c 60.90 to arrange re billets etc. Inclined to	
			arrangements unable for night to take place on. and all gas cleared up, usual	see Jun 81
			on leaving over.	
BAC ST MAUR	20/3/18		Coy moved in accordance with attached Sheet Order no.18. move complete by	APPENDIX A
Sheet 36				see Jun 81
H13 c 60.90			12 noon. although little up favourable time by attack expected in the near	see Jun 81
	21/3/18		Capt Danvers to IV Corps for orders Lieut Fletcher attended CRE's conference	

WAR DIARY
or
INTELLIGENCE SUMMARY

Army Form C. 2118.

Place	Date	Hour	Summary of Events and Information	Remarks and references to Appendices
BAC ST MAUR Sheet 36 H.13.C.6090			at CRE's office during Capt Dawson's absence. By attached numbers new sector. No3 outpost line wild brigade No.19H on main defences system. and No3 on rear work. Good till bombardment was a exception at 4am. to 11 am.	Front 2.7.19 S4
	22/3/18		Sive wire instructed as gas casualties, ing Sappers Legge & Watson 7. Milk. R. Smith E. & 2/o Jeffery R. Apparently these men were gassed away by each Morgl. accompanying Inspector.	time report 84
	24/3/18		Lieut Helder. Col Chambers & 1 OR. Left for t Dury School at WISCOUES. Bire his parties, 100 in number started working on Castle gas, employed in sectors of sappers of this Coy	work very cold
	24/3/18		Received instruction of cancellation of all leave. Men Egan & Townsend give leave to U.K. 3 OR going on leave to U.K. returned to unit from Reinforcement camp.	
	25/3/18		CRE calls re work. OC to Horn lines and HQo RE	True etc.
	26/3/18		OC to front system inspecting, Lieut Pearce's work, also to Sibuit Lui re "Strato" work. Lt Pearce & Sutton working on supporting HQo in line. During completion of posts behind Support line. Blowing up road junction RUE PETILLON	

WAR DIARY
INTELLIGENCE SUMMARY.

(Erase heading not required.)

Army Form C. 2118.

Place	Date	Hour	Summary of Events and Information	Remarks and references to Appendices
BAC ST MAUR H.13.c.6.9	26/3/18	(Cont.)	RUE DES FIEFS to form Tank obstacle. Lieuts Shiel & Bohrman with their Sections working on Subsid^y Line ("Battle Zone") which is composed of front line in fair order for 500 yds. a support line (unrevetted p.o.b. & trenches) + a reserve line only partially laid out. Spillwha- Ihner Section with 100 Inf^y working Party each, working on support line, mainly trenches & wire. 1st Sect beginning construction of new Battle Btn HQrs. Down 5-9" but dug out — Lieut J.N. Fincher arrived having been recalled from Inf^y Course at WISQUES, run STOMER- Has only been here 2 days—	sent C.Ros
	27/3/18		C.R.E. could u work— Have to concentrate on Subsid^y Line gone arrived WINDY POST- Burying & & o told of. on practising sweeping bridges C.S.M Rolfe with cadre took out men & other practising felling demolition charge ESTAIRES BRIDGE	
	28/3/18		O.C. with 1st Peace to Right Bn in Line - inspected No 2 Sections work & fires p.o.b. reports complete behind Support Line most broken at 12 midnight Peace blew 2 craters at junction of RUE DELVAS PETILLON	

Army Form C. 2118.

WAR DIARY
—or—
INTELLIGENCE SUMMARY.
(Erase heading not required.)

Instructions regarding War Diaries and Intelligence Summaries are contained in F. S. Regs., Part II. and the Staff Manual respectively. Title pages will be prepared in manuscript.

Place	Date	Hour	Summary of Events and Information	Remarks and references to Appendices
BAC ST MAUR H13 c 6.9	28/3/18 (cont)		One crack (100 lbs ammonal) 50' down, 12ft deep. Two Shurtmore&Co (charge) 50'x30'x10' deep. Charges were in holes 5' deep. The craters are to act as tank obstacles – HQ packing trial in case of sudden move.	wet Cht
	29/3/18		O.C. to Support Line (Subsect) Spoken with 1st 2nd Divisions. O.C. to 173rd Bde. re Dumps, Reserves. 1st Division went to St. Pol via Doulieu to be specialed. 1st Division returned. Specialed having left St. Pol.	fine Cht
	30/3/18		O.C. along river LYS to see Light Bridge being put across by Lt Burrell. Saw arc to carry Infy. in file & to act as Emergency Bridge, being shelved in N. Bank normally. Consist of cork rafts 15ft long. Received orders to move tomorrow. To hand over to 231 Field Co. R.E.	
	31/3/18		Left Billets at 12 noon. Stopped at SAILLY hill 3.30 pm. arriving via ESTAIRES & NEUF BERQUIN at a billet 2 miles west of ESTAIRES which we occupied on 15/11/14 – No billets available but found accepted there which is a very good one. Operator MacMathews June handed over to 231 Field Co. R.E. 40th Div.	APPENDIX B APPENDIX C

Copy of Army Standing orders attached.

C. A. Day
MAJOR,
COMMANDING 500th
WESSEX FIELD Co. R.E.

SECRET.

APPENDIX A

Copy No..........

57th DIVISION.

C.R.E's. OPERATION ORDER No. 18.

Map reference - Sheet 36 N.W.

1. The Field Companies R.E. of 57th Division, and attached Infantry, will relieve the Field Companies R.E., of 12th Division, and attached Infantry, on 20th March, 1918, as follows :-

57th Divn. Unit.		12th Divn. Unit.	Headquarters.	Horse Lines.
421 Coy.	relieves	70 Coy.	G.18.b.8.8.	G.18.b.8.8.
502 ,,	,,	87 ,,	H.13.c.60.90.	G.5.b.central.
505 ,,	,,	69 ,,	H.13.b.3.6.	G.10.b.9.5.

2. Field Companies 57th Division will come temporarily under the orders of C.R.E., 12th Division, till C.R.E., 57th Division takes over.

3. Officers concerned will arrange details direct, and will take over all work in hand, documents, plans, &c., relating to the same, together with all bridging schemes and demolition schemes.

4. Lists of all Area Stores and numbers of all Secret Maps taken over will be submitted, in duplicate, to this Office by 22nd instant.

5. O.C. 421 Field Company will hand over all gum boots received for work on LYS Line to O.C. 70th Field Company and receipt for same will be sent to this Office. O.C. 421 Field Company will send to this Office a statement showing number of barrows, tools, etc., taken over from 38th Division, number since drawn from Corps Park, and numbers actually handed over to O.C. 70th Field Company.

6. The relief of 421 Field Company R.E. by 70th Field Coy. R.E. will not take place until the afternoon of the 20th inst., so that work may be carried on as usual on the LYS Line.

7. **Main Divisional Dump.** (G.11.c.3.0.)

Personnel for this Dump will be as follows :-

H.Q.R.E.
- 9471, R.S.M. Cook, W.F. i/c Dump.
- 241864, Pte. Jones, S. Clerk. (2/5 K.O.R.L.R)
- 21842, ,, Jones, P. Painter. (2/7 K.L.R.)
- 203728, ,, Buckley, J. Carpenter. (- do -)
- 48303, ,, Morris, T. - do - (- do -)

421 Fd.Co.
- 430066, L/Cpl. Wood, H. Clerk.
- 430024, Sapper Bower, W.L. Painter.
- 430089, ,, Hughes, E. Fitter.
- 430187, ,, Simms, C. Tinsmith.
- 67097, ,, Sharp, W.D. Carpenter.
- ,, Riley, J. Signwriter.

502 Fd.Co.
- One Serjeant or Senior Corporal - Carpenter.
- 508368, L/Cpl. Cottrell, W. Checker.
- 508401, Sapper Littlejohn, A. Carpenter.
- 508034, ,, Hatcher, W.H. Sawyer.
- 508425, ,, Pearce, W.J.B. Signwriter.
- One Sapper Engine Driver (Oil).

SECRET.   APPENDIX B
                                                                Copy No. ...

57th DIVISION.

C.R.E's. OPERATION ORDER No. 19.

Map Reference:- Sheet 36 N.W. 1/20,000 and HAZEBROUCK 5A, 1/100,000.

1. (a) 57th Division (less Artillery) will be relieved by 40th Division (less Artillery) between 31st March and 2nd April.
    (b) On relief 57th Division (less Artillery) will leave XV Corps Area by train. Entrainment to begin on April 2nd.

2. (a) The Field Companies R.E. will be relieved on 31st March as follows :-

    502 Field Company, H.Q., H.13.c.6.9, Transport Lines G.5.b.central, By 231st Field Company, 40th Division, H.Q., at SAILLY.
    505 Field Company, H.Q., H.13.b.3.6, Transport Lines G.10.b.9.5, By 224th Field Company, H.Q., at RUE MONTIGNY.

    (b) 421 Field Company, H.Q., G.18.b.8.8., Transport Lines G.18.b.8.8, will move in accordance with attached March Table on April 1st, and will be prepared to hand over details of work to O.C. 229 Field Company, 40th Division, when latter arrives.

3. Details of Reliefs will be arranged direct between opposite numbers and 57th Divisional Field Companies will hand over all work in hand, all maps, air photos, plans, documents etc., of work in hand or proposed. All Demolition Schemes, Bridging Schemes, Defence Schemes, Trench and Area Stores, R.E. Material in R.E. Dump, etc. Receipts for all Trench and Area Stores handed over and also Receipts for all Secret Maps and other Secret Papers to be sent to this Office in duplicate by 4th inst April.

4. The Attached Infantry will rejoin their respective Brigades on 31st instant under arrangements made by C.R.E. with Brigades concerned.

5. (a) Attached Infantry and R.E. Personnel at the R.E. Dump will rejoin their Units on 31st instant, viz :-

    To 505 Field Company by 8.30 a.m.
       502   - do -   by 8.45 a.m.
       421   - do -   by 5.0 p.m.

    (b) L/Cpl. Cottrell and the 8 O.R. Attached Infantry of 502 Field Company at LA GORGUE will rejoin their respective Units on the 1st April in the ESTAIRES AREA. These men to take unexpended portion of that day and the following day's rations.

6. The 2 G.S. Wagons on loan from A.D.M.S., 57th Division will be collected from the Field Companies on the morning of 31st instant.

7. On Relief, the 502 and 505 Field Companies will be grouped with the 172 Infantry Brigade, and the 421 Field Company with the 171 Infantry Brigade.

8. (a) Moves in connection with and after Reliefs will be carried out in accordance with the attached March Table.
    (b) Orders concerning entrainment will be issued separately.

9. On the March the following intervals will be observed:-

    Between Companies — 500 yards.
        ,, Sections — 100 yards.

10. Completion of Moves, giving Map locations will be notified to this Office daily by wire.

11. C.R.E's. Office will close at CROIX DU BAC at 10.0 am. on 2nd April and reopen at a time and place to be notified later.

12. ACKNOWLEDGE.

Issued at 11 a.m.   *[signature]*   Capt. & Adjt.,
31.3.1918.   for C.R.E., 57th Division.

DISTRIBUTION:

Copy No. 1 - 57th Division "G".
        2 - 57th Division "A" & "Q".
        3 - O.C. 421 Field Coy., R.E.
        4 -   - do -
        5 - O.C., 502 Field Company R.E.
        6 -   - do -
        7 - O.C., 505 Field Company R.E.
        8 -   - do -
        9 - 171 Infantry Brigade.
       10 - 172   - do -
       11 - 231st Field Company R.E.
       12 - 224th Field Company R.E.
       13 - 229th Field Company R.E.
       14 - C.R.E., 40th Division.
       15 - C.R.E., XV Corps Troops.
       16 - C.E., XV Corps.
       17 - 57th Divisional Train.
       18 - 57th Div. Signals.
       19 - A.D.M.S., 57th Division.
       20 - D.A.D.V.S., 57th Division.
       21 - D.A.D.O.S., 57th Division.
       22 - R.S.M. Cook, R.E.
       23 - Area Commandant, ESTAIRES.
       24 - War Diary.
       25 -   - do -
       26 - File.
       27 - Spare.
       28 - Spare.

MARCH TABLE TO ACCOMPANY C.R.E's. OPERATION ORDER No. 19.

Serial No.	Date.	Unit.	From.	To.	Route.	Remarks.
1.	March 31st.	502 Field Co.R.E.	Coy. H.Qrs.	ESTAIRES AREA.	No Restrictions.	Not to enter ESTAIRES before 4 p.m. and to be clear of Cross Roads BAC ST MAUR by 2.30 p.m. An Advance Party to be sent forward to arrange for billets with Area Comdt. ESTAIRES.
2.	March 31st.	505 Field Co.R.E.	FORT ROMPU.	ESTAIRES AREA.	- do -	Not to enter ESTAIRES before 4 p.m. and to be clear of FORT ROMPU by 2.30 p.m. An Advance Party to be sent forward to arrange billets with Area Comdt. ESTAIRES.
3.	March 31st.	251 Field Co.R.E.	SAILLY.	H.13.c.6.9.	- do -	Advance Parties to be sent forward to H.Q. 502 Field Co.R.E.
4.	March 31st.	224 Field Co.R.E.	RUE MONTIGNY.	FORT ROMPU.	- do -	Advance Party to be sent forward to H.Q. 505 Field Company R.E.
5.	April 1st.	502 & 505 Fld. Coys. R.E.	ESTAIRES AREA.	HAVERSKERQUE AREA.	- do -	(a) To be clear of ESTAIRES by 12 noon. (b) To march under orders of 172 Inf. Bde.
6.	April 1st.	421 Field Co.R.E.	CROIX DU BAC.	ESTAIRES AREA.	CROIX DU BAC and thence North Of River LYS.	Billets to be arranged by 171 Infantry Brigade.

502nd Wessex Field Co. R.E. **APPENDIX C**

STANDING ORDERS. *by Major C[...]*

October 1917

1. PRELIMINARY REMARKS - VALUE OF PREPARATION.

   In all arms of the service at least 9/10ths of fighting consists of careful preparation, but this is exceptionally true of Sappers with their mass of technical tools, explosives and bridging materials.
   One arricle missing at the critical moment might cause failure of R.Es work and possibly the failure of an Army's operation. The absence of a detonator may let the enemy in at a vital point, the sickness of a horse or the rotten state of his harness, or a hole in a pontoon may prevent our Artillery establishing itself at a vital point on the far bank of a river.

2. GENERAL DUTIES OF OFFICERS AND N.C.Os.

   Every Officer and N.C.O will study, all the time, to:-
   (a) Keep the men in good condition, both mentally & physically.
   (b) Keep their technical equipment (including wagons & horses) ready for use.
   (c) Perfect all their men in the use of their technical equipment so that they can go into action confident that if they fail there will be someone else to carry on.

3. OFFICERS' WORK.

   The Officers' work is never finished. He must "think ahead" all the time. Constant forethought is essential. He will, thereby, ease his men, relieve himself of anxiety, improve the organisation of his Section avoid unneccessary risks and casualties, and double the work done by his Section. The practise of forethought appears often to be the chief characteristic of the Sapper Officer, and the lack of it is inexcusable.
   At the end of the day he has to go on thinking over details and nothing can be too small to escape his attention and action. But he must not do everything himself. Every N.C.O must take his share in the work, and it is the Officers' duty to see that he trains his N.C.Os to do their share.

4. PREPAREDNESS FOR ACTION.

   All ranks will bear in mind that the three objects to be aimed at are that all ranks should be :-
   (a) Able to fight at all moments.
   (b) Able to march.
   (c) Able to exist without further supplies for at least 24 hours.
   To secure the above three objects, Section Commanders and N.C.Os will carefully note the following paras.

5. ABILITY TO FIGHT AND TO WORK.

   In a Sapper this means :-
   (a) Rifle and bayonet in good order.
   (b) Ammunition sufficient.
   (c) Gas protectors in good order.
   (d) Tool carts fully equipped & horses & harness in good order.

6. ABILITY TO MARCH.

   This means that :-
   (1) Men's feet, socks and boots are good and kept good.
   (2) Men's bodies are hard and as clean as water available will permit.
   Note. A unit that does not shave is a unit that does not wash.

7. ABILITY TO EXIST.   This means that :-
   (1) Unexpended portion of provisions is carried.
   (2) Iron ration is carried.
   (3) Water bottles are filled at beginning of march and ½ full at end, with the Water cart full and not drawn on during the day.

8. BILLETS.   Billetting Party.

(a) The usual procedure is that on marching days a billetting party reports to the billetting Officer (usually a Staff Officer) at a place and hour named in orders.
(b) The party will usually consist of :-
   The Subaltern on duty on day of arrival in new billets,
   1 N.C.O.

The Subaltern will be responsible for finding from his N.C.O.:-
(1) The Officer he is to report to.
(2) The rendezvous.
(3) The hour.
(4) The route by which the Co. marches.
(5) The strength of the Company.

9. SELECTION OF BILLETS.

F.S.R.I.
Sec 51.   The staff Billeting Officer will either allot an area or certain buildings to the Company. The Subaltern will then select :-
(1) Quarters for each section.
(2) Quarters for Co. H.Q. (Close to C.Os Quarters.)
(3) C.Os Quarters.
(4) Park for wagons and horses, if possible together.
(5) Watering place for horses.
(6) Place for Guard Room.

N.B. (1) The Captain's Quarters should be with the C.O.
     (2) The Officers' Quarters should be with their Sections.
     (3) The C.Os Quarters must include his Office and the Officers' Mess if possible.
     (4) All details must be chalked on doors.

10. GUIDING TO BILLETS.

On completion of Section Billets the Sec. Subaltern will come back or send the N.C.O. back to meet and report to the C.O.

11. HOT WATER.

Arrangements should be made, if possible, for hot water for tea to be prepared by the time the Compant arrives.

12. MAPS.

The Subaltern will draw a rough map showing the disposal of the Co. and will meet the C.O. with it before the latter enters the area.

13. ARRIVAL IN BILLETS.

On the Co. arriving in camp, any Officer or N.C.O. already in the camp will report at once to the C.O.
   Before the Co. is dispersed to its quarters the C.O. will :-
(1) Fix and point out the parade ground and Alarm post to all ranks.
(2) Inform the C.S.M. of strength of Guard and Fire picket, time and place of Guard Parade and No. of Section for next duty.
(3) Inform Sec. Commanders of position of their respective billets.
(4) Fix hour for drawing rations.
(5) "   "   " foot and rifle inspection.
(6) Orders re water.
(7)   "   re bounds and lights.
(8) Any special orders.

14. SETTLING IN.

The Captain will then proceed to park horses and wagons: get under trees and hedges and avoid symmetry, if near enemy.
   Sec. Commanders will lead Sections to Section Quarters.
   Senior N.C.O. will lead Co.H.Q. to their quarters with Cooks cart and G.S.wagon.
   Orderly room Sergt and Pay Corpl. will set up Office.

14. SETTLING IN. (Continued)

Cooks will at once set to work to prepare tea for immediate consumption and to cook dinners.

Fatigue parties will prepare latrines and incinerators, if there is not time for the latter, a hole to bury refuss near cooks fire.

Fires should be lighted in places concealed from enemy's view and if possible from aeroplanes.

Each Sec.Commander will point out to all his men the position of his own billet, and will point out to his N.C.Os and cyclists the position of the Cos' Quarters.

" On occupying billets, Sec.Commanders, (Officer or N.C.O. as the case may be) will, within 2 hours of a Section being billeted, render a return to the Orderly Room stating number (if any) of Billet, Name of Owner, and number of men billeted."
) -C.O.382 (amended).

15. GIVING THE ALARM.

The Alarm Signal is a series of long and short blasts on the whistle.

16. ACTION ON ALARM.

(1) All ranks will put on equipment at once.
(2) Drivers will fall in under their N.C.Os and double to the Park, harness horses, hook in and stand by.
(3) Sec.Sappers will fall in under Sec.Sergtts who will tell off men for fatigues as ordered; remainder will double to Alarm Post.
(4) H.Q. Sappers and Cook Corpl. will report to Orderly Room and load G.S.Wagon & Cooks' Cart. Majors' and Captain's batmen and Officers' and N.C.Os Mess Cooks will load Mess Cart.

17. STATE OF PREPAREDNESS.

It is of the utmost importance that Troops should be prepared to move off at any time of the day or night, at the shortest possible notice.

The following orders must therefore be rigidly observed:-
(1) By night all men will sleep with their equipment, rifles, boots, puttees etc. next to them in such a position that they can be found and put on in the dark.
When in the presence of the enemy, men will sleep fully clothed with equipment loosened.
(2) Harness & saddlery will invariably be kept ready to put on the horses. After every feed nosebags etc will be placed by saddles.
(3) Wagons will be kept parked with everything that is not in actual use.
(4) Batmen will have their arms and ammunition ready at the place where they are working.
(5) Batmen will see that Officers' saddlery is complete and ready to put on.
(6) As marches may have to be started at a moments notice (as in the case of an alarm) it is essential that the state of preparedness as laid down above, should be carefully observed by all ranks.
It is only by paying the most careful attention to these details that Sec.Commanders cam expect to get their Sections off without leaving behind more pr less valuable stores.

18. BOUNDS, HOURS IN BILLETS, and LIGHTS OUT.

" No man may leave his billet, except on duty, without first ascertaining from C.S.M., or senior N.C.O. at the billet, what bounds have been fixed." - C.O.323.

Within the Co. Billeting area belts need not be worn but men must be properly dressed.
No man will be out of his billet after 9.0 pm without a pass.
Lights out - 9.30 pm.
All lights necessary after dark to be screened.

19.   ROUTINE IN BILLETS.

The following points will be attended to by Sec. Commanders, but are subject to Co. arrangements :-
(1) Overhaul war equipment and clothing and report deficiencies to Captain, in accordance with orders in force.
(2) Men to bathe and wash clothes.
(3) Horses to go out for walking exercise, to be generally trimmed up and grazed.
(4) Daily inspection of rifles, ammunition, smoke helmets, respirators and feet.
(5) When a Sec. is on detachment or in separate billets, the only personnel normally left in billets by day will be- 1 cook, 1 O.R. to act as sanitary man, guard etc, and 1 bayman.

20.   PAYMENTS.

No payments will be made for billets. A form is provided (A.B.397) and regulations are given in G.R.O.

21.   SECTIONS ON DUTY.

The Section on duty will provide :-
The Officer on duty.
The Guard.
Any fatigue parties required.

22.   MARCHING WITH DUE NOTICE.

When several hours notice is received the C.O. will inform the Capt. of hours of parade and marching off, and the latter is responsible for all arrangements.
These arrangements should be on the following principles, Z being the hour of marching off.

At Z. - 3h. 30m.   All ranks warned.

By Z.- 1h.   All packs will have been packed and will, with arms and equipment, bt piled by each section (except H.Q.) neatly in one of its Section billets, under guard of one man. Billets and neighbourhood of billets will have been cleaned up by each section, and billets vacated by men. Latrines and refuse pits filled in. Chalk marks removed from doors The Section on duty will also have done this for H.Q., billets, stables, and horse lines, Offices, Messes & Stores.

Between Z. - 1h, & Z - 30m.
Section Officers will inspect all their section billets, latrines, etc, and report to O.C. that billets are quite clean. Section on duty will also do this for H.Q. section billets, stables or horse lines, messes, offices, stores etc.

By Z - 30m.
All transport will be loaded, animals watered and fed, and hooked in, but with girths slack, and pack mules off loaded. Brakesmen and pack mule loaders standing by.

At Z. -30m.
Sappers (less pack mule loaders and brakesmen) resume arms and equipment etc.

At Z.- 20m.
Sappers parade ready to move off.(Co. parade).

At Z.
Move off. Pack mule loaders rejoining sections.

Longer warning than 3h 30m will be given if move is taking place in the dark and much loading of transport is required, or if a meal is provided before moving off.

23.   ORDER OF MARCH.

(a) Usually in ordinary Column of Route, No.1 Section leading, Co.H.Q. in rear.
(b) If the Sappers all march in front with all wagons in rear of Sections, Sec.Comr of No.1 Sec. marches behind No.2 Sappers,

23. Order of March (continued)

No.2 behind No.2 Section wagons, No.3 behind No.4 Sappers, No.4 behind No.4 Sec.wagons. The Capt. marches in rear of the column. All pack mules together immediately in rear of Sappers.

MARCH DISCIPLINE.

(1) A Unit that marches badly will arrive at its destination more tired and depressed than one which marches well. It will have more stragglers, will delay the march of other troops, and is as likely as not to cause the failure of an operation. On other words, a unit that marches badly is a bad unit and brings discredit on the Reg. or corps to which it belongs.

(2) The following are the chief points to be observed in actual marches. General instructions are contained in F.S.R. Part 1. page 40 et seq.

- i. Keep to the right of the road and leave plenty of room for traffic to pass on the left.
- ii. Never more than 4 men to march abreast, or 2 animals.
- iii. Keep close up.
- vi (4) Keep each section of fours properly dressed. Bad dressing is the chief cause of a column opening out on the match.
- v (5) Always march by the right unless otherwise ordered.
- vi (6) At halts, men to lie or sit down beside the road to the right and drop off their packs. Drivers to dismount, ease girths, and see to harness, wagon men to look over their wagons, before resting. All riding and led animals to be turned to face the centre of the road. Officers, N.C.Os and men are not to wander on the left of the road at halts.
- vii (7) Never block side roads at halts; close up sufficient men and wagons to leave an opening.
- viii (8) Section Commanders must march at the rear of their Section transport except as in 23(5). It is impossible to keep an eye on ones' command from in front.
- ix. Mounted Officers & N.C.Os. must not ride alongside the wagons or their men. Periodically they must ride down the column to check that they must not take longer than is necessary to put their vehicles in.
- x (9) On the march, halts are to be made always for 10 minutes at 10 minutes to every clock hour. Watches will be synchronised beforehand. At 11 minutes to the hour, all ranks will march to attention by order of the C.O.
At 10 minutes to the hour, the C.O. will blow a whistle once which means "Halt", Fall out by the side of the road, Packs Off Pack mule loaders will off load pack mules.
At two minutes to the hour pack mule loaders will load.
At 1 minute to the hour, the C.O. will blow a whistle once which means "Put on your packs and fall in"-at the slope". Fall in at the same spot where fell out, not closed up.
At the clock hour Section Commanders will step to the left of the column and signify to the C.O. that their sections are ready to move. The Capt. will do the same for the transport. A third whistle will then be blown, and the C.O. will give the order "By the right, quick march".
- (xi) Rifles and equipment are to be on the men always during marches, except that drivers of all vehicles will carry their rifles in clips provided. Wagon men of pontoon and trestle wagons will put their rifles on the wagons.
- (xii) If a Sec.Com. considers that the pace is too fast or too slow he will immediately send a cyclist to the head of the Co. to report to that effect.
- (xiii) Troops will always be marched to attention for 5 minutes before and after passing the Starting Point, and for at least 1 minute after each clock hour halt.
- (xiv) Smoking will not be allowed before the first clock hour halt, nor for the forst 15 minutes after each clock hour halt.

3. A man cannot march properly unless his boots are good and well repaired and fitted, his socks good and constantly washed, his feet washed at the end of the day's march.
Nor can he march properly if he is overloaded woth unauthor--ised articles of kit, or if his pack is nor properly put on.

4. Socks must be frequently washed. Feet must be washed at end of a day's march.

23.(contd)
5. Rifles must be slung when marching at ease; they are not to be carried with the butt in the air.
6. Pack mules to be off loaded at halts by 2 Sappers specially told off for the purpose from the section. These sappers at halts should automatically drop back and off-load panniers.

24. CYCLISTS.

Cyclists march in front of their Sections normally but until the Brigade Column is joined, will form advance guard as follows. When with Brigade Column, if units march at 500 yards interval, cyclists will form connecting files in similar order and distances. -

    Point 2 Cyclists of leading Section
      100 yards.
  Ad.Guard 2 Cyclists of leading Section
      100 yards.
    2 Cyclists of leading Section
      100 yards.
    Head of Company.

25. SICK ON MARCH.

Men falling out sick will remain on right hand side of road. They will be given a falling-out slip by the Section Commander.

The Orderly Room Sergt., marching in rear of G.S.Wagon, will check each mans' slip, and if he has not got one will give him one. At the end of the march he will hand a list of men who have not rejoined to the Capt.

All Officers giving a man a falling out slip will note in his book his name and time and place of falling out.

Men falling out will report themselves to the first F.A. that passes. A F.A. usually moves at the end of the column. After being attended to they will do their best to rejoin the Co. unless they are sent to hospital by the M.O. with the F.A.

      FALLING OUT SLIP

No...... Rank..... Name............

Unit.......   Cause (Sick, sore feet, etc.)..........

Place..........

Place to rejoin........

Time..........   Date..........

        (Signed)............

Officers should prepare a number of falling out slips as above.

26. UNFIT FOR MARCHING.

Officers will report early to Capt. names of any men unfit for marching, so that he may take steps to hand them over to F.A.

27. HORSES.

Officers will report at once to Capt. any sickness or injury to horses. The Capt. is in sole charge of the Vet. Chest and nothing will be taken from it without his permission.

28. POSTAL.

(1) The number of the Co., Brigade or Div. to which a man belongs must not be put at the head of his letters. It may, however, be placed in the body of the letter.
(2) Address. All ranks must warn their correspondents that their address is :- No. Rank... Name....
    502 Wessex Fd.Co.R.E. Brit. Ex. Force.
No other address must be given.

29. BOOKS TO BE CARRIED.

(a) All Officers will carry on them:-
 (i) The F.S.Pocket Book or Man. of Fd. Eng.
    The latter is the more useful in the trenches.
 (ii) A.B.153 (Fd Message & Sketch Bk) with envelopes (A.F.C.398)

(b) N.C.Os will carry a note book (A.B.153) and M.F.E. if in possession.

30. MAPS TO BE CARRIED.

(a) Officers and as many N.C.Os as possible will have the maps of the locality, Officers carrying two, one to be given to men detached from the Column for any reason.
The Cyclist N.C.O. must have a map.

31. PRESERVATION OF DOCUMENTS etc. FROM ENEMY.

(a) All ranks are forbidden to carry on them any map or document that contains information of use to the enemy when going into our front line area & especially when going into action.
All ranks are to destroy at once any envelope bearing their name and Unit as soon as received. Also postcards. Officers are to see that this order is carried out by constant inspections.
(b) All documents must be destriyed by fire.
(c) A messenger with a written message must destrot it if in danger of capture.
(d) All waste paper in the Office or drawing offices of the Co. must be destroyed daily by fire under the supervision of the C.Os clerk.

32. SECRECY AND SPYING.

(a) All ranks are warned to be constantly on the look-out for pleasant strangers anxious for information. It is often impos--sible to tell a German Spy from a BRITISHER, FRENCHMEN, or BELGIAN.
(b) The Germans have learned useful information from hearing our Officers talking in the trenches and in billets. Military matters must therefore not be discussed.
(c) When requested to give information by Telephone make sure of the identity of the speaker. If not certain tell him nothing.
(d) Look out for spies dressed as British or French Officers.
In the trenches regard all Officers with suspicion that do not belong to the Battalion with which you are working.

33. PUBLIC HOUSES.

ESTAMINETS & RESTAURANTS are out of bounds except between 12 noon and 2.0 pm and 6.0pm to 8.0pm, whereever the soldier may be.

34. HORSES & VEHICLES ON ROADS.

(a) N.C.Os or men in charge of horses or vehicles will never halt them outside an Estaminet, and will never leave them unattended by the roadside.
(b) Horses are never to be exercised on main roads or roads used by Supply Columns, or on streets through towns. On arrival in every new billet the Capt. will arrange roads for exercising horses.
(c) Animals, whether led, driven, or ridden, are not on any account to be trotted on the pavement.
(d) No other than the driver is to ride on any cart, wagon, or transport animal without a written order from an Officer.
                                                              -C.O.35.
(e) Horses & mules are to be bitted in cases where they have to be taken along main roads to or from water, and strict march discipline is to be enforced. Care is to be taken that the bits are removed when the animals are drinking.   - C.O.335.

35. CASUALTIES.   When on detachment duties all Officers or N.C.Os in charge of detachments are to report casualties to emn & horses to the C.O. in writing daily. If in action, at the end of the action.

36. SENTRIES.

(a) Occasionally, as after a long march or when fighting is in progress, it may be necessary to mount a sentry who is tired out. If so he must be relieved every hour.
Under ordinary circumstances, Section Commanders will see that men are not overworked before going on guard.

(b) It is essential that the N.C.O of the Guard should relieve every sentry personally. In cases of extreme fatigue 2 N.C.Os should be mounted in order to divide the relieving work between them.

(c) It is absolutely forbidden for a Sentry to call his relief; he must call the N.C.O. if necessary.

(d) The harder the previous day's work, the more necessary for visiting the Sentries on the Officer's part.

(e) Sentries in Trenches.
  (i) Sentries to be posted in pairs when attack is likely.
  (ii) Relief every hour.
  (iii) Constant inspection & supervision by Officer & N.C.O.

37. CLAIMS FOR DAMAGE.

Damage done by the Co. must be brought home to the persons or persons who did it and Sec. Comrs. and N.C.Os are to be constantly on the alert to prevent damage being done and to report offenders at once.

38. RANKS OF N.C.Os and PROMOTION.

(a) All N.C.Os must be given their substantive rank (with their acting or lance rank in brackets) in all returns rendered to the C.R.E.
Examples:—   Pioneer, (Lce-Cpl)   A.
            Sapper   (Lance Cpl Unpaid)   B.
            Sapper   (Lce Cpl & Acting 2nd Cpl)   C.
            2nd Cpl (Acting Corpl.)   D.

(b) Provisional rank will be similarly treated: e.g.
            2nd Corpl (Provl. Sergt.)   E.

(c) Acting rank carries pay of that rank; provisional rank does not, a man being given provisional rank to vest him with necessary authority for some particular work.

(d) Appointments and promotions by the O.C. are made subject to the provision of G.R.O.2373, according to which N.C.Os may be sent to the Unit from the Base. Such appointments or promotions being therefore liable to be cancelled.

(e) All N.C.Os must understand that promotion will not be made by seniority but by merit.

39. COMPANY DAILY ORDERS.

(a) The Capt or Orderly Room Sergt. is responsible for a copy of Co. Daily Orders being sent to each Section Commander, who is responsible for seeing that their N.C.Os and men know the contents.

(b) Nothing useful to the enemy will be put in Co. Daily Orders.

40. WATER.

(a) Washing in or close to the roadside ditches is prohibited as it fouls the water and renders it useless for watering horses.

(b) Sec. Commanders will arrange for water to be boiled or chlorinated before it is put in water bottles, unless otherwise notified.

41. GAS.

(a) Helmets & Respirators. All ranks will carry the Box Respirators slung over right shoulder; P.R. Helmet over left shoulder. A packet of spare respirators & helmets will be kept by Capt. as a reserve in G.S. Wagon.

(b) Alarm signal. Every Sec. Com. who goes into the trenches is responsible for knowing the nature of the Alarm and Signal for "Gas" and for telling it to all the men, especially the Sentry.

(c) Sleeping alone. He will never allow any of his men (nor will he himself) sleep alone.

41.   GAS. (Contd).

(d) Anti-Gas Precautions. After a Gas attack the N.C.O. or Senior Sapper in charge of any isolated party may give the order to remove Gas Helmets, in the absence of an Officer only when he has satisfied himself it is safe to do so. The N.C.O or senior sapper concerned must report to his Sec.Officer at the first opportunity, stating composition of his party, nature of Gas attack, and precautions taken to satisfy himself that it was safe to remove the Gas Helmets. -C.O.271.

42.   ABSENTEES & STRAGGLERS.

After 36 hours absence the name of absentee (with full description) will be sent to the A.P.M.
The A.P.M. will be at once informed if the man's return.

43.   SALVAGE.

All ammunition, arms, equipment etc. found by anyone is to be handed to the C.Q.M.S.
The Capt. will arrange for any salvage to be handed to Divl. Salvage Company.

44.   BATHS & CLEAN CLOTHES.

(a) When the Co. goes to the Divl Baths, the men's dirty underclothes will be exchanged there for clean underclothes, so that clean clothes need not be carried there.
(b) When the Co. is unable to go to the baths on the dates arranged the Capt. will indent on O.i/c Laundry for clean underclothing and will send transport to remove it.
An equivalent and similar number of soiled articles for replacing them (including unserviceable articles) will be sent by the Capt. within 48 hours.
(c) The Capt. will endeavour to arrange baths at convenient dates at the Baths, but this does not mean free Sec, Commanders of the responsibility of seeing that their men get hot baths at least once a week by Section arrangements.

45.   CAPTAIN'S RESPONSIBILITY.

The following illustrates the general distribution of the Captain's work and his Staff.
The Capt. is responsible that the work of each of his Staff is understood by at least one other N.C.O. of his Staff.

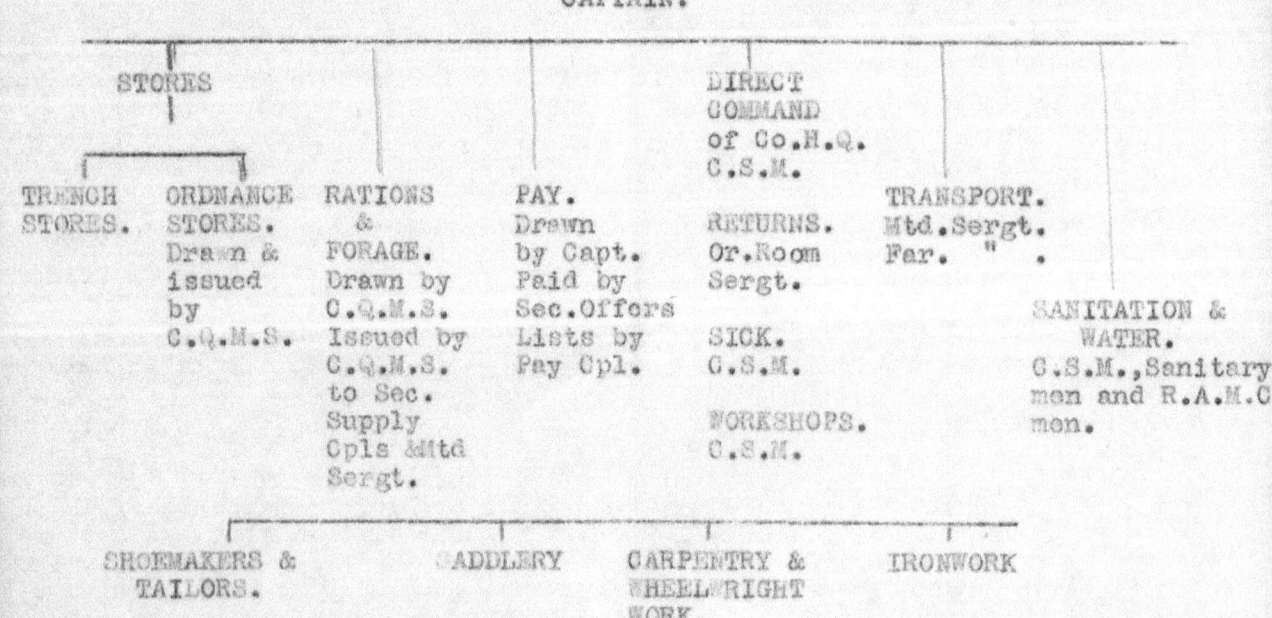

45. (Cont'd). Returns.

  (a) The Ord.Room Sergt is responsible for the compilation of all Returns in time for signature and despatch and for their despatch.
  (b) The Capt.(if not on detachment) is responsible for their accuracy.
  (c) If the Capt. thinks the O.C. will be unable to sign them in time for despatch he will sign them himself.

46.   CONCEALMENT OF MOVEMENTS IN THE FORWARD AREA.

  (a) Moving in Groups. Men moving in groups of 2 or 3 do not attract much attention, and if they do, it is usually not worth while opening fire on them. Larger bodies are easily seen and often shelled, consequently it is an order that no parties should move in larger groups than 5 men, with 50 yards between groups, and each group in file, with a few yards between the men.
  (b) Groups in Trenches. In the trench area men will not congregate when breaking off work for lunch. Never more than 4 Sappers should remain for this purpose in the same bay or arm of a trench or in the same spot.
  (c) Looking up. Men will not look up at aircraft.
  (d) Work in Front & Support Lines. When working in the front & support Lines by night, the Officer, N.C.O. or Sapper in charge of every party of men will see that one man at least is posted as a sentry, unless the work is being done within 10 yards of a Sentry Post or of another Sentry. Such Sentry, when posted must be relieved every 2 hours, and visited at least once in his spell by the Officer or O.R. in charge of the party.
  The Officer, N.C.O. or man in charge of a Working Party in front of the Support Line will invariably report before starting and after finishing work, to the Co.Com. in whose portion of the line they are at work. Neglect to do this involves the likelihood of being shot at from the Support Line.
  When at work forward of the Support Line, Sappers will invariably act as Infantry, and in the event of an attack will man the nearest Fire Bay or cover and offer a stout resistance to any attack.   - C.O.250.

47.   WORKING DRAWINGS.

  (a) Officers & N.C.Os will always be provided if possible, with a working drawing of the work they are on. If not they must make one. A copy of all sketches that are made by Officers, of work proposed, or in hand, should be submitted to the C.O.
  (b) When a Co. is relieved, working drawings will be handed over to the relieving Officer.
  (c) The Capt. is in charge of the work of preparing working drawings. The original will not be sent into the Field, but only tracings, and these must not show the general defences-only portions of them.
  (d) Plans- details of. All plans must contain:-
    (i) Heading.
    (ii) Magnetic North.
    (iii) Scale,-if not to scale it must be stated on plan.
    (iv) Signature and Date.
    (v) Descriptive remarks, which must not be written so as to confuse detail, but in the margin with a line & arrowhead
    (vi) Illustrative Sections, a Section Line being shewn on the plan and clearly marked 1,11,111 etc.

48.   ARMS & AMMUNITION.

  (a) Arms. N.C.Os and men proceeding on leave to the U.K. will take their rifles with them.
  (b) Ammunition. All ammunition will be collected before any man proceeding on leave is given his pass.

49.   CYCLES.

  (a) Sec.Officers will detail one N.C.O. to take charge of the Sec. bycycles. He will be personally responsible to the Sec.Officer

49. **Cycles. (Contd)**
that all his bicycles are clean and in good order, and that all deficiences can be accounted for. He must report at once if a bicycle is returned to him short of any accessory that was on it when issued.
- (b) Any Officer, N.C.O. or man using a Gov. bicycle, or other vehicle, is responsible for its safe custody, and if he has to leave it in the cause of his duty he is responsible that it is left in a safe place or under the care of a responsible person.

50. **DISCIPLINE.**

- (a) N.C.Os and men joining a detachment will immediately report on arrival to the Officer in charge; similarly N.C.Os and men joining H.Qs will report at once to the Co. Office. Sections moving will send in "marching-in" states". -C.O.375.
- (b) When a N.C.O. or man is on parade or on the works and is called for by name by an Officer, he will invariably fall out at the double. Officers will do the same if called by Senior Officers.
- (c) (i) It is the duty of every man to read Co. Daily Orders. Ignorance of Co. Orders will be no excuse for non-compliance.
    - (ii) When meeting an Officer or passing a Sentry on the road, NCOs & men marching with tools or marching at ease, will be given "Eyes Front" by the Senior N.C.O. who will then come to the slope, give "Eyes Right" or "Eyes Left" as the case may be, and himself salute.
    When in small parties without tools, of men alone, each man will slope arms and salute.
    When without arms, all N.C.Os and men will salute Officers.
    - (iii) When proceeding to work, parties consisting of more than 4 men will be marched there by the Senior N.C.O or man of the party.
    - (iv) When passing a sentry all ranks, if smoking, whether on duty or not, will remove pipe or cigarette and stop smoking, temporarily - C.O.221
- (d) **LOOTING.**
    - (i) On no account are troops to enter any unoccupied house or building other than their own or other billets or buildings used for military purposes.
    - (ii) Should occasion demand it, and troops are required to enter buildings which are not billets or used for military purposes they will do so only on receipt of a direct order from an Officer.
    - (iii) Property of Civilians, in any form, which is left behind in billets or buildings, hitherto occupied by civilians, is to be left untouched and on no account any articles of furniture or personal belongings to be removed on any conditions whatever. - C.O.280
- (e) **RIFLES & REVOLVERS.**
    - (i) No man is, on any account, to clean a rifle either outside or inside while there is a cartridge either in the chamber or the magazine. The bolt will, therefore be removed and the magazine detached before any cleaning takes place. (C.O.42)
    - (ii) Officers? N.C.Os and men will invariably empty the magazines of their revolvers and rifles before entering any building where they are billeted. - C.O.167.

51. **SPECIAL ORDER TO OFFICERS.**

- (a) Officers requisitioning gor articles to replace those lost by their Sections will invariably investigate the loss personally and state on the requisition if the articles in question were lost by neglect or lost owing to the exihencies of the service. All articles lost through lack of reasonable care & precaution will be replaced on repayment only. (No.11)
- (b) In normal cirstances only the Officers and Sergts should be needed for supervision. All N.C.Os should work with the Sappers and Pioneers. Work should be arranged for Section Clerks so that they are kept empoyed throughout the day. (No.26)
- (c) All Officers will make a note of any N.C.O. or man doing a good piece of work at the trade for which at he was enlisted, with a view to increasing his trade rating in the future. (No.27)

51. Special Orders to Officers. (Contd.)

    (d) Reports of reconnaissance, or of any work, report on which is asked for by C.R.E. or Brigade H.Q., will be rendered to this Office in duplicate. (No.28)

    (e) The Censor stamp impression will in future always be made on the top left hand corner of the envelope, to avoid obliteration by subsequent postmarks. (No.35)

    (f) Cards of recognition of bravery, or good service under difficult circumstances, are granted by the Division. In future, Officers will submit to the O.C., immediately after the service or work in question, the name of any man whom they consider worthy of a card. Full details, with names of witnesses, date & place etc., should also be rendered. Similarly with cases where Officers wish N.C.Os or men recommended for immediately honours. (No.39)

52. WORKING PARTIES.

    As some misunderstanding seems to exist, the following regulations as to the position of R.E. in charge of Working Parties must be followed:-

    Working Parties work for 4 hours only and it is up to the R.E. in charge to get the most work obtainable from them while they are on the job.

    When a N.C.O. or Sapper is in charge of a Working Party, however small, it is his duty to see that each man in the party has plenty of work allotted to him.

    As a rule any purely Sapper work is of secondary importance compared with the necessary supervision of the Infantry.

    Overcrowding must be avoided at all costs. It is not advisable to shift men about from place to place; rather, give each man a task that will last 4 hours, and that, when finished, will give him something to show for his labour.

    It is not an R.E. job to give orders to the Infantry to work harder - that is for the Infantry Officer or N.C.O i/c Working Party to do. It is our job and our interest to get the work done and if a party, or a man of the party, does not work well or has moved from the allotted task, it must be reported at once to the Infantry Officer or N.C.O. i/c Working Party. If the matter is not then put right, the R.E., N.C.O. or man i/c must report it at the first opportunity to any R.E.Officer or Senior N.C.O visiting the works, or on returning to Co.H.Q., to his Sec.Officer.

    The nature and the distribution of the work, and the giving to each man plenty of work to do, is essentially the work of the R.E. and this demands <u>constant personal attention,</u> that good work and much work can be obtained from any party. -C.O.308

53. PROGRESS.

    (a) The C.O. wishes to bring to notice points referring to this Co. commented on by Higher Authorities. The O.C. has been highly complimented on the good discipline and the good work of the Co. It was appreciated that all ranks work hard and steadily. At the same time it was considered that with the same amount of effort more valuable results could be achieved if less attention was paid to neatness and nicety and more to quickness of work. Strength of construction and rapidity of construction were the distinguishing features of the work of the R.E. of the original Ex. Force, and this Co. can follow no higher example. In future the ability of a N.C.O. or man to get work done strongly and rapidly will be taken largely into consideration in the appointment or promotion of N.C.Os. It should be kept always in mind that we are out here not only to work hard, but to work damned hard, as it is only by work that we shall beat the Bosche and end the War. C.O.223 dated 5-7-17

    (b) The O.C. wishes all ranks to know that their work in the field has given great satisfaction, not only to him, but also to the C.R.E. and the Brig.Gen.Commanding 170th Inf.Brig, from whom the O.C. has received expressions of keen appreciation. Arduous and often dangerous work has been carried out cheerfully and well by all

53. PROGRESS (Contd)

ranks, and we can look back on the past seven months in the knowledge that we have played our part to the best of our ability, and to the satisfaction of higher authority.

The Company has been on trial and has made good. Its achievements in France have established a tradition for doing good work of which it may well be proud. The O.C. is confident that every Officer, N.C.O and man of the Co. will see to it, by his utmost endeavours, that this tradition and reputation is maintained and enhanced by everything we undertake in the future. -C.O.322½

17.9.17.

(c) PROGRESS (Contd)

1. The O.C. is informed by the C.R.E. that Major-General F.W. Barnes was very pleased with the work of the Field Companies when in the Line recently.
2. The O.C. considers this Company can congratulate itself on its efforts there. He is proud of the determination and grit of all ranks to "carry on", and of their coolness under fire, which latter was particularly noticeable. Sappers supported their N.C.O's, and N.C.O's and Sappers supported their Officers loyally; one and all, in fact, pulled together splendidly. The Transport Section, no less than the Sappers, bore a large share of the risk and heavy work and helped materially in the Company's success.
3. The Company has been bound together closely in a severe trial by common hardship and sorrows. It will go into any future action more sure of itself and with each man more confident in his own and his comrades' ability to "stick it".
4. We read of other Divisions fighting, some of them throughout the year, in battles such as VIMY, MESSINES, PASSCHENDAELE and CAMBRAI, and of the glory and satisfaction in their achievements felt by the Allied Armies and by people at home.

Let us determine never to fail to "do our damnedest" whenever our chance comes. (C.O. 475 of 5.12.17.)

57th Divisional Engineers

WAR DIARY

502nd (Wessex) FIELD COMPANY R.E.

APRIL 1918

Vol 15

Confidential
War Diary
of
502 (Wessex) Field Coy R.E.

From:- 1/4/18   To 30/4/18.

(Volume 15)

C.h.M. MAJOR.
COMMANDING 502nd
WESSEX FIELD Co. R.E.

Army Form C. 2118.

WAR DIARY
~~INTELLIGENCE SUMMARY.~~
(Erase heading not required.)

Instructions regarding War Diaries and Intelligence Summaries are contained in F. S. Regs., Part II. and the Staff Manual respectively. Title pages will be prepared in manuscript.

Place	Date	Hour	Summary of Events and Information	Remarks and references to Appendices
ESTAIRES L32.6.7.6	1/4/16		Left Huts billet at 11.0 AM marched at Head of 172nd Inf. Bde Group to	APPENDIX A & B Bn' Entraining train 172nd Bde Group to
(HAZEBROUCK) inside 28-B-Coy			STEENBECQUE. Loaded pack on transport. Arrived 4 pm	28-B-Coy Ord
STEENBECQUE F.4.9.2	2/4/16		An easy day, cleaning up. inspection o.c. Read Mn Coy, G.O.C's letter re the Bn & more Ch.r.	more Chr.
	3/4/16	6.30 AM	Left STEENBECQUE Station; Arrived DOULLENS 12.30 AM. left Station 3 PM	Showing Ch.r
(Shell LENS. W.) WARLUZEL 4.F.6.6	4/4/16		Arrived WARLUZEL 6.30 PM. Good march discipline kept, + men cheery. C.R.E. called. Inhabitants very truculent & grumpy. Had to change billets	
	5/4/16		of 2 Sections. Day spent in cleaning up kit, harness &c. CAPT O'KRYGER 2/Lt ORR Showers (attached to coy for to any instruction to Stoff Course) Shy	Showers Ch.r
			Drew money at AVESNE LE COMTE. Paid men. Sections shortbouts inn kit + inspection by Section officers. Coy hrs to be ready between 8 oAM + 12 noon	
			to move at one hours notice after that at 3 hours notice: Hrs to daily	Snow Ch.r
	6/4/16		Shortroute march - Sections at drill. Hrs to r lectures, explosives &c in A.M.	
			Football in p.m. C.R.S called	
	7/4/15		Knill, o.c.no 4 platoon - abv lecture to officers & N.C.O.s on outpost defence by Lt	
			BURRELL O.C. with Lieut B & Capt. NOORKNYR (attached to Instruction)	
			2/Lt KORLR working out tactical scheme for afternoon which was cancelled	wet in p.m
			later owing to rain	C.A.Inn

Army Form C. 2118.

WAR DIARY
INTELLIGENCE SUMMARY.
(Erase heading not required.)

Instructions regarding War Diaries and Intelligence
Summaries are contained in F. S. Regs., Part II.
and the Staff Manual respectively. Title pages
will be prepared in manuscript.

Place	Date	Hour	Summary of Events and Information	Remarks and references to Appendices
(LENS II.) WARLUZEL 4.F.6.6.	9/4/18		Left this place at 2.0 p.m. Good march discipline to MONDICOURT. Moved into 170 Bde operation area.	Wet Ch.1
MONDICOURT 54.F.6.1.			Distance 5 miles.	APPENDIX "C" 170 Bde operation order
	9/4/18		Left here 10.0 A.M. Good march discipline. 9 1/2 miles to AMPLIER. Marches recently have been made easier for men by packs or blankets being carried on toolcarts + meascart. All surplus kit gear cut down to a minimum so mules (horses are doing work easily. Very little extra to establishment carried, and our establishment (meascart) to do it. Horse lines at AMPLIER a quagmire approached by very steep heavy road.	sorry APPENDIX "E" cby 3 Ch1 (Bde of any)
AMPLIER 5.E.7.6.	10/4/18		Moved to HALLOY on 170 Bde orders - O.C.(all) on Bde HQ.	Cby 3 Ch1
HALLOY 5.F.1.8.	11/4/18		Mill + mules try in A.M. Fixed up baths blacks + Coybathed in P.M. O.C.called on Bde H.Q. Saw AAQMG. re toothbrushes as we have none. On your holding mules ready to move at 2 hours notice.	fine cht Fine cht
	12/4/18		Moved to SUS ST LEGER in P.M. Marches past Coc Div. r 19 G.C. 170 Bde.	Fine Ch1
SUS ST LEGER 4.F.2.8	13/4/18		Good billets. Bde group ordered to PAS. Moved in P.M. Very bad march held up & stopping constantly. On arrival at PAS ordered on to AUTHIE. Arrived there 9.30 P.M. Bivouacked in wood. rained all night.	cold Ch1

Army Form C. 2118.

WAR DIARY
INTELLIGENCE SUMMARY
(Erase heading not required.)

Place	Date	Hour	Summary of Events and Information	Remarks and references to Appendices
(57) d. I.440 ovo) AUTHIE I.10.a.9.3.	14/4/18		Spent day in fixing up Camp, cleaning harness & chewits tents for Coy. O.C. twice to C.R.E. in P.A.S. re work to be done on RED LINE	Saturday Cht
	15/4/18		Coy marched to SOUASTRE. The three Field Coys supervised work by 170 & Inf Bde on RED LINE. ½ N.L. + 1 Coy of Pioneer Bn (2/5 N.L.) dug about one mile of trench for us. Good work. Work done for Corps minus direction of LtCol Neville R.E. O.C. Capt Dawson to P.A.S. to see C.R.E. re move & work tomorrow.	Shgnnry Cht
	16/4/18		Moved to near SAILLY-AU-BOIS. Took over Camp on side of chalk hill from 439 Field Coy (42nd Divn) O.C. reconnoitred work. Met O.C. 2/5 K.O.R.L.R. 2.O.C. 2/4 W. + C.R.E. re work required. In P.M. officers + men reconnoitred taped out work for Bde next day – Enlarging posts in front line	Dull Cht
SAILLY-AU- BOIS J.16 & 8. S.	17/4/18		2/5 K.O.R.L.R. + Pioneer Bn working on right of Bde line under O.C. Renwick. ½ N.L. and shortage of tools. Fair progress considering weather. Work to 4/15 L.N.L.R working under me. on the PURPLE SWITCH running from S.W. of SAILLY-AU-BOIS North to CHATEAU DE LA HAYE thence Northwards a mile. Total length of line over 3 miles.	Cold Cht

WAR DIARY
INTELLIGENCE SUMMARY

(Erase heading not required.)

Army Form C. 2118.

Place	Date	Hour	Summary of Events and Information	Remarks and references to Appendices
SAILLY-AU- BOIS J.16.d.8.5.	18/4/18		Bde not working, reconnoitring new dispositions as 2 Corps & 172 Bde are to take over line N. of CHAT^u DE LA HAYE & 170 Bde take over charge of line W. of SAILLY-AU-BOIS. Sappers completing previous days work & continuing own work for next day.	Wet & cold
	19/4/18		Work and distribution of Inf^y hindered by Prussians starting work in part of our line. This was soon profuse. Coy moved in evening (with transport) to CHATEAU grounds COUIN - foot camp & near Bde H.Q. Last table camp likely to be shelled as very close to 6" how. & 9.2" in firing. O.C. attended Conference at Bde H.Q. at 11 p.m.	snowing showers
COUIN J.L.b.7.5.	20/4/18		O.C. reconnoitring whole line to report to C.R.E. constructing detached posts for one platoon & 2 platoons in support of Front Line where it is almost untenable. also C.T.s from these posts to front line. O.C. attended 170 Bde Conference as possible counter attack to retake HEBUTERNE. if lost. 170 Corps Comm^d arr^d along line - Lieut DUIGENAN	fine & cold
	21/4/18		C.R.E. on line, says Corps Comm^d considers disconti^s of trench all i/O as wide as Corps frontage. R.G.C. 170 Bde. sat. Bde satisfied with line as a fighting line.	fine & cold

WAR DIARY
INTELLIGENCE SUMMARY

Army Form C. 2118.

Place	Date	Hour	Summary of Events and Information	Remarks and references to Appendices
COUIN J.16.J.5	22/4/18		Started wiring new trenches to Coy/Battn - OC with CO 2/5KOR	
			L.R. selecting small posts he required for flank defence south of CAILLY	fine
			attended Bde HQ Conf: re M.G. Forward Defence. Capt ORTNER left	
	23/4/18		Started from Hqts posts and wire for defence of forward M.G.s having	
			sites same with M.G.C. officers of B.C.C. 170 Bde. 170 Bde only	
			firing 2 Coys for work today. Most of Sappers staying in Camp	dull day
			finished excavation for forward M.G.s. OC to Bde Conference re	
	24/4/18		assembly lines for possible counter attack on GOMMECOURT	dull day
			Draft of 13 arrived. Coy now 7 under strength. 5 animals	
			shot OC - Lieut. Widdrin with CRE B&C (7) Bde (Longden)	
	25/4/18		+ MGC officers siting 16 splatoon posts to form new switch	
			covering BAYENCOURT + joining PURPLE SWITCH at CHAT 4th DE	
			LA HAYE - Still carried rapid 6x6 R.Street picketing	
			crawling lines fixed on by Bde. (see last entry 24/4/18)	on til
	26/4/18		Wish all new posts on new SWITCH started. Working party	Silver
			from 2/9 K.L.R. worked very well. 170 Bde firing 6 Coys only	

Army Form C. 2118.

WAR DIARY
or
INTELLIGENCE SUMMARY.
(Erase heading not required.)

Instructions regarding War Diaries and Intelligence Summaries are contained in F.S. Regs., Part II. and the Staff Manual respectively. Title pages will be prepared in manuscript.

Place	Date	Hour	Summary of Events and Information	Remarks and references to Appendices
COUIN	26/4/18 (cont.)		fa work on PURPLE SWITCH, being a daily infixture	Showery cho
	27/4/18		NEW SWITCH. 14 out of 16 posts completed by 2/7 K.L.R. Work on PURPLE SWITCH going well. Some wiring done every day but cannot get enough wire. O.C. saw M.G.C. H.Q. re their Bn HQ. Work on PURPLE SWITCH interfered with by shellfire	
	28/4/18		Posts of NEW SWITCH completed. Work on PURPLE SWITCH being carried on with. Existing frontline towards our S. div? Boundary also connecting up front line where gaps exist & putting in new supporting posts	dull cho
	29/4/18		Started wiring in pob to NEW SWITCH. O.C. met Gen. Longbourn (172 Bde) + C.O. M.G. Batt. re wiring M.G.s. re Work on part of PURPLE SWITCH interrupted by shellfire	dull cho
	30/4/18		170 Bde. wiring parties cancelled by Acte HQ after Coppice had left for work. Section of trench to be dug in thus Copse area 74 b 97/119 wire at top. Trace of trench constantly altering. Finally fixed at 7° Friebay. 7° sided & covered	wet cho APPENDIX E

[signature]
COMMANDING 502nd
WESSEX FIELD Co. R.E.

C O P Y.

S.638.

APPENDIX A

SECRET.

ADMINISTRATIVE ARRANGEMENTS REFERENCE 57th DIVISIONAL ORDER
NUMBER 77.
----

1. Troops will entrain from STEENBECQUE, CALONNE and MERVILLE in accordance with the Table attached.

The average interval between trains at each Station will be 3 hours.

2. ARRANGEMENTS AT ENTRAINING STATION.

The vehicles and horses of each train load will be at the Station named 3 hours, and the personnel one and half hours before departure of the train.

3. Entraining strengths shewing (a) Officers and Other Ranks
(b) Horses and Mules
(c) Vehicles and number of wheels.
will be handed to the R.T.O. or Officer detailed to assist at least 2 hours before departure of trains.

4. Units will not enter the Station precincts previous to the 3 hours mentioned in para 2. Roads leading to the Station will not be blocked by Units, and to ensure this strict punctuality must be kept.

5. The D.A.Q.M.G. 57th Division will superintend the entrainment generally and will be at STEENBECQUE Station. Officers as under will assist him as assistant R.T.Os.

(a) AT MERVILLE - 171st Brigade Group - 2 Officers.
(b) AT STEENBECQUE - 172nd Brigade Group - 2 Officers.
(c) AT CALONNE - 170th Brigade Group - 2 Officers.

These Officers will report to the R.T.O. at their respective Station at least three hours before the departure of the first train, and will entrain with the last train. They are to reconnoitre at once their respective Stations, in order to get acquainted beforehand with the loading, etc., facilities, and the approaches to the Station.

6. The O.C., 57th Divisional Signal Company will detail a Motor Cyclist Orderly at each Station.

7. Each Brigade Group will detail one Company and one Cooker and Team to be at their entraining Station 3½ hours before departure of the first train, and report to the R.T.O. These will act as loading party for all Units. They will entrain on the last train and will be under the orders of the Officer detailed above.

8. BILLETING.

Advance Parties for billeting will be sent on in the first train from each entraining Station, under Staff Captains of Brigade Groups. Two days' rations will be taken.

9. Entrainment will be completed half-an-hour before the departure of the train.

10. Breast ropes for horse trucks must be provided by Units. Ropes for vehicles will be provided by the Railway.

11. All doors of covered trucks and carriages on the Right hand side of the train when on the Main Line must be kept closed.

12. Arrangements at detraining Station.

The D.A.A.G. 57th Division will be in general charge at the most central Station.
Staff Captains, with billeting parties, will go by first train and will get into communication with the D.A.A.G., as early as possible.

13. ARRANGEMENTS AT DETRAINING STATION (Contd.)

Each Infantry Brigade will detail one Company, and one Cook and Team to go in the first train and to report to R.T.O. at detraining Station. The Officer in command of this Company will act as Detraining Officer.

14. GENERAL INSTRUCTIONS.

One blanket per man will be taken. All troops will move with the normal Field Service Scale of Transport. No extra transport will be provided but arrangements will be made for the conveyance of extra blankets.

15. RATIONS.

Rations to accompany troops will be :-

(a) Iron Rations.
(b) Current Day's Rations.

In addition, two days' Rations will be taken, one in Supply Vehicles of the Divisional Train and one by Divisional Mechanical Transport Company.

All supply vehicles of the Divisional Train will move full.

16. RAILHEAD.

Railhead up to 1st April, inclusive, will be BAC ST MAUR and on 2nd April LESTREM NORTH.

D.H.Q.
31st March, 1918.

(Sd.) W.M. Stewart, Lieut.-Colonel,
A.A. & Q.M.G., 57th Division.

Officer Commanding,

50 Field Company R.E.

Forwarded for your information and necessary action.

31.3.1918.

Lieut.-Colonel,
C.R.E., 57th Division.

TRAIN ARRANGEMENTS FOR MOVE OF 2ND DIVISION THE BETHUNE.

No. of Train	Time	173rd Infantry Bde. Group.	No. of Train	Time	171st Infantry Brigade Group.
1.		1st Coy. R.E. Bde. H.Q. Sig. 1 Coy., 1 Cooker and Mess Batt. F.A.C.T., R.A.M.C. 172 L.T.M.B.	3.		171 Bde H.Q. Bde. Sig. Sec. 1 Coy., 1 Cooker and Mess Batt. 1 Coy. R.E., Pnrs. 171st L.T.M.B.
4.		"A" Batt. less 1 Coy. and Cooker.	6.		"A" Batt. less 1 Coy. and Cooker.
7.		"B" Batt. less 1 Coy. and Cooker.	9.		"B" Batt. less 1 Coy. and Cooker.
10.		"C" Batt. less 1 Coy. and Cooker.	12.		"C" Batt. less 1 Coy. and Coker.
13.		H.Q., Fld. Train. 1 Coy. and Cooker "A" Batt. Bde Fd Id Company "B" Batt.	15.		Bde 3 Coy., 172 Brain. 471 Field Coy. R.E. 1 Company and Cooker "B" Batt.
16.		Bde. S Adv. Dre. 282 Field Coy. R.E. 1 Coy. & Cooker "C" Batt.	18.		Divl. H.Q. 248 Adv. Dre., Sup. Coy. No. 1 Sec. Div. Sig. Coy. M.G.B.N.

SECRET   172nd Infantry Brigade Operation Order   Copy No.
                              No. 45

APPENDIX B

1. Troops will entrain at STEENBECQUE Station on April 2nd/April 3rd in accordance with attached time table.

2. ARRANGEMENTS AT ENTRAINING STATION
   Vehicles and horses of each unit will be at the station of entrainment three hours and the personnel one and a half hours before departure of the train. All entrainments to be completed half an hour before train departure.

3. ENTRAINING STRENGTHS showing:-
   (a) Officers and Other ranks
   (b) Horses and Mules
   (c) Vehicles and Number of wheels
   will be handed to the R.T.O. three hours before departure of trains; loading parties will be shown separately.

4. Units will not enter the station precincts previous to the times shown in attached table for entrainment.

5. The D.A.Q.M.G. 57th Division will superintend the entrainment at STEENBECQUE Station. The following officers will report to the Staff Captain 172nd Inf.Bde at Bde Hd Qrs at 10-0.a.m. April 2nd:-
   Lieut J.Sillavan 2/10th Bn Lpool Regt
   1 Officer to be detailed by 9th Bn. Lpool Regt
   These officers will act as assistant R.T.O's and will be rationed up to and inclusive of April 4th. The name of the officer detailed by the 9th Bn Lpool Regt will reach Bde Hd Qrs by 10-0.a.m. April 2nd. Both these officers will travel to destination by the train no:19 and will keep their kits with them.
   The Staff Captain will explain to these officers the facilities for loading and the method to be employed.

6. LOADING PARTIES consisting of 1 Company, 1 cooker and team, will be detailed as follows:-

To load train number	Report at station at	Unit	To travel by	To unload
1	April 2nd 11-30.a.m.	9th Bn Lpool R.	No: 1 Train	Nos: 1, 4, 7, and 10.
4	2-30.p.m.	2/10th Lpool R.	No:13 Train	No:13.
7	5-30.p.m.	ditto	do.	--
10	8-30.p.m.	ditto	do.	--
13	11-30.p.m.	2/4th Bn S.Lan R	No:16 Train	No.16
16	April 3rd 2-30.p.m.	ditto	No:16 Train	--
19	5-30.a.m.	2/3rd Wessex F.A.	No:19 Train	No:19

(x) Party to be at least 40 strong.
Units detailing loading parties will make all arrangements for feeding their personnel. The cooker and team of each company acting as loaders will travel on the train with their respective Companies.

7. BILLETING PARTIES.
   Advance parties for all units in the Brigade Group will travel by train no: 1. They will be rationed up to and including of April 4th. Each Battalion will detail two cyclist orderlies to proceed with advance parties, and other units one each.

8. Breast ropes for horse trucks will be provided by units. Ropes for vehicles will be provided by the railway company.

9. All doors of trucks and carriages on the right hand side of the train when on main lines must be kept closed.

10. Units will enforce strict discipline during the journey, and during entraining and detraining.

11. ARRANGEMENTS AT DETRAINING STATION.
All advance parties will report to the Staff Captain at station of detrainment immediately on arrival.
The Officer in command of the Company of the 9th Bn Lpool R. proceeding by train no: 1 will report to R.T.O., station of destination and will act as detraining officer for all trains.
Unloading parties will be found as shown in column 5 para 6 above.

12. GENERAL INSTRUCTIONS
One blanket per man will be taken for which special transport will be provided at station of detrainment. No other transport will be provided.

13. All baggage wagons and supply wagons will report to units in their present locations at 6-0.a.m. April 2nd. They will entrain with units and will remain with them until further orders.

14. RATIONS
Rations to accompany troops will be:-
 (a) Iron ration
 (b) Current day's rations.
In addition, one day's supply will travel in the vehicles of the Divisional Train and one by Div.M.T.Column.
All water bottles will be filled before entraining.

15. All billets in the present area will be left scrupulously clean. Billet certificates must be completed and handed in to the Mairies of the respective Communes before leaving.

16. ACKNOWLEDGE.

                        Captain
                    Brigade Major
            173nd Infantry Brigade

Issued by Signals
1/4/1918.
Distribution:-
Copy No: 1   9th Bn Lpool R.
 2. 2/10th Bn Lpool R.
 3. 2/4th Bn S.Lan R.
 4. 173nd L.T.M.Batty
 5. Bde Signalling Offr
 6. 57th Division "G"
 7. 57th Division "A"
 8. H.Q.Divnl Train ASC
 9. 4 H.T.Coy A.S.C.
 10. S.S.O.
 11. Bde Supply Officer
 12. 502nd Field Co. RE.
 13. 505th Field Co. RE.
 14. C Coy 57th M.G.Bn
 15. 2/3rd Res...
 16. 57th Mobile Vet.Sec.
 17. Area Commdt HAVERSQUERQUE
 18. Area Commdt STEENBECQUE
 19. R.T.O., STEENBECQUE
 20. 9th Lpool R. Entraining Officer
 21. Lieut J'Sillavan
 22. 9th Lpool R. Detraining Officer
 23. G.O.C.
 24. Brigade Major
 25. Staff Captain
 26/27. War Diary
 28. File
 29/30. Spare

TRAIN ARRANGEMENTS FOR ENTRAINING OF 172ND INFANTRY BDE. AT STEENBECQUE STATION APRIL 2ND & 3RD 1918.

No. of train	Units	Time of entrainment Transport	Time of entrainment Personnel	Time & date of departure.	Remarks.
1	172nd Bde H.Q. 172nd Bde Signal Sect. 9th Bn. K.L.R.(1 Coy, 1 cooker & team) "G" Coy. 57th Bn. Machine Gun Corps 172nd L.T.M. Bty.	Apl 2nd 12 noon	Apl 2nd 1-30 p.m.	Apl 2nd 3-0 p.m.	
4	9th Bn. K.L.R. (less 1 Coy, 1 cooker & team)	Apl 2nd 3-0 p.m.	Apl 2nd 4-30 p.m.	Apl 2nd 6-0 p.m.	All loading parties will report with cooker and team three and a half hours before train is due to depart.
7	2/10th Bn. K.L.R. (less 1 Coy, 1 cooker & team)	Apl 2nd 6-0 p.m.	Apl 2nd 7-30 p.m.	Apl 2nd 9-0 p.m.	
10	2/4th Bn. S.Lan.R. (less 1 Coy, 1 cooker & team)	Apl 2nd 9-0 p.m.	Apl 2nd 10-30 p.m.	Apl 2nd/3rd 12-0 midnight	
13	H.Q. Divisional Train 2/10th K.L.R. (1 Coy, 1 cooker & team) 505th Field Co. R.E.	Apl 2/3rd 12 midnght	Apl 3rd 1-30 a.m.	Apl 3rd 3-0 a.m.	
16	No. 4 Coy. Divl Train 502nd Field Co. R.E. 2/4th Bn. S.Lan.R. (1 Coy, 1 cooker & team)	Apl 3rd 3-0 a.m.	Apl 3rd 4-30 a.m.	Apl 3rd 6-0 a.m.	
19	2/3rd Wessex Fld Amb. 57th Mobile Vet. Sect.	Apl 3rd 6-0 a.m.	Apl 3rd 7-30 a.m.	Apl 3rd 9-0 a.m.	

SECRET. 170TH INF. BDE. ORDER NO. 115.

Copy No. 6.
APPENDIX C

R.I. LENS 11. 1:100,000.

1. 170th Inf. Bde. Group will move on April 5th to the MONDICOURT Area where units will occupy the following billets :-

    170th Inf. Bde. H.Q.   ...   GRENAS.
    1/5th L.N.L. Regt.   ...   GRENAS.
    2/4th L.N.L. Regt.   ...   MONDICOURT.
    2/5th K.O.R.L. Regt.   ...   WARLINCOURT.
    170th L.T.M. Batty.   ...   MONDICOURT.
    No.2 Coy. Divl. Train.   ...   do
    502nd Fld. Coy., R.E.   ...   do
    3/2nd W.L. Fld. Amb.   ...   POMMERA.

2. Units will move as follows :-
   (a) 1/5 L.N.L.R. pass starting pt. 4.F.43.49. at 1.45 p.m.
       170th L.T.M.B.   "   "   "   "   " 2.0 p.m.
       No.2 Coy. Divl. Train. pass starting pt. 4.F.43.49 at 2.15 p.m.
       3/2nd W.L. Fld. Amb.   "   "   "   "   " 2.25 p.m.
       502nd Fld. Coy. R.E.   "   "   "   "   " 2.35 p.m.
   Route for above units :- 4.F.37.29 - 4.F.57.15, thence to respective billets.
   (b) Bde. H.Q.   pass starting pt. 4.G.67.04. at 2.00 p.m.
       2/4 L.N.L.R.   "   "   "   "   " 2.10 p.m.
   Route :- Main ARRAS - DOULLENS Road to 4.F.57.15, thence to billets.
   (c) 2/5th K.O.R.L. Regt. pass starting pt. 4.G.44.44. at 2.45 p.m.
   Route :- 4.G.24.36 - 4.G.18.21 - billets.

3. Distances of 200^x between Coys., 500^x between units, and 100^x between a unit and its transport will be maintained on the march.

4. Bde. H.Q. will close at BAVINCOURT at 3.00 p.m. and will reopen at GRENAS at the same hour.

5. Immediately they have arrived in their new billets units will notify Bde. H.Q. by runner.

6. ACKNOWLEDGE.

Issued through Signals
at 1 p.m.

                                              Captain.
                                              Brigade Major.
                                              170th Infantry Brigade.

COPIES TO :-

    1. 502 Fld. Coy. R.E.
    2. 2/5 K.O.R.L. Regt.
    3. 2/4th L.N.L. Regt.
    4. 1/5th L.N.L. Regt.
    5. 170th L.T.M. Batty.
    6. 3/2nd W.L. Fld. Amb.
    7. No. 2 Coy. Divl. Train.
    8. 57th Div. "G".
    9. 57th Div. "Q".
    10. 171st Inf. Bde.
    11. Town Major, BAVINCOURT.
    12. Sub-Area Comdt., MONDICOURT.
    13. Bde. Signal Offr.
    14. Bde. Transport Offr.
    15. Bde. Major.
    16. Staff Captain.
    17. File.
    18. War Diary.

SECRET.

Copy No....

170TH INF.BDE. ADMIN. INSTRUCTION NO. 23.
With reference to 170th Inf.Bde. Order No. 115.

7th April 1918.

1. (a) Billeting parties will proceed in advance and take over from units of the 171st Inf.Bde. which they are relieving. These parties will arrive in the new billets by 9 a.m. 8th inst.
(b) Each billeting party will send a representative to report to the Staff Captain at the Area Comdt's. Office, MONDICOURT, at 12 noon 8th inst. to report on the billets.

2. (a) Lorries will be provided to move blankets etc., as under:-
    Bde. H.Q. ... 1.
    Battalions. ... 1 each.
    T.M.B. ... 1.
(b) These lorries will report to their respective units billets at 11 a.m. 8th inst.
(c) O.C. Units will arrange to have guides at a central place in the village to meet their lorries.

3. Billets will be left clean and a certificate to that effect obtained from billet wardens or incoming units.

            Captain.
            Staff Captain.
Copies to all recipients of   170th Infantry Brigade.
170th Inf.Bde. Order No.115.

APPENDIX D

SECRET.

Copy No. 1.

170TH INF. PDE. ORDER NO. 116.

8.4.18.

Ref: LENS 11, 1:100,000.

1. 170th Inf. Bde. Group will move to the ORVILLE Area on April 9th in accordance with the following :-

Unit.	Starting Pt.	Time passing Starting Pt.	Route.	Destination.
1/5 L.N.L.R.	5.F.29.92.	9.35 am.	HALLOY.	HALLOY or AMPLIER.
2/4 L.N.L.R.	do	10.0 am.	5.F.15.77.- 5.E.97.58. ORVILLE.	P.O.W. Camp.(5.E. 82.41)
No.2 Coy. Div.Train.	do	10.15 am.	do	ORVILLE.
502 Fld.Coy. R.E.	do	10.25 am.	do	do
3/2 W.L.Fld. Amb.	do	10.35 am.	do	do
Bde. H.Q.	do	10.45 am.	do	ORVILLE.
170 L.T.M.B.	do	11.00 am.	5.E.85.77- 5.E.08.72.	CAUMESNIL.
2/5 K.O.R.L.	4.F.92.00.	10.00 am.	do	SARTON.

2. On completion of the move the Division will be in Army Reserve; all units will be ready to move at 1 hour's notice between 8 a.m. and 12 noon daily, and at 3 hours notice for the remainder of the day.

3. (a) Distances of 500^x between battns, 100^x between Coys., and 100^x between a unit and it's transport will be maintained on the march.
(b) Transport will accompany it's unit.

4. Billeting parties will report on 9th inst. as follows :-
2/5 K.O.R.L. report to Town Major, MARIEUX at 9.30 a.m.
1/5 L.N.L.R. & 170 L.T.M.B. report to Town Major HALLOY at 9.30 am.
502 Fld.Coy.R.E., No.2 Coy.Div.Train, Sec.D.A.C., 3/2 W.L.Fld.Amb., & 2/4 L.N.L.R. report to Staff Capt.at Village Wardens Office, AMPLIER (Billet No.7) at 8.30 a.m.

5. Lorries will be provided to convey blankets etc., as follows :-
Battns., L.T.M.B., and Bde.H.Q.   1 each.
Units concerned will send guides to Bde.H.Q. at 8 am. to take over their lorries.

6. All billets will be left clean and a certificate to that effect obtained from Billet wardens.

7. Bde.H.Q. will close at GRENAS at 10.15 am. and will reopen at ORVILLE at the same hour.

8. Immediately on arrival in new billets units will report the fact by cycle orderly to Bde.H.Q. at the same time giving the map ref. of their new Headquarters.

9. ACKNOWLEDGE.

Captain.
Brigade Major.
170th Infantry Brigade.

Issued through Signals at
9.45 p.m. 8.4.18.   COPIES TO :-
1. 502 F.Co.RE. 6. 3/2 W.L.Fd.Amb. 11. S.Area Cdt.MONDICOURT.
2. 2/5 K.O.R.L. 7. 2 Co.Div.Train   12. Town Major,MARIEUX.   15. Bde.Major.
3. 2/4 L.N.L.R. 8. 3 Sec.D.A.C.   13.   "   "   HALLOY.   16. Staff Capt.
4. 1/5 L.N.L.R. 9. 57 Div. "G"   17. File.
5. 170 L.T.M.B. 10. 57 Div. "Q"   14. Bde. Sig. Offr.   18. War Diary.

SECRET.

APPENDIX E

Copy No. 1

170TH INF. BDE. ADMIN. INSTRUCTION NO. 24.

1. The following moves will take place on 10th inst. :-

Unit.	From.	To.	Route.	Remarks.
502 Fld. Coy. R.E.	AMPLIER.	HALLOY.	AMPLIER - HALLOY Road.	To clear AMPLIER at 2.15 p.m.
3/2 W.L. Fld. Amb.	AMPLIER.	HALLOY.	do	To clear AMPLIER at 2.30 p.m.
2/5 K.O.R.L. Regt. (less 2 Coys)	HALLOY.	AMPLIER.	HALLOY-CAUMESNIL - AMPLIER.	To clear HALLOY 2.15 p.m.
H.Q. 3 Sec. D.A.C.	Present billets in AMPLIER.	H.Q. vacated by 3/2 W.L.Fld.Amb. AMPLIER.	-	-

2. Billeting parties will report as follows :-

Unit.	To report to :-	Time.
502 Fld. Coy. R.E.	Town Major, HALLOY.	11.30 a.m.
3/2 W.L.Fld.Amb.	do	do
2/5 K.O.R.L.R.	Staff Capt. at Village Warden's Office, AMPLIER.	10.30 a.m.
No. 3 Sec. D.A.C.	do	do

3. (a) Distances will be maintained on the march as laid down in 170th Inf. Bde. Order No. 116 para 3 (a).
   (b) Transport will accompany units.

4. Blankets will be carried on the man.

5. All billets will be left scrupulously clean.

6. Immediately on arrival in new billets units will report the fact to Bde. H.Q., at the same time giving map ref. of their new H.Q.

7. ACKNOWLEDGE.

9.4.18.

Captain.
Staff Captain.
170th Infantry Brigade.

COPIES TO :-
1. 502 Fld. Coy. R.E.
2. 2/5th K.O.R.L.R.
3. 3/2 W.L. Fld. Amb.
4. 3 Sec. D.A.C.
5. 2 Coy. Divl. Train.
6. Town Major, HALLOY.
7. 57 Div. "A".
8. Bde. Signal Offr.
9. Bde. Major.
10. Staff Captain.
11. File.
12. War Diary.

APPENDIX F.

METHOD OF COMPLETING RED LINE TRENCHES.

FIG.1. Shows section of RED LINE TRENCHES when completed round Traverses or as C.Ts. Section of 'BB' or CTs.

FIG.2. Shows section of Red Line Trenches when completed as Fire Trenches. Section at 'AA' or Fire Bays

FIG.3. Shows plan of Double Section Post.

HEAVY LINE SHOWS EXISTING WORK.
DOTTED "   "   WORK TO BE DONE.

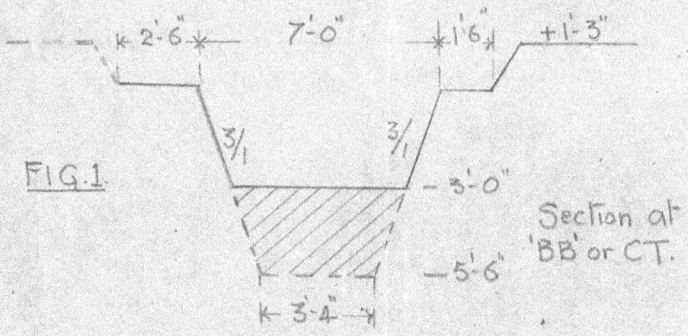

FIG.1. Section at 'BB' or CT.

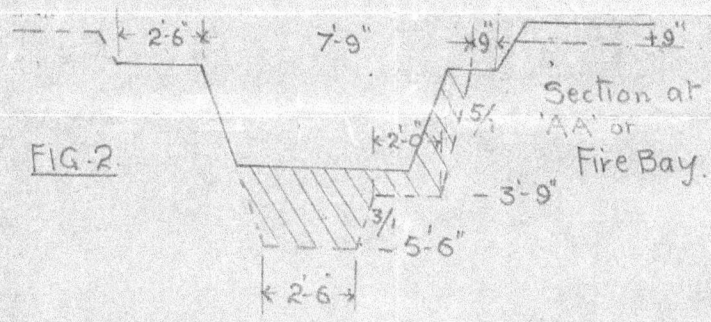

FIG.2. Section at 'AA' or Fire Bay.

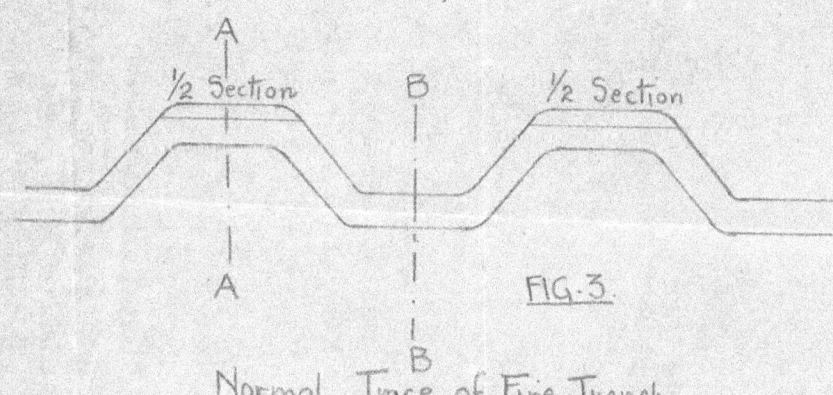

FIG.3.

Normal Trace of Fire Trench.

CONFIDENTIAL.

WAR DIARY

of

502nd (WESSEX) FIELD COY. R.E.

From: 1st May 1918   To: 31st May 1918.

Volume 16.

WAR DIARY
INTELLIGENCE SUMMARY
(Erase heading not required.)

Army Form C. 2118.

Place	Date	Hour	Summary of Events and Information	Remarks and references to Appendices
COUIN T.1.b.9.6 (57D)	1/5/18		Work on front line of PURPLE SWITCH completed to CORPS PATTERN. Putting in new supporting posts + more wire. Front Line (only wired) thoroughout.	Col Cdr
	2/5/18		Erecting stage in CHATEAU grounds COUIN for open air RED (1708 to 19 Bde) Concert party. Natural amphitheatre providing fireplace. No 3 Section with our two platoons wiring posts in NEW SWITCH (in front of BAYEN COURT) New C.S.M. arrived on account of application to BASE to make our A/CSM BARLOW substantive. Barlow has been acting of this Coy 12 months. O/C with C.R.E. 210.I. + B.G.C. 170 Bde. Siting six new posts to protect flank on (SAILLY) South End.	First Cdr
	3/5/18		OC taped out new posts South of SAILLY with Lieut PEARCE whose work began. Met OC 429 Sub to (CAPT JONES) whose in relieve. Showed him over PURPLE SWITCH + saw his work in BEER TRENCH (Wired) British Front + Support Lines) South of FONQUEVILLERS. Lewis Gun Instructor coming daily to instruct 4 NCOs + 12 men in Lewis Gun	Done C.R.

Army Form C. 2118.

WAR DIARY
~~INTELLIGENCE~~ SUMMARY
(Erase heading not required.)

Instructions regarding War Diaries and Intelligence Summaries are contained in F. S. Regs., Part II. and the Staff Manual respectively. Title pages will be prepared in manuscript.

Place	Date	Hour	Summary of Events and Information	Remarks and references to Appendices
COIGN J.1.b.9.b.	4/3/18		O.C. 429 visits called a hurried over. C.R.E. called re new work & dispositions of R.E. Inf'y	Insp chd
	5/9/18		Work started on Divl. HQ. Ruined Dug out. COIGN & Visual signal Station. Lieut TROTMAN left for Hospital having broken small bone of leg playing football yesterday. No.2 en 12 month with	Foot ball Coy
	8/9/18		Coy. two 2 Sections moved to sidings N.E. of COIGNEUT. to being over Camp of 429 Co (42 ANZ) for accommodation in early Inner Hr5 ra No.3. No1 Section (Lieut R.E. BURRELL) no Section (Major GEE & TROTMAN) moved to SAILLY no. Hrys av. to work in BEER TRENCH in old pre-somme front line between FONQUEVILLERS & HEBUTERNE now held by us Routine. (at present 170th) Lieut STREET supervising work being done by 6th R.A. of H.L. 42 & 62 Divisions checking, in link to- O.C. to Corp't H.Q. O.R.E s re working parties + c. Then to CHAT DE LA HAYE. Where work on temporary stores are NO.G.2. Believes to be started. Letter to Tunnel Bu re this with S.G.	

Army Form C. 2118.

WAR DIARY
INTELLIGENCE SUMMARY.
(Erase heading not required.)

Instructions regarding War Diaries and Intelligence Summaries are contained in F. S. Regs., Part II. and the Staff Manual respectively. Title pages will be prepared in manuscript.

Place	Date	Hour	Summary of Events and Information	Remarks and references to Appendices
COIGNEUX T.36.b	6/5/18		Col° Bolitho (170 Tr.) + C.R.E. at work in BEER TRENCH, working parties out – material over	out Obs
	7/5/18		O.C. to work started on B&SHQ in front of CHAT' DE LA HAYE, to 'BEER' wet in A.M. TRENCH + to detachment at SAILLY.	wet in A.M. Obs
	8/5/18		OC with C.R.E. siting section posts to be made in old french let. Tr. 29. CHAT' DE LA HAIE + FONQUEVILLERS. Then to BEER TRENCH + SAILLY posts B.G.C. 170 Bde laying down order of importance of work to him, + wishes four new posts. Work in D.H.Q. Dugout, Coun, house one to 429 Co. News received that Major JANE died of wounds.	
	9/5/18		Work on CRD and Bde HQ foregoing – Site shell WBy13 Bde let outskirts. Work on BEER TRENCH also going well. Received draft of 7 men, Cap notes 1 Officer + 7 O.R. under strength. Men now sleep in bunks with wire lines by shrubs between lot, much less than when on the ground.	w/drg Obs
	10/5/18		Work + forging well – Have totally used 2 all B + R of sub-train piled	

Army Form C. 2118

WAR DIARY
INTELLIGENCE SUMMARY
(Erase heading not required.)

Instructions regarding War Diaries and Intelligence Summaries are contained in F. S. Regs., Part II. and the Staff Manual respectively. Title Pages will be prepared in manuscript.

Place	Date	Hour	Summary of Events and Information	Remarks and references to Appendices
COIGNEUX J.3.b.1.6.	10/5/18	(Cont)	by Bde Gas Officer who found a large number of small dugouts mainly among mounds of ruins. Also interrogated by RE Enquirer who spoke very highly of cleanliness of Coy's billets.	Fine cns
	11/5/18		Working on new post B.61, at K7C3.6. Work on post going well. CTs being cleared out but there are few dug-outs. Worked rapid movement in CTs not possible.	Chilly cold
	12/5/18		2 Gas Casualties last night. Capt Mackenzie (2 i/c M.G.) also Capt Aylee (Bde M.O.) amongst latest but casualty. A dug-out for Bde HQ - completed but only one man went into it with orders to live in them, only 6' of earth + on top of a hill - there probably dug - have not seen any Boche	Dull ens
	13/5/18		Two forward sections staying in CRUMPETERY owing to Bde Relief - Several gas casualties in Hd Bde has been night of 11th - CRE called in A. & Q. Mess.	Wet cns
	14/5/18		Shelling on BEER TRENCH interfering with work. Called on B.G.C. Mainly for property of dugouts in BEER TRENCH + running of posts.	Fine cns
	15/5/18		Started for property dugouts (hunnel) in BEER TRENCH. MAJ. VIVIAN D.S.O. signals called re his dugouts	Fine cns
	16/5/18		Explored several old mine systems in BEER TRENCH. No troops except L.T.M. B. in BEER TRENCH now. A Sapper severely wounded by (supper store) one Spoad R.F.A. found as field (Supper Store)	Very hot cns

WAR DIARY
INTELLIGENCE SUMMARY
(Erase heading not required.)

Army Form C. 2118.

Instructions regarding War Diaries and Intelligence Summaries are contained in F.S. Regs., Part II. and the Staff Manual respectively. Title pages will be prepared in manuscript.

Place	Date	Hour	Summary of Events and Information	Remarks and references to Appendices
Sheet 57D COIGNEUX J.36.3.6	17/5/18		Draft of 5 OR arrived. Started section. Going on arrange on admin etc. Went to Camp. Orders to extend range to take 24 horses	
	18/5/18		Enemy shelling SAILLY daily. Detachment therefrom find it hard to enter village at times. Overlynnen Sergeant checking Proof marker. Nos of guns to mm:o on 31/12/17 finds errors on 25% of same on representation their to Payson, error admitted in 75% or 12 cases	
	19/5/18		Started dismantling ST MARTINS LANE. Work on BEER TRENCH going well. Old mine systems being filled in	
	20/5/18		Moved to new by camping of Nº 6. Leave obtained to move Nº 1 Section to this Camp. They moved in today two of their billets at SAILLY having been blown in by shells. Detailed Lieut Gilchrist to act as S/B for RARE % of complete section of Rd. R.A. to do constructional work for R.O.D. 12.Db arrived. Inspection of Harness. All in very good order. 17 horses & 7 ufle arrived	
	21/5/18		OC to BEER TRENCH, to SAILLY, to C.R.E. w/future work.	

WAR DIARY
INTELLIGENCE SUMMARY

Army Form C. 2118.

Place	Date	Hour	Summary of Events and Information	Remarks and references to Appendices
Sheet 57D COIGNEUX T 36	22/8/16		O.C. with C.R.E. seeing overhead (4 chains) shafts blown by explosive near COVIN. Then with Lieut STREET reconnoitred new Emergency Track. 1st Section arrived from SAILLY. 2 Lieut L. DIXON reported from No.1 section arrived from K1a. 40 to COIGNECOURT WOOD for duty with the Coy. Has not been out before. 12 months England. Late Sgt Instructor of Musketry in England (of WEST YORK). S.B. Respirators to be worn by all ranks for an hour continuously every few days & next few days.	every few 2/h
	23/8/16		O.C. + Lieut STREET working for old tunnel system at ROSSIGNOL FARM, above COIGNEUX - C.R.E. called.	saw CRE
	24/8/16		Lieut FLETCHER, Sergt BONIFACE + 7 others starting on RARE Section (about 30 O.R. from 2nd RA form not yet of personnel). Above R.E. personnel detained from transit from lorry. 2 Sects & 2 Sappers left for 14 days at army Rest Camp, detailed by M.O.R.E. LIEUT. T.W.T. STREET was attached temporarily yesterday to 5th/S Co. as they are short of officers.	W.F.C.W? Saw C.R.E.

Army Form C. 2118.

WAR DIARY
INTELLIGENCE SUMMARY
(Erase heading not required.)

Instructions regarding War Diaries and Intelligence Summaries are contained in F. S. Regs., Part II. and the Staff Manual respectively. Title pages will be prepared in manuscript.

Place	Date	Hour	Summary of Events and Information	Remarks and references to Appendices
Sheet 57D COIGNEUX J.16.3.6	26/5/18		R.E. An American Sgt is allotted to us for 3 days; another comes when he goes. Much reopening of dugouts being done.	See Ch.3
	27/5/18		C.R.E. inspected work at ROSSIGNOL FARM, where we have opened up a blocked entrance to an old subterranean tunnel 30+ long. Same can be entered also from a well. Are making it fit for a Bde HQ.	See Ch.3
	28/5/18		OC called on Major JORDAN, new OC 575 Co. Work on BREWERS TRACK proceeding.	See Ch.3 Div.Ch.3
	29/5/18		BEER TRENCH ness in good order. CJs being duckboarded.	See Ch.3
	30/5/18		Coy having a day in Camp. Inspections & interviews to hand over work on first relief to 428 Coy. OC 428 Coy called & officer & NCOs arrived to take particulars of work.	
	31/5/18		WESSEX TRACK to GOMMECOURT WOOD put in order. OC to CRE re Bn.HQ in BEER TRENCH.	See Ch.3

C. A. Poole
MAJOR,
COMMANDING 502nd
WESSEX FIELD Co. R.E.

C O N F I D E N T I A L.

W A R   D I A R Y

of

502nd (WESSEX) FIELD COY., R.E.

From: 1st June 1918   To: 30th June 1918.

VOLUME   17.

Army Form C. 2118.

WAR DIARY (JUNE 1918)
INTELLIGENCE SUMMARY

(Erase heading not required.)

Place	Date	Hour	Summary of Events and Information	Remarks and references to Appendices
Sheet 57D COIGNEUX T.3.b.3.4.	1/6/18		Order to relieve 429 Div to be cancelled. Now ordered to relieve 505 Coy in COMMIE COURT WOOD. Carrying on work on VALLEY AVENUE clearing out old trench & digging 150′ new trench between K.29.95 & K.7.81. This will make valuable protected communication from Bde HQ in K.7.81.	
TRENCHES REFERRED TO see MAP ATTACHED (APPENDIX 1)			Road to BEER TRENCH system, to COMMECOURT WOOD. Our getting in four wiring party. Doing work with sappers.	Four Chn
	2nd		Infr working party. Doing work with sappers. Received orders to take over from & hand over to 505 Coy with 2Lt DIXON & Emergency A.D.S. on SOUASTRE - BIENVILLERS road which he is constructing. To 505 Coy + our Major JORDAN to move - 2Lt PEARCE + 3 NCOs acting as advanced party reported to him. O.C. to C.R.E. work in new Sector (Right Bde forward area.) 505 Coy suffered much sickness. Wrote in time C.R.E. arranging for field Coys in line to do less of Bde's work so as to enable some sappers to be looking at hostilities.	APPENDIX "A"
	3rd		No work. With Lt BURRELL went round wire with O.C. 505 Coy. Then wired BEER TRENCH system. Present distribution of Sappers, two sections	Inst Chn

WAR DIARY
INTELLIGENCE SUMMARY
(Erase heading not required.)

Army Form C. 2118.

Instructions regarding War Diaries and Intelligence Summaries are contained in F. S. Regs., Part II. and the Staff Manual respectively. Title pages will be prepared in manuscript.

Place	Date	Hour	Summary of Events and Information	Remarks and references to Appendices
57D COIGNEUX	3/6/17	Cont'd	under Right Bn. took over working on 1 Bn Front, remainder on work under CRE. Shall have about 1½ sections with Co. FLETCHER	
F.3.b.3.4.			& 5 OR remain on RARE Scheme, & some men on wk w Hugh mex. Work of forward schemes forward of and including GONNECOURT TRENCH consists mainly of supervising Infantry wiring, duckboarding + clearing trenches. Chief of further work will consist of dugouts. Inf'y parties for all forward work. 3 Coys. of Reserve Bn. Work in rear consists mainly of enlarging & constructing Baby Elephants in GRAYLING TRENCH (by moving in back of traverses + wiring Baby Elephants) strengthening ADS & constructing Tank Boot by Trap. Also wiring & improving trenches RUM TRENCH, GRAYLING TRENCH &c. for which 1 Coy working party is provided by Res. Bn. 2/Lt PEARCE + L/EDSON in STOUT TRENCH had narrow escape. Both badly shaken. CAPT DAVISON left for England on leave. HQrs + Nos 1.2.+4. Sections moved to STOUT TRENCH in GOMMECOURT WOOD	Ingh CRE

4

WAR DIARY
INTELLIGENCE SUMMARY
(Erase heading not required.)

Army Form C. 2118.

Place	Date	Hour	Summary of Events and Information	Remarks and references to Appendices
GOMMECOURT WOOD E.28.c.9.6	4/6/18		Transport, Hoadwies sleeping in same camp though moving Sect. No J	
	5/6/18		Section in civvies part of Hoad line part with R.A.R.E. had extremely wet busy day in GOMMECOURT WOOD. Exchanged hostings with notes with OC 58 Coy, E.L. Dixon excursions at Hoadways. Called on OC Rouge Bks + RA in line. Work started - Coy in wire dug into an old Block front line very dirty end of night shift. Am gassed one or two spl. into bomb proof shelter to flush host in Slo to flush.	Sect CWS just ches
	6/6/18		Quietest time of day early morning when one can move about anywhere at wish. Watering party from Reserve Bks drawing work HEBUTERNE SWITCH. Via GOMMECOURT TRENCH + HEBUTERNE SWITCH is only latent communication between forward areas. Extreme right to left + time in Coy in places + wires so low as to be dangerous after dark. Confident Reserve Bde do not do (so?) work owing to shot horses work not in equipment re Sh. all numbers + CRE. Approved Lt J.E PEARCE returned MC. (Birthday Honours)	

WAR DIARY
INTELLIGENCE SUMMARY

Army Form C. 2118.

Place	Date	Hour	Summary of Events and Information	Remarks and references to Appendices
Sheet 57D GOMIÉCOURT E.28.C.9.6	7/6/18		OC ammunition column night of line. Communication out in front without going outside our wire. Running GOMIECOURT TR. HEBUTERNE SWITCH need clearing out. 171 Bde relieved tonight by 170 Bde.	
	8/6/18		CRE called re organization of work. Digging & wiring except when absolutely necessary to be done by Bde. under their own organization. This is to relieve Sapps officers & NCOs from responsibility with regard to parties. Thus saving them night work. Called on BGC 170 Bde & drew up programme of work showing responsibility of Inf. & RE. He is continuing 171 Bde policy & programme. Visited ROSSIGNOL WOOD shelled heavily tonight in hopes of silent trench fire but without any visible result except the stopping of all parties for nearly dark tonight.	APPENDIX B Programme of work
	9/6/18		CO's and I went to AIRE to look for our surplus kit & brought most of it back with him to our employees. Working parties started.	

WAR DIARY
INTELLIGENCE SUMMARY

Army Form C. 2118.

Instructions regarding War Diaries and Intelligence Summaries are contained in F. S. Regs., Part II. and the Staff Manual respectively. Title pages will be prepared in manuscript.

(Erase heading not required.)

Place	Date	Hour	Summary of Events and Information	Remarks and references to Appendices
GOMMIE-COURT WOOD E.28.c.9.6	10/6/18		Boch shelling W end of STOUT TRENCH very effectively. G.S.W. nearly hit mostly shaken. Boch was violent nervous fires on his shells. Fragmentation is good + splinters fly hundreds of yards. Decided to mend mask pond old Boch wire dugout which much remains. This will encourage 100 nave, pickets - taken but mainly a sapping job in the dark.	True (L.L.)
	11/6/18		Went by Inf. Corps. on the own proceeding very slowly - have had to employ in. They were in their equipment plentifully reported this to R.G.C. 170 Bde who save orders to the contrary at once. Went on Baby Elephant Dugouts which are handled 5th below ground level with side of traverses. These are very popular with Inf'y. Cpl. called October time.	C.L.L.
	12/6/18		Lt. PEARCE still suffering from headache as result of shelling near him recently, so sent him to H.O.e.lines. Lt P. DIXON taking on his wk here. No 2/3 Lt. joining. Attended big drive conference at H.Q. 170 Bde re dispositions of accommodation & arms.	C.L.L.

D. D. & L., London, E.C.
(A7853) Wt. W80/M6672 — 50,000 4/17 Sch 52a Forms/C/2118/14

WAR DIARY
INTELLIGENCE SUMMARY

(Erase heading not required.)

Army Form C. 2118.

Instructions regarding War Diaries and Intelligence Summaries are contained in F. S. Regs., Part II. and the Staff Manual respectively. Title pages will be prepared in manuscript.

Place	Date	Hour	Summary of Events and Information	Remarks and references to Appendices
GONNELIEU WOOD E.28.c.9.b.	13/4/18		Wiring of GRAYLING TR completed. Have started clearing up trench at S.W. end of GONNECOURT WOOD. B&C 170th Bn making fresh dug-outs & traverses of their men on their front, involving deepening & open- ing up of old trenches.	
	14/6/18		Sending men to Horseshoe for 48 hours rest work (CRE orders) about 14th Sapping Mine not. Breastwork or putting in Batty Elephants Dug outs. We have 6 to 12 nightly contributions continually, mostly working parties stopped by shellfire last night. #171 relieved 172 Bde in line on left. 50'3 Coy relieved 421 Coy in line. MAJOR LLOYD (recently Capt in 503 Coy) now in 253rd Div & reported killed. CC to Horseshoe.	
	15/6/18		16.170 Bde.	
	16/6/18		Till now I have had three cases of P.U.O. + no other sick. (or nearly a fortnight) Today we have sent three to Hospital and to Horselines all sick. Fever apparently comes on very suddenly.	
	17/6/18		Rode the left sub sector up to Gonthrue with B.G.C. 170 Bde - fairly wet. Nothing doing to straighten line from alley coming up along BUCKSMITH RD STREET to HORSESHOE.	

WAR DIARY or INTELLIGENCE SUMMARY

Army Form C. 2118.

Place	Date	Hour	Summary of Events and Information	Remarks and references to Appendices
FONQUE-VILLERS COURT HOOP B25.C.8.5.	18/6/18		Work on erecting BLITZ switched strong defences flank started.	
			Leave to Divny. Hope 4 allotments in next week.	
	29/6/18		Surveyed trenches round K.10 Central for B.O.C. 170 Bde with a view to entrenching strong point. Lt BURRELL with a Coy of Infy here done very good work at S.W. corner of GOMMECOURT PARK clearing up out & deepening old Boche front Line.	
	30/6/18		Lieut STREET at Hirochire developed P.U.O. about 125 O.R. at Horse Lines sick with P.U.O. (temperatures n.d.) About 20 gone to Hospital with the same. Working strength of a Section 15. but much good work being done, largely due to Section Officers energy in getting all available men for work. Form Baths "Batt" organization administration seems b.d. & after seeing Bnde & Officers see Coy. Pploons. Commanders to fix up. necessitates work re. Minimal baths for estroy, everything that conf. wiring duties. Bathus own work on trenches fatigues & encouraged by R.E. Officers. Little would be done. All this Corps officers very tired, form of organizing themselves to this work CRE	

WAR DIARY or INTELLIGENCE SUMMARY

Army Form C. 2118.

Place	Date	Hour	Summary of Events and Information	Remarks and references to Appendices
GONNECOURT E.23.a.6.	26/6/18		170 Bde to be relieved by 172 Bde tomorrow night. A few shuttles take place today. C.F. post pushed forward using broken cart ruck as covering. During 14 days 170 Bde have been under an hour continual old 25% baby elephants, duckboards & stands. five tons of mud & wet clothes in trenches carried out by MINENWERFER (and D company) trench to the front of (78/6) in front of the British front line. FELTRICH TRENCHES, BIEZ SWITCH. O.C. to RAID (170) re cleaning out GOMMECOURT & a round MUSKETEER GOMMECOURT with the 2 M.L.R. journey out that reported to be dire. Work being carried out by Trenches very muddy and Bottes taking up year operational. CAPT DAVISON returned from leave.	
	27/6/18		C.R.E. called. CAPT DAVISON to hospital. A few bootytraps when RWM TR over to GOMMECOURT - PUISIEUX Road at RAP in GOMMECOURT occupied today. 1st BUFFS R.H. Relief (12 men) to Hochwaldgraben west	

WAR DIARY
INTELLIGENCE SUMMARY.

(Erase heading not required.)

Army Form C. 2118.

Instructions regarding War Diaries and Intelligence Summaries are contained in F.S. Regs., Part II and the Staff Manual respectively. Title pages will be prepared in manuscript.

Place	Date	Hour	Summary of Events and Information	Remarks and references to Appendices
Sheet 57d GOMMÉCOURT E.28.c.9.6.	23/6/18		Called on B.G.C. 170 Inf Bde who to handed me to 172 Bde & who arranged with B.M. 172. Programme of work. Went up & found movement of 172nd Bde which was approved. Work to start tomorrow night. Bde to keep tonight & late tonight. Do them intend to be best tonight. Harness — bellies and their time althought inspected was a surprise & caught them unprepared.	
	24/6/18		Renewed the tests with B.M. 172 showing him work in hand & re-rates on 3 Bath's Command 2n0. Much food spade work has been done by 170 Bde & such bearing over chiefly required. Dumb loading GOMMÉCOURT — GUINNESS TR. begun. Also making a new reserve walk/point near ST MARTIN'S LANE E25 d 46.	
	25/6/18		B.M. 172 called. Rus Bn can only supply 20 yds for work & must belong. As they want to use our by improving G.C.T. & wiring.	
	26/6/18		No working parties provided owing to Rhine stop or ROSSIGNOL WOOD. Officers carried out "HEICHER" reports, returned [?] tohrAKE — O.C. round Truce Baths & this work. Received orders re relief by N.Z.E. on 1/7/18	APPENDIX C

WAR DIARY
INTELLIGENCE SUMMARY.
(Erase heading not required.)

Army Form C. 2118.

Place	Date	Hour	Summary of Events and Information	Remarks and references to Appendices
GOMMECOURT Shef 57c.9.6	Feb 28/4/18		L PEARCE + OC relieved 2/Lb HOSKINS. Lt BURRELL to Bde HQ as wiring officer (unfortunately killed). He took charge of 60 Inf. from 2/4 SLR and completed 450x double apron, including carrying materials. Tonight a very good piece of work. K/D NOR West wired at RIVAGE to make tank obstacle. Crater 12ft deep with 250lb charges & 2 ammonal. New Zealand Officer called re harrying ours - facing to hand over to 2 Coys 2nd NZ Inst Bde - Officer in different Officer + 2 CO's arrived here with NZE Officers + NCO's. More wiring down in front of RUM TR. Intro. FROOT TR. + NAMELESS CT. where practically none existed previously.	1 + 48 ORs June end APPENDIX D
	29/4/18			
	30/4/18		Officers of N.Z.R. called retaking over dug outs re Map of Which [?] Bryant area.	

Chr To
MAJOR.
COMMANDING 502ND
WESSEX FIELD Co. R.E.

SECRET.   Copy No. 4

APPENDIX "A"

57th DIVISION.

C.R.E's. OPERATION ORDER No. 21.

Reference Map:- 1/20,000 57D. N.E.

1. The 505 Field Company R.E. in the Right Sector, 57th Divisional Forward Area, with H.Q. at E.28.c.98.70 and Transport Lines at J.9.a.4.2. will be relieved by 502 Field Company R.E.

2. The 502 Field Company R.E., in 57th Divisional Reserve Area, with H.Q. and Transport Lines at J.3.b.3.4. will be relieved by 505 Field Company R.E.

3. Arrangements for relief will be made direct between Os.C. Units concerned, who will get in touch with one another as soon as possible and take over billets and all work of their opposite number.

4. O.C. each Field Company will provide an Advance Party of One Officer and three N.C.O's to report to the opposite Company before 9 p.m. on 2nd June.

5. O.C. 505 Field Company R.E. will detail an Officer to take over 57th Div. R.A.R.E. Section. This Officer should get in touch at once with Lieut. Fletcher at D.22.c.3.0. and make himself thoroughly conversant with all details of this Section's programme, so that there may be no break in the continuity of work.

6. The relief of the Transport will be completed by 4 p.m. on June 4th.
   The remainder of the relief will be carried out on the night of 4/5th and will be completed by 3 a.m. on 5th June.

7. The usual March Intervals will be observed.

8. Completion of relief must be notified to this Office by wiring the code word "OVER".

9. ACKNOWLEDGE.

Issued at 12 noon.   Capt. & Adjt.,
2nd June, 1918.   for C.R.E., 57th Division.

DISTRIBUTION :

Copy No.		Copy No.	
1.	57th Div. "G".	12.	O.C. Div. Train 57 Div.
2.	57th Div. "A" & "Q".	13.	D.A.D.V.S.
3.	O.C. 502 Field Coy. R.E.	14.	D.A.D.O.S.
4.	,, 505 ,, ,,	15.	A.D.M.S.
5.	,, 421 ,, ,,	16.	M.O.R.E.
6.	,, 2/5 L.N.L.Regt. (P).	17.	R.S.M. Cook, R.E.
7.	170th Infty. Bde.	18.	War Diary.
8.	171st - do -	19.	-do-
9.	172nd - do -	20.	File.
10.	C.E. IV Corps.	21.	Spare.
11.	O.C. Sigs. 57 Div.	22.	-do-

170TH INFANTRY BRIGADE INSTRUCTION No. 52.

WORK PROGRAMME. 8.6.1918.

1. The attached table shows the work that will be started on 9th June in addition to any other items which Bn. Comdrs. can carry out.

2. The strength of parties given is the number that the Brigadier orders Bn. Comdrs. to supply.
   A proportion of Officers and N.C.O's will attend.

3. Daily reports will be **furnished** to reach Bde. H.Q., by 12 noon to show the total amount of work completed up to date (percentage).

4. All arrangements for parties and tools will be made direct between O.C. Field Coy. R.E., and Bn. Comdrs. concerned.
   Tools will be kept at the site of the work until the latter is completed.

5. As far as possible Bn. Comdrs. will tell off the same parties for each item. If finished before the date given, the parties will not be required to work on the remaining days.

6. All parties in attack order, except carriers behind the main green line, who will carry rifle and a bandolier of cartridges.

                                                Captain,
                                                Brigade Major,
                                          170th Infantry Brigade.

COPIES TO:-

    502 Field Coy. R.E.
    2/5th K.O.R.L.R.
    2/4th L.N.L.R.
    1/5th L.N.L.R.
    War Diary.
    File.

APPENDIX B

WORK PROGRAMME – BEGINNING 9th June 1918.

Item.	Place.	Nature of work.	Offr. responsible.	Unit finding party.	Morning by which completed.	Remarks.
1.	MAIN GREEN LINE. WOMAN, FUSILIER, GOMMECOURT Tr. from Juncn. of WOMAN and RICHMOND to EEL ALLEY.	Deepening and widening where necessary.	O.C. 1/5 L.N.L.R.	1 Coy. (68 diggers.) 1/5 L.N.L.R.	16.6.18. (7 nights.)	Depth and width to be indicated by O.C. 502 Fld.Co. Coy.Condr. will be in charge of working parties.
2.	FUSILIER from RUM at K.10.a.25.85. to GOMMECOURT Tr at K.10.b.18.00.	Make into C.T. Depth 5'6" below ground level, 2½' wide at bottom, 6' wide at ground level.	O.C. 1/5 L.N.L.R.	1 Coy. (68 diggers.) 1/5 L.N.L.R. & 3 R.E.	16.6.18. (7 nights.)	To be brought through No.3 Post at K.10.b.05.10. The Coy. Condr. will be in charge of working party.
3.	GOMMECOURT TR.	Improve wire until equal to 2 double aprons.	O.C. 2/4 L.N.L.R.	2 Platoons. (34 carriers.) 2/4 L.N.L.R. & 10 to 12 R.E.	16.6.18. (7 nights.)	R.E. will wire: infantry carry.
4.	GOMMECOURT TR., EEL, PIKE, & BIBZ Switch as far forward as COD Tr.	Improve wire until equal to 2 double aprons.	O.C. 2/5 K.O.R.L.R.	2 Platoons. (34 carriers.) 2/5 K.O.R.L.R. & 10 to 12 R.E	16.6.18. (7 nights.)	R.E. will wire: infantry carry.
5.	All Posts in GREEN System.	Complete marking. Improve wire until equal to 2 double aprons and extend wire from ROACH to FISH.	C.Os of Rt. & Lt. GREEN Bns.	Garrisons and Reserve Coys.	16.6.18. (7 nights.)	Inf. will wire and carry.
6.	GOMMECOURT TR. (About K.5.c.2.2.)	Complete elephant dugout for Rt.Bn. Post.	O.C. 502 Fld.Co.R.E.	4 R.E., 12 O.R 2/4 L.N.L.R. from local Coy.	12.6.18. (3 nights.)	4 Inf. per shift of 4 hours for 12 hours. Any carrying to be done by Reserve Coy.

- 2 -

Item.	Place.	Nature of Work.	Officer responsible.	Unit finding Party.	Morning by which completed.	Remarks.
7.	WOMAN ST. (About K.10.d.3.7.)	Complete elephant dugout for Rt.Bn. Post.	O.C. 502 Fld. Coy. R.E.	4 R.E., 12 O.R. 2/4 L.N.L.R. from local Coy.	12.6.18. (3 nights.)	4 Inf. per shift of 4 hours for 12 hours on end.
8.	GRAYLING TR.	Complete 4 elephant dugouts.	do	16 R.E., 48 O.R 2/5 K.O.R.L.R. from local garr.	12.6.18. (3 nights.)	4 Inf. per shift on each dugout of 4 hours, working continuously night and day until finished. (i.e. Each party comes on twice in 24 hours.)
9.	NAMELESS TR. (About K.11.a.3.4.)	Timbering Coy. H.Q. in Rt.Bn.area.	do	4 R.E.	—	Small carrying party when required, from Rt.Bn.
10.	NAMELESS TR.	Improve and make fire bays.		2 R.E., 2 Platoons.(34 workers) 1/5 L.N.L.R.	16.6.18. (7 nights.)	—
11.	BIEZ switch as far forward as NEW TR.	Deepen and duckboard Clear a straight and make a block in BIEZ switch forward of NEW TR.	do	4 R.E., 2 Platoons.(34 workers) 1/5 L.N.D.R.	16.6.18. (7 nights.)	

Item.	Place.	Nature of Work.	Officer responsible.	Unit finding party.	Morning by which completed.	Remarks.
12.	R.E. Dump. E.28.d.5.1.	For coiling wire in lighter loads.	O.C. 502 Fld. Coy. R.E.	3 men 1/5 L.N.L.		Permanent Party. Attached to & rationed by R.E.
13.	R.E. Dump. E.28.d.5.1.	For unloading R.E. Stores.	-----do-----	1 N.C.O. & 6 men 1/5 L.N.L.		Daily at 10-30 a.m.
14.	All C.T:s and Trenches.	Improve the marking especially in Rt.Bn. area.	-----do-----			

170TH INFANTRY BRIGADE INSTRUCTION No. 99.

10.9.1918.

Brigade Instruction No. 99 is cancelled and the following substituted.

1. In continuation of No. 1 programme issued with Bde. Instruction No. 92 the attached programme will come into force on the dates stated therein.

   Any item in No. 1 programme not likely to be completed by the time given will be notified at once to Bde. H.Q.

2. The Bde. programme will not in future, contain any reference to elephant dug-outs. These will be constructed as follows:-

   (i) At least two dug-outs in every Coy. area in the MAIN GREEN Line will be in construction at one time (excluding Counter Attack Coys).
   (ii) The Bn. Comdr. will inform the O.C. Field Coy. where he wishes these dug-outs, and will provide the men who should be furnished by the local garrison, to enable the work to proceed continuously, in shifts of 4 men, 4 hours on and 8 hours off. A maximum of 4 night's work or 2 day's if work is possible during the day, is to be allowed for each dug-out.
   (iii) The O.C. Field Coy. will provide the necessary n.c. skilled labour, and will be responsible for the work.
   (iv) The Bn. Comdr. will provide the party required to carry up material.
   (v) The O.C. Field Coy. will inform Bde. H.Q. on his daily report of the progress on each dug-out, giving trench, number of post and map square.
   (vi) In selecting positions, Bn. Comdrs. will aim at providing every section with a dug-out, until each section in a post has one. Then to add a second dug-out for the section. Every 2 section post will thus eventually have four dug-outs.

3. It is noticed that Bn. Comdrs. are asking for E.D.O., where they already have a deep-dug-out within 50 to 80 yds. of their fire positions. They should first consider whether it would not be possible to shift the fire position nearer the dug-out. If not possible the E.D.Os must must be put in.

                                         Captain,
                                 A/Brigade Major,
                                 170th Infantry Brigade.

COPIES TO:-

                 O.C. 2/5th K.O.R.L.R.
                 O.C. 2/4th L.N.L.R.
                 O.C. 1/5th L.N.L.R.
                 O.C. 502nd Field Coy. R.E.
                 War Diary.
                 File.

WORK PROGRAMME - BEGINNING 17th JUNE, 1916.

Item.	PLACE.	NATURE OF WORK.	OFFICER RESPONSIBLE.	Unit furnishing party.	TO BEGIN ON.	TO BE COMPLETED BY.	REMARKS.
15.	MAIN GREEN LINE from Junc. of GYMNECOURT A WE to Junc. of PIKE & PIKE SWITCH.	Continue deepening until passage behind firestep is 6 ft. below ground level.	O.C. 1/5th L.N.L.	1 Coy. 63 diggers. 1/5 L.N.L.	15/17th June.	23rd June. A.M.	Party from item 1. Programme 1. To dig at Junc. of A & PIKE, and clear PIKE first. All earth to be piled in trench on slope of crossover one.
16.	TROUT TRENCH.	Wire up.	O.C. Field Coy. R.E.	1 Plat. 17 workers 1/5 L.N.L.	22nd June.		Plan will be given Fld. Coy. by Bde. H.Q.
17.	NAMELESS TR. (defensive flank) from RUM TO PIKE.	Improve old Boche wire on both sides, and make fire-bays.	O.C. Field Coy. R.E.	2 Plat. 34 workers. 1/5 L.N.L.	At once.	23rd June.	Begin at RUM Trench end.
18.	PIKE SWITCH (def. wire between PIKE SW. ensive flank) and PIEZ SUPPORT. from PIKE TO TROUT Trench.		O.C. Field Coy. R.E.	1 Plat. 17 workers. 1/5 L.N.L.	At once.	23rd June.	
19.	PIKE SWITCH (def - Fire bays facing N.E. ensive flank) from PIKE TO TROUT.		O.C. Field Coy. R.E.	1 Plat. 17 workers. 1/5 L.N.L.	15/17th June.	23rd June.	As indicated by Bde. H.Q.
20.	PIKE SWITCH from RUM to ROACH.	Continue deepening but not overlapping. Fat block front of RUM Trench.	O.C. Field Coy. R.E.	1 Plat. 17 workers. 1/5 L.N.L.	15/17th June.	23rd June.	
21.	MUSKETEER (RUM to GYMNECOURT TR.)	Continue clearing and improve part already cleared. Dig through ross at A.10.a.7.8.	O.C. 1/5th L.N.L.	1 Coy. 63 diggers. 1/5 L.N.L.	Continue.	21st June.	Repeated from programme No. 1.

SECRET.   Copy No. 6

57th DIVISION.

C. R. E's. OPERATION ORDER No. 23.

Reference Map:- 1/20,000,   57D.

1. 57th Division (less Artillery) will be relieved by New Zealand Division (less Artillery) in the Centre Sector, IVth Corps Front, between 1st and 3rd July.

2. On relief, 57th Division will be in Corps Reserve. Units will be in readiness to move at 1 hour's notice between 9 p.m. and 9 a.m. and at 2 hour's notice between 9 a.m. and 9 p.m.

3. Field Companies R.E. and 2/5 L.N.L.Regt. (P) of 57th Division will be relieved by Field Companies R.E., and N.Z. Maori (Pioneer) Battalion of New Zealand Division, and corresponding Units of 57th Division will take over from opposite numbers of N.Z. Division as below :-

57th Div.Unit.	N.Z.Div.Unit.	Headquarters.	Horse Lines.	Date of Relief.
421 Fld.Co.R.E.	1st Fld.Co.R.E.	I.24.a.7.5.	I.24.a.8.4.	July 1st.
502 - do -	2nd - do -	J.20.c.3.9.	J.20.c.3.9.	- do -
505 - do -	3rd - do -	I.24.a.cent.	I.24.a.4.2.	- do -
2/5 L.N.L.R.(P) (less 1½ Coys.)	N.Z.Maori(P)Bn.	I.24.b.6.2.	I.24.b.6.2.	- do -
1½ Coys. 2/5th L.N.L.Regt.(P).	-	-	-	Under orders of G.O.C. Rt Infty. Bde.

4. Details of reliefs will be arranged direct between opposite numbers and Units 57th Division will hand over all work in hand, all maps, air photos, plans, documents, etc., of work in hand or proposed, all demolitions schemes, trench and area stores, R.E. Materials in Dumps etc.
   Receipts for all Trench and Area Stores, Secret Maps and Papers to be sent to this Office in duplicate by 4th July.

5. Field Company Commanders will prepare for the incoming Unit detailed Handing Over Notes, shewing both work in hand and proposed and all other information that may be necessary for the incoming Units.

6. Os.C. Field Companies and 2/5 L.N.L.R.(P)., 57th Division, will take over all work at present undertaken by corresponding Units of N.Z. Division which they relieve. They should get in touch with their opposite numbers as early as possible and make themselves acquainted with all present work.

7. An Advance Party of 1 Officer and 3 N.C.O's. from each Unit of 57th Division will report to their opposite number at 12 noon on 30th June, and will remain at their billets until relief takes place. All Parties will take with them unexpired portion of that and following days' rations.

8. The Personnel at R.E. Dump, SOUASTRE, will be relieved by a Party from N.Z. Division by Noon 1st July.

9. R.S.M. Cook R.E., with Corpl. Cottrell and 2 Attached Infantry will take over the N.Z. Division Dump at AUTHIE by Noon on 1st July.

10. The attached Pioneers and Battle Surplus Personnel of Infantry and R.E., except Corpl. Cottrell and 1 Sapper 502 Field Coy., R.E., will rejoin their Units at Noon on 1st July.

P.T.O

Sheet No. 2.

11. Water Supply Officer, 57th Division, will get in touch with W.S.O., N.Z., Division, with whom he will exchange work in hand and duties in the respective areas.

Roads Officer 57th Division will get in touch with Roads Officer, N.Z. Division, and hand over all work and duties in his present Area.

12. The usual March Intervals will be observed.

13. Command of the Centre Sector, IVth Corps Front, will pass to G.O.C., N.Z., Division at 4 p.m. on 2nd July.

14. Completion of Reliefs will be reported to H.Q.R.E., using B.A.B. Trench Code.

15. C.R.E's. Office will close at COUIN and open at AUTHIE at 4 p.m. 2nd July.

16. ACKNOWLEDGE

Issued at 5 p.m.
27th June, 1918.

Capt. & Adjt., R.E.
for C.R.E., 57th Division.

D I S T R I B U T I O N :

Copy No.		Copy No.	
1 - 57th Div. "G"		14 - C.R.E., IV C.T.	
2 - 57th Div. "A" & "Q"		15 - C.R.E., N.Z. Divn.	
3 - O.C., 421 Field Co. R.E.		16 - O.C. 57 Div. Sigs.	
4 - do -		17 - O.C. 57 Div. Train.	
5 - O.C., 502 Field Co. R.E.		18 - A.D.M.S.	
6 - do -		19 - D.A.D.V.S.	
7 - O.C., 505 Field Co. R.E.		20 - D.A.D.O.S.	
8 - do -		21 - R.S.M. COOK, R.E.	
9 - O.C., 2/5 L.N.L.R. (P)		22 - 2nd Lieut. BICKLEY.	
10 - 170th Inf. Bde.		23 - War Diary.	
11 - 171st - do -		24 - do -	
12 - 172nd - do -		25 - File.	
13 - C.E., IV Corps.			

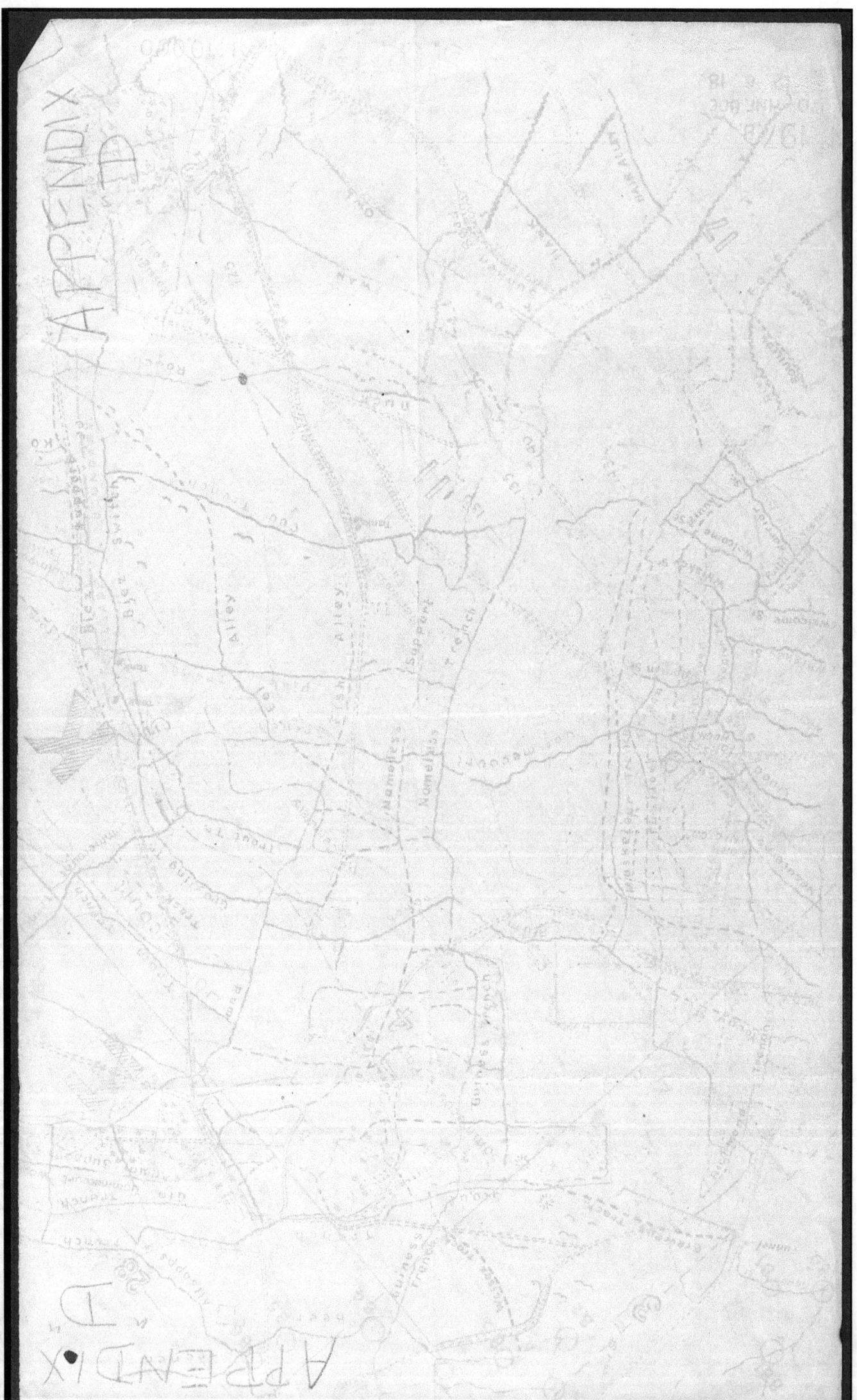

ORIGINAL
Vol 18

CONFIDENTIAL

WAR DIARY of
502 (Wessex) Field Coy RE

Volume XVII

Army Form C. 2118.

WAR DIARY
~~INTELLIGENCE SUMMARY.~~
(Erase heading not required.)

Instructions regarding War Diaries and Intelligence Summaries are contained in F. S. Regs., Part II. and the Staff Manual respectively. Title pages will be prepared in manuscript.

Place	Date	Hour	Summary of Events and Information	Remarks and references to Appendices
RUSSIEN-ARTOIS 37.OC.3 9	1/7/18		Coy. moved out of billets in CONTECOURT, handing them over to N.Z.R.	
		4.30 AM	Left 4.30 AM. Arr? HOPLINES 8 AM. Whole Coy billeted there 9 AM	
			Arrived BUS 10.0 a.m. Taken over Camp occupied by NZ	tus Chd
			Coy. NZE very good accommodation, very pretty site	
	2/7/18		Coy. resting & cleaning up &c. Received message for G.O. to all	
			field Coys. meeting them for their visit. Reassurance for work	
	3/7/18		of english Purple Reserve Line where I section to work with	tus Chd
			one Batt" men cleaning wagons & CRE WF & English eng.	
			on leave. Major Jordan (A/CRE) called	
	4/7/18		Started Training - Inf" drill, musketure	tus Chd
	5/7/18		Officers started using Tennis court. All ranks comfortable in Camp.	tus Chd
	6/7/18		Started work on PURPLE RESERVE LINE. Lt PEARCE & section and 1 Bn" daily	tus Chd
	7/7/18		Work mainly erection of high wire entanglement	tus Chd
	8/7/18		Work delayed by shortage of pickets - wire - owing to shortage of lorries	tus Chd
			unable send them in there in their turn according to orders	tus Chd
			O.C. with Lieut PEARCE meeting 2 Corp or line - work going well	

Army Form C. 2118.

WAR DIARY
or
INTELLIGENCE SUMMARY.
(Erase heading not required.)

Instructions regarding War Diaries and Intelligence Summaries are contained in F. S. Regs., Part II. and the Staff Manual respectively. Title pages will be prepared in manuscript.

Place	Date	Hour	Summary of Events and Information	Remarks and references to Appendices
BUS-EN-ARTOIS J.20.c.5.9.	8/1/18	Cont	Called on Major ARMSTRONG (late Glercoux R.E.) now commanding 547 Field Co. R.E. (Errol Laughin "B" Categ. men) at THIEVRES	
	9/1/18		Have to submit leave roster for 24 more men: this will clean off all sappers who came out with the Coy on 12/2/17 + all but 12 drivers.	wet cld.
	10/1/18		Reconnoitred trenches nrue S.J. BERTRANCOURT + work rt which is going satisfactorily. L/BURRELL r No 1. Section having own farm from L/PEARCE today. Sports Committees meeting. No wire available for wiring CAIRO AVE. so working party driving in pickets only	wet cld.
	11/1/18			wet cld
	12/1/18		Major FOX proceeded on leave to to PARIS and FLETCHER proceeded on leave to ENGLAND. Very bad weather for work, heavy rain all the morning, afternoon dried off but top stick of mud.	
	13/1/18		Work found satisfactory. Rumour was Lieut STREET to say to La.	wet cld. wet

WAR DIARY
or
INTELLIGENCE SUMMARY.

Army Form C. 2118.

Instructions regarding War Diaries and Intelligence
Summaries are contained in F. S. Regs., Part II.
and the Staff Manual respectively. Title pages
will be prepared in manuscript.

(Erase heading not required.)

Place	Date	Hour	Summary of Events and Information	Remarks and references to Appendices
BUS-EN -ARTOIS J.20 c 39.	14/7/18		Work on wiring very satisfactory. Coy Sports held in afternoon and in spite of the wet were most successful. Bicycle, Relay, & Steeplechases were most enthusiastically received by sappers. Programme attached.	Cool. RbB APPENDIX A
	15/7/18		All working parties were cancelled owing to a movement of units.	Cool. RbB
	16/7/18		Cooks again held up by lack of packets and all sappers soaked through by thunderstorm of over 1" of rain fell in the night	Cool. RbB
	17/7/18		Commenced training Cpl Kings loose for Dwd Scarpe. 5 drivers posted to Coy from 505 Fild Coy	Fine. RbB
	18/7/18		Very satisfactory work on works. Divnl RE Sports & efficiency competition. Coy won squad drill section easily, also got highest marks for class of work in wiring, but lost on time. Judges stated turn out was the best in case of mule team but mules were not well enough matched. Sr James won jumping competition with a mule & rode admirably.	Storms RbB.
	19/7/18		Working up for packets. No 1,2 & 3 sections firing on range. 11 Sappers reported as reinforcements.	Fine RbB

Army Form C. 2118.

WAR DIARY
or
INTELLIGENCE SUMMARY.
(Erase heading not required.)

Instructions regarding War Diaries and Intelligence Summaries are contained in F.S. Regs., Part II. and the Staff Manual respectively. Title pages will be prepared in manuscript.

Place	Date	Hour	Summary of Events and Information	Remarks and references to Appendices
BUS-EN-ARTOIS J30c39	20-7-18		LIEUT T.W.T. STREET returned from leave & Coys for Coy Sports. however conditions were perfect. Trees bare for elm'l Scurvy Monthly DRILLS are most fortunate in lines as length & here stone work at a coaches looks very satisfactory, most of important uning now completed.	Col in Sh
"	21-7-18		Capt. MARSHALL arrived and took over the Coy. Din' Sports 1st Coy Sports Second boys for turn out (4 marches GS) h. works comp h Sports	Post Cpl 3
"	22-7-18		No work going on Dir Sports. Reconnoitred roads with Lieut Lt Street and "Lt Pierce in morning. Started mongaring hose lines. Attended Divl Sports	Orders Conf Ord
	23/7/18		MAJOR FOX arrived from leave in PARIS.	
	24/7/18		CRE calls re MOIR PKRD to be erected. O.C. inspected squad Divo non drill competition in DisL R.E. Sports Monthly inspection of Animals & Harness. Good in spite of bad weather & other adverse circumstances.	
	25/7/18		Board held re loss of Cold Squadrons horse "Starlight". Coy on range target practice. Reconnoitred site for new MOIR (MOIR) Received	Shoveo Cto

D. D. & L., London, E.C.
(A-88)) Wt. W80/M672 350,000 4/17 **Sch. 82a** Forms/C/2118/4

WAR DIARY
or
INTELLIGENCE SUMMARY.

Army Form C. 2118.

Place	Date	Hour	Summary of Events and Information	Remarks and references to Appendices
Staff 457-D BUS EN- ARTOIS	25/7/18		(Cont.d) order from CRE to take over Camp of 428 Coy. (MAJOR ENTWHYZE) not	Showery
J.20.C.9 R.	26/7/18		on 29/7/18 — Could not C.R.E. as work i.e.	
	27/7/18		MOIR Pill Box started OC 428 Co. out: Coy. buing in camp of one. Round work of 428 Coy. with OC. Work is chiefly localities, pillboxe. Capt MARSHALL to CREs in conference re Carrihenne work.	
	28/7/18		Orders to take over from 428 Coy cancelled — four more lewis guns have been issued to Coy. Training of Section L.G. teams being carried on. Received orders to hand over to 63rd (R.N.) Div + more showing attacks has a not talk for grupas.	over APPENDIX B.
(Sheet LENS(1) #24 # BOUQUE- MAISON (4.E.05.50) WANQUENTIN (3.A.30.70)	29/7/18 30/7/18	8.30 A.M. 3.30 P.M. 6.30 P.M.	Tomorrow to BOUQUEMAISON AREA no.th. of DOULLENS. CRE's Open, Left BUS 8.30 A.M. arrid here 3.30 P.M. good march. no casual. Left 10.30 A.M. and here 6.30 P.M. Marched with Bde P.W.O. to'd much, many halt. four men marched without horses so kept fairly cool. they marched very well — 16 miles	
	31/7/18		Turned out of billets by Town Major. So Coy. moved to Noradenes Avroached OC. with Lt. FLETCHER + 4 N.C.O.s to ARRAS to take over from 3rd Fd Canadian Engineers (C.R.E.s Operation order attached) This is now CE.?	APPENDIX C

Army Form C. 2118.

WAR DIARY
or
INTELLIGENCE SUMMARY.
(Erase heading not required.)

Place	Date	Hour	Summary of Events and Information	Remarks and references to Appendices
WANQUETIN 3. H.	31/7/18		Two Coys. doing hurdling work almost entirely. One Coy working found with Bde. and one on demolitions etc. Propose putting 2 sections on forward work + two on demolitions rob jobs temporarily. Went round line with OC Major PEPLER – very quiet. Our work up to front line (not behind outposts) above ground. Saw Divn. Commander and fixed billets.	

Ch. M.
MAJOR,
COMMANDING 502ND
WESSEX FIELD Co. R.E.

APPENDIX A

COMPANY SPORTS.
Sunday, July 14th 1918.
PROGRAMME OF EVENTS.

Company Sports will be held on Sunday, July 14th, and the following events are open for competition:

1.	100 yards flat race.	Prizes - 10 frs., 5 frs., 2 frs.
2.	220 " " "	Prizes - " " "
3.	440 " " "	Prizes - " " "
4.	High jump.	Prizes - " " "
5.	Long jump.	Prizes - " " "
6.	Bicycle race.	Prizes - " " "
7.	Mule steeplechase.	Prizes - " " "
8.	Horse steeplechase.	Prizes - " " "
9.	Band race.	Prizes - " " "
10.	N.C.O's race.	Prizes by Officers.
11.	Tug-of-War (Teams of 8). Open.	Prize - 3 francs per man.
12.	Inter-section Relay Race.	Prize - 5 francs per man.

    (a) Run 100 yards.
    (b) Run 220 yards.
    (c) Cycle 220 yards.
    (d) Ride 220 yards on horse back, over jumps.
    (e) Ride 220 yards on mule back, over jumps.

Mules and horses from Section teams only.

13. Sappers v Drivers. Wrestling on mule back.
    (Teams of six.)   Prize - 3 francs per man.

ALL ENTRIES TO BE IN BY 8 p.m. ON THE 19th INSTANT.

11-7-18.

Ch. Fox Major
O.C 502 Wessex dist to R.E

APPENDIX B

SECRET.　　　　　　　　　　　　　　　　　　　　Copy No. 6

57th DIVISION.

C.R.E's. OPERATION ORDER No. 24.

Reference Maps :- 57D. and 51.C. 1/40,000.

1. 57th Division will be transferred to VI Corps on July 29th and be in G.H.Q. Reserve in the LUCHEUX Area.

2. Field Companies will move with Infantry Brigade Groups to which they are affiliated, in accordance with March Table issued by Brigades.

   Moves to be completed by 6 p.m.

3. 63rd Division (less Artillery) is being transferred to G.H.Q. Reserve in IV Corps Area on July 29th, and will take over all billets, camps and tents of 57th Division.

4. Field Companies will leave an Officer behind to hand over to Advance Parties of 63rd Divisional R.E. and will rejoin Units later. All defence Schemes, Maps, programmes of work and training facilities will be handed over together with all tents and Area Stores, and receipts, in duplicate, will be obtained and forwarded to this Office by July 31st.

5. Usual March discipline and March Intervals will be observed.

6. Completion of Moves will be reported to H.Q.R.E. stating locations.

7. C.R.E.'s Office will close at PAS and open at BOUQUEMAISON at 11 a.m.

8. ACKNOWLEDGE.

H.Q.R.E.　　　　　　　　　　　　　　　　　　　　　Capt. & Adjt. R.E.
28-7-1918.　　　　　　　　　　for C.R.E., 57th Division.

Issued at 10 p.m.

DISTRIBUTION :-

```
Copy No.  1  -      57th Div. "G".
          2  -      57th Div. "A".
          3 & 4.-   O.C. 421 Field Coy.R.E.
          5 & 6.-   O.C. 502   - do -
          7 & 8.-   O.C. 505   - do -
          9  -      170th Infantry Brigade.
         10  -      171        - do -
         11  -      172        - do -
         12  -      C.E. VI Corps.
         13  -      C.R.E., IV Corps Troops.
         14 & 15.-  War Diary.
         16  -      File.
         17 & 18.-  Spare.
```

SECRET.

57th DIVISION.

C.R.E's OPERATION ORDER No. 25.

Map Reference :- 51.B.NW. 1/20,000, 51.C. 1/40,000. All Map references are on Sheet 51B. NW. except where otherwise stated.

1. (a) 57th Division will relieve parts of the 4th and 1st Canadian Divisions in the line North and South of River SCARPE on nights 31st July/1st August, and 1st/2nd August.
    Relief to be completed by August 2nd.
   (b) 171 Infantry Brigade and 172 Infantry Brigade relieve 12th Canadian Brigade, 4th Canadian Division, on nights July 31st/Aug.1st and 1st/2nd August respectively, North of River SCARPE, 171 Brigade in Centre and 172 Brigade in Left.
   (c) 170th Brigade will relieve Left Brigade, 1st Canadian Division, South of River SCARPE on night 1st/2nd August.

2. (a) 421 Field Company R.E., will relieve "B" Coy., of 12th Battalion Canadian Engineers, 4th Division, on night 31st/1st August.
    "B" Coy. H.Qrs. - G.18.a.7.3.
    Relief to be arranged direct between O.C. 421 Field Coy. R.E., and O.C. 12th Batt. Canadian Engineers whose Headquarters are at A.27.c.3.5.
   (b) 505 Field Company R.E., will relieve "C" Coy., of 12th Batt. Canadian Engineers of 4th Canadian Division, on night of August 1st/2nd, and will move into billets now occupied by "D" Coy., 12th Batt. Canadian Engineers at H.13.b.2.5.
    Reliefs to be arranged between Os.C. concerned as in para. (a).
    Advance Party will be sent tomorrow, 31st July.
   (c) 502 Field Coy., R.E., will relieve 3rd Batt. Canadian Engineers, 1st Division, after 6 p.m. on August 1st.
    3rd Batt. Canadian Engineers H.Qrs. - Red brick house, PLACE ST CROIX, ARRAS - G.22.c.65.55.
    Billets of the 3rd Batt. Canadian Engineers will be taken over subject to approval of Town Commandant, ARRAS.
    An Advance Party of 1 Officer and 3 Other Ranks will be sent up July 31st.
    O.C. 502 Field Coy., R.E. will get in touch with O.C. 3rd Batt. Canadian Engineers as soon as possible and make himself acquainted with all works in hand, and particularly demolition schemes.

3. The Transport Lines of all three Field Companies will be at the Sugar Factory LOUEX L.10.a. (Sheet 51.C.).

4. Os.C. Units will make themselves acquainted with the line and will carry on at present with the most important works, till a re-adjustment can be made.

5. 57th Div. R.Es. will come under the orders of the C.R.Es. 4th and 1st Canadian Divisions in their respective Sectors till C.R.E., 57th Division takes over.

6. (a) All Secret Maps, documents, trench and area stores, &c. will be taken over as usual and copies of receipts sent to this Office.
   (b) Os.C. Units will also take over any R.E. Dumps in their respective Areas (being the Areas of the Brigades to which they are affiliated).

P.T.O.

- 2 -

7. (a) O.C. 2/5 Bn. L.N.L.Regt. (P) will move his "C" Coy., into billets now occupied by "C" Coy., 12th Batt. Canadian Engineers at G.16.b.7.7. on night July 31st/1st August - Details of relief being arranged direct between Battalion Commanders.

   (b) H.Qrs. and remainder of 2/5 Bn. L.N.L.Regt.(P) will move and take over portion of billets now occupied by 3rd Batt. Canadian Engineers, 1st Canadian Division, in ARRAS, about G.22.c.6.5. subject to approval of Town Commandant, ARRAS, after 6 p.m. on August 1st.
   Arrangements of relief to be made direct between O.C. Battalions concerned.

   (c) Transport Lines for 2/5 Bn. L.N.L.Regt. (P) will be at ANZIN ST. AUBIN about 8 A.

8. Completion of reliefs will be wired to this Office.

9. C.R.E.'s Office closed BOUQUEMAISON and opened at HERMAVILLE at 11.0 a.m. July 30th.

10. C.R.E.'s Office will close HERMAVILLE and open ETRUN at an hour and date to be notified later.

11. ACKNOWLEDGE.

H.Q.R.E.
30th July, 1918.

Capt. & Adjt. R.E.,
for C.R.E., 57th Division.

Issued at 11 p.m.

DISTRIBUTION:

Copy No. 1-57th Div. "G".
2-57th Div. "A" & "Q".
3-421 Field Co.R.E.
4- - do -
5-502 Field Co.R.E.
6- - do -
7-505 Field Co.R.E.
8- - do -
9-2/5 Bn.L.N.L.Regt.(P).
10-170 Infty. Bde.
11-171 - do -
12-172 - do -
13-C.R.E. 4th Canadian Div.
14-C.R.E. 1st   -do-
15-C.E.XVII Corps.

Copy No.16-C.R.E.XVII C.Troops.
17-Field Engineer Tramways, XVII Corps.
18-Town Comdt. ARRAS.
19-O.C.57 Div.Signals.
20-O.C.57 Div.Train.
21-A.D.M.S. 57 Div.
22-D.A.D.O.S., 57 Div.
23-D.A.D.V.S., 57 Div.
24-M.O.R.E., 57 Div.
25-War Diary.
26- - do -
27-File.
28-Spare.
29-Spare.

C O N F I D E N T I A L.

W A R   D I A R Y

of

509nd (WESSEX) FIELD COMPANY R.E.

From: August 1st 1918.   To: August 31st 1918.

VOLUME: XIX.

Army Form C. 2118.

WAR DIARY
or
INTELLIGENCE SUMMARY.
(Erase heading not required.)

Sheet 51 B N.W.

Place	Date	Hour	Summary of Events and Information	Remarks and references to Appendices
ARRAS	1/8/18		OC shint BURRELL to OC 3rd Bn. C.E. Took over papers etc. Lt B. investigating ST. SAUVEUR set demolitions. CRE called. Arranged to show Bde Signals Officer where explosives are placed in Caves. Also to take over Water Supply. Coy moved in. 6 P.M. Lt PEARCE Section went to Horterius with Capt MARSHALL & Transport at LOUEZ. 1 P. to take over C. Group Demolitions near ETRUN. Coy is in food billets S. side of GRANDE PLACE - large roomy cellars three storeys deep under some houses. 170 Odr. relive (remaining) me C.L.O. tonight. Called on new Brigadier (B.Genl. BOYD) re work.	
	2/8/18		Took over Bush dump yesterday (BULL DOG DUMP near Station) Inspected it today. It is to be shifted to STE. CATHERINE. NW of ARRAS. O.C. Lt FLETCHER down SCARPE VALLEY from BLANGY to FEUCHY - very wet & boggy. Called on forward Bn. Bde. CAPT DAVISON returned from BASE, after a month at CON-VALESCENT CAMP with "flu" etc. CAPT. MARSHALL will hand-over to 305- Coy - a very efficient Officer.	Wanted Coy?

Army Form C. 2118.

WAR DIARY
or
INTELLIGENCE SUMMARY.
(Erase heading not required.)

Instructions regarding War Diaries and Intelligence Summaries are contained in F. S. Regs., Part II. and the Staff Manual respectively. Title pages will be prepared in manuscript.

Place	Date	Hour	Summary of Events and Information	Remarks and references to Appendices
ARRAS	3/9/19		Chose of tunnels + caves at ST SAUVEUR & arrangements for demolition of same. Looked for new billets near swimming baths at ST NICHOLAS. Cpl. called - says Sect. Coy to work for Bde. Cine men on special jobs. To start work on completion of 2 dug-outs. L/ PEARCE with him over demolitions to KEDSON OP's &c. Lt FLETCHER wiring across S. of SCARPE VALLEY behind FEUCHY all clear. Tunnels are undefined but wire	stopping Cable?
	4/8/18		Started Recce in Train Line Tunnels. Accommodation fair. Searched for dug-outs is pretty fair. Accommodation fair. Searched for dug-outs to be worked on & for Glbstmitts to connect M.G. tunnels & emplacements in Rly Embankment behind ATHIES MILL. Saw Billets & programme of work.	give C.R.E.
	5/8/18		Investigated ST SAUVEUR Tunnel; advised CAVE MAJOR to block with wire so to cut off 2-4 exits, so as to facilitate clearing tunnel. To Divnh. Lieut PEARCE left for course at ROUEN.	showing old
	6/8/18		Reconnoitred FEUCHY FEUCHY RESERVE TRENCH with Lt FLETCHER	

Army Form C. 2118.

WAR DIARY
or
INTELLIGENCE SUMMARY.
(Erase heading not required.)

Place	Date	Hour	Summary of Events and Information	Remarks and references to Appendices
ARRAS.	6/8/18 (Cont.)		This trench to be main line of resistance in forward system - Called in forward Bn HQ	showing enemy
	7/8/18		Reconnoitred FEUCHY REST with Brig. 170th Bde. who wants new trench dug to command 2 high mounds by Railway Cutting in J.21.C. Also were in SCARPE VALLEY in front of ATHIES MILL which is now very foul. Lt. DIXON & Sergt. BONIFACE returned from course at ROUEN - report course to be a poor one.	first class
	8/8/18		Reconnoitred work acquired by Div. with L. FLETCHER. To forward Bn HQ. To Horse Lines up in - there are at LOUEZ near ETRUN - are fair.	Some CHE
	9/8/18		With CRE along FEUCHY RESERVE & part of BLANGY TRENCH. Boche more active than usual.	Very CHT
	10/8/18		Inspected dugouts being worked on by no. 10 forward Bn HQs -	very CHT
	11/8/18		Arranging to further tunnelled dugouts in BLANGY TRENCH. To Brigade daily re work. parties.	ours

WAR DIARY or INTELLIGENCE SUMMARY

Army Form C. 2118.

Place	Date	Hour	Summary of Events and Information	Remarks and references to Appendices
ARRAS @ 22.c.7.9	12/8/18		Inspected 1 week's infirmed men - Men from 8 weeks signal class received. Sappers "extra good", Sapper sergts. "fair - poor". Tunnelling instruction - are to take over dug out work today. N.D arrived.	D. Bulf. C.R.E.
	13/8/18		With C.R.E. & adjutant inspecting BABY ELEPHANT dug outs - work construction by Pioneers - not being well done. To Bn HQ the BULLDOG DUMP - Supn. C.R.E adjt. all Coy officers bathing in swimming pool ARRAS.	hot
	14/6/18		Reconnoitred FEUCHY, & front support line on left. There are very little shelled. Trench well wired but in fair condition. With line so lightly held, Sopa in each Firebay - wire every 100' so too frequent. Wire roughly 80 Kilms on night 8/11/12th. got 2 Germ men - west 4 of Mericoups Commander (FERGUSON) round line yesterday. Works front line more strongly held. B'dier called.	
	15/9/18		Conference at Bde HQ. American Colonel present. B'dier explained tactical features of defensive system.	

WAR DIARY
or
INTELLIGENCE SUMMARY.
(Erase heading not required.)

Army Form C. 2118.

Place	Date	Hour	Summary of Events and Information	Remarks and references to Appendices
ARRAS G.22.c.7.9.	16/8/18		Round line with COL. POPHAM new C.O. of 2/5 K.O.R.L.R. showed him dug outs I recovered suitable for Coy HQ with which much pleased.	see Ch 2
	17/8/18		Warned to be prepared to be relieved. Received orders from C.R.E. to this effect but cancelled later. Round line with Brigadier.	See Ch 2
	18/8/18		Reconnoitring FEUCHY VILLAGE for defence. Carrying on work. In p.m. told by Brigadier to stop all work. Decide captured last night state Hun is retiring. We are to take his 2 front lines & hold same with a Coy in each.	
	19/8/18		Detailed to Sappers to follow each Coy to spot booby traps. Inf. obtained 3 their objectives which were not occupied. CAPT. TWADDLE 1/5 L.N.L.R. captured M.G. & crew of six. XVth Div. on our right failed to keep in line making sharp opposition. Up to now trenches twice. 2 Coys detailed to work river line to were to dig right flank defence - boiled down to 2 platoons & they could do nothing but carry out Inf 1/4 both the new trench line tonight INDIAN TR. were	APPENDIX A new gas see Ch2 see Ch2
	20/8/18			

WAR DIARY or INTELLIGENCE SUMMARY

Army Form C. 2118.

(Erase heading not required.)

Place	Date	Hour	Summary of Events and Information	Remarks and references to Appendices
ARRAS G.22.c.7.	20/9/18	cont	continually counter-attacked & had to withdraw to MORAY T.R. Up to present with-drawn from scrapping with Boche last night. Arranged with Pr 2 Coys again to make night-patrolling route. At 7.30 p.m. to C.Worf Coys have orders return to our old front line — then cancelling work. Arranged wiring etc. of front line & FEUCHT RES. to the 2 Coys - have 1 Coy taken away — so only employed 1 Coy wiring front line — a very good job done, the ship actual wiring 100ft wire erected. obsolescene repaired — Lt BURRELL VC will + R.E. Am in charge of 1 Coy of Pioneer Batt. They followed trench dug by them previous 2 nights.	Pre. CRE.
	21/9/18		CRE 51st Divn (NAPIER CLAVERING) called — took him round line. Orders to carry on normal work.	v. to CRE
	22/9/18		Last night received word that 13de to be relieved tonight — by Batt: of M.G. Life Guards. (Batt. of Cyclists. phoned CRE 57 Divn who sent an officer from 404 Co. to take over/for one	

Army Form C. 2118.

WAR DIARY
or
INTELLIGENCE SUMMARY.
(Erase heading not required.)

Instructions regarding War Diaries and Intelligence Summaries are contained in F. S. Regs., Part II, and the Staff Manual respectively. Title pages will be prepared in manuscript.

Place	Date	Hour	Summary of Events and Information	Remarks and references to Appendices
ARRAS G.22.c.7.9	22/6/18		(day only) 175th Cy. C.E. + a Canadian Bde expected to take over sector tomorrow. Officer arrived, took over documents.	APPENDIX
			He party took over Dumps, Water Patrol + Demolitions.	v. Int. Cat.
			Received orders to proceed to WANQUETIN from Bde.	
			Whole Coy. bathed at swimming Baths. This has been best sector we have been in in every respect. Swimming baths a great addition.	
WANQUETIN K.32.b.5.0	23/6/18		Left ARRAS 7.30 p.m. yesterday. Arrived here in field where previously billeted 10 o/c a.m. Men, mules + lorries in transport	fine, clear
WARLUZEL Sheet LENS 11	24/6/18		Arrived here 6.0 p.m. yesterday. Goods trucks attended Corps at Bde H.Q.	fine, cool
BASSEUX LENS 11. B.H	25/6/18 26/6/18		Arrived here 6.0 p.m. Bivouacked in fields - some lorries from Bde. Very wet last night. Men went to cover. Received orders to proceed to	Rain wet cool
			West of BOISLEUX-AUMONT with Bde Group. Left 10.30 p.m. Staying behind for night, sick.	
BOISLEUX AO M.ONT J4.0.5	27/6/18		Good march last night. J up. m received orders from Bde to proceed to MERCATEL. Also orders from C.R.E. to relieve 417 Co R.E. (52 nd Div) at once	showery cool

WAR DIARY or INTELLIGENCE SUMMARY

Army Form C. 2118.

(Erase heading not required.)

Place	Date	Hour	Summary of Events and Information	Remarks and references to Appendices
LENS 11				
BOISLEUX-AU MONT J.14.0.5	27/8/18		Reported at once to Rde who were on march Went forward to follow up 2/R.E. Scouts. Unable to find 413 Coy. at map reference given — anywhere near	Showery day
	28/8/18		Found 413 Coy at their new lines, early. Proceeded with officers reconnoitring HENIN-BOIRY r. to fix place to move to — Reported to RHQ who stated must find work on our own. Initiative on work supply, wardrobes & Coy. moved to ST. MARTIN SUR COJEUL in p.m. Reconnoitred & reported on work COTEUL between ST MARTIN & BOIRY.	Showery day
ST. MARTIN SUR COTEUL K4.Q.57.5	29/8/18		Coy. in new area here as in back weather cold. 172 Rde attacked yesterday, 170 Rde mopping up & now in front of FONTAINE LES CROISILLES. Dark & dry. Rde hunting villages of HENDECOURT. 170 Rde attacking RIENCOURT today at 1 p.m. L/s FLETCHER & DIXON on water supply near ST MARTIN, & MAJOR BOIRY, clearing roads COJEUL. Also C/s, 2 mens water troughs repairing bridges. L/t BURRELL & Rest engineering FONTAINE. Also SENSEE RIVER Co. for work supply. O.C. also Mr SENSEE

WAR DIARY or INTELLIGENCE SUMMARY

Army Form C. 2118.

Place	Date	Hour	Summary of Events and Information	Remarks and references to Appendices
ST MARTIN K.4.03-7.55	29/8/18		10 dry. Ransacked FONTAINE for wells &c - but found only one burst well - in poor order. Found food Boche wells - pump at V1.a.4.7 FONTAINE very unhealthy. R. Stretcher stopped putting culvert in road at HENIN by O.C. Coy. O.C. 2nd Siege Coy. bringing steam roller O.C. 2nd Siege Coy. called; lending him fortnum [?] uniform. Am intending to keep half a section or so on light duty in Camp by day in case some urgent work by night demanded. Two parties in FONTAINE heavily shelled slightly gassed. O.C. L. STREET reconnoitred for water, then above the SENSEE, where he Cpl. ISGER "told" water with divining rod in several places close to old dry river bed. Dug down 7ft at one spot (in the HINDENBURG FRONT LINE trench, then 10ft R, then 15ft R heard running water. 16 men working on shelters for men B.W. HQ Officer running COYEUL &c. Enemy counter attacking & drove 17th Div. who took RIENCOURT yesterday, out of it south of HENDECOURT	See C.W.D.
	30/8/18			
	31/8/18			See C.W.D.

WAR DIARY
or
INTELLIGENCE SUMMARY.

Army Form C. 2118.

Place	Date	Hour	Summary of Events and Information	Remarks and references to Appendices
ST MARTIN SUR COTEAU 14.05.15	31/8/15		O.C. 1st Half. Sqn Serving water in JENSEE VALLEY. Envied by a stream of water flows down valley underground seven to river bed. Have found a 6 inch earth auger, + with this bored down to 16ft below ground level + obtained 2ft of water in hole – (at spot dug open yesterday)	Lieut Cuy
			#6 List of two Corporals since arrival in France attached. Same is co Sept by Orderly Room Sergt.	APPENDIX B

Ch. ?N
Major
Commanding 2nd
Wessex Field Co. R.E.
1/9/15

SECRET   APPENDIX A
                                                 Copy No. ...7...

170TH INF. BDE. ORDER NO. 145.

                                                 18th Aug. 1918.
Ref: Sht. 51 B.N.W. 1/20,000.

    1. 170th Inf. Bde. will attack the enemy positions S. of River SCARPE on August 19th.

    2. The attack will be carried out by 1/5th Bn. Loyal North Lancs. Regt.

    3. Objectives.

    1st Objective - ICELAND and IONIAN TRENCHES, from the ARRAS - DOUAI Railway (inclusive) to an E. and W. line through H.28.c.4.7.

    2nd Objective - A line H.22.d.7.4 (Railway inclusive) - MORAY TRENCH as far S. as H.28.d.4.9 with posts in INDIAN TRENCH.

    4. Method of Attack.

    (1) The attack will be carried out by 2 Coys. 1 Coy. will capture the 1st objective and will establish posts at the S. end of ICELAND and IONIAN TRENCHES.

    (2) When the 1st objective has been captured the 2nd Coy. will leap-frog and capture the 2nd objective.

    When the barrage has lifted off INDIAN TRENCH posts will be pushed forward and established in that trench.

    5. Forming-up.

    (1) The leading Coy. will be formed up on a taped line H.27.b.9.8 - H.27.d.9.6 by Zero minus 30 mins., with the 2nd Coy. about 100 yds. in rear of this line.

    (2) O.C. 2/5th Bn. King's Own (R.L.) Regt. will arrange:-

    (a) To keep No Man's Land clear of the enemy, with strong fighting patrols from Zero minus 3 hrs. to Zero minus 5 mins. All such patrols will be W. of the forming-up line by Zero hour.

    (b) To establish a post in SCAPA TRENCH at H.27.d.9.6 until attacking troops are formed up when the post will withdraw.

    (c) To establish a platoon post at BROKEN MILL. This post will remain in position until orders are issued by Bde. H.Q. for its withdrawal.

    (d) To cut gaps in the wire in front of BROKEN LANE by Zero minus 2 hrs.

    6. The remaining 2 Coys. of 1/5th L.N.L. Regt. will be in support in FEUCHY TRENCH and FEUCHY SUPPORT.
    Advanced H.Q. 1/5th L.N.L.Regt. will be at H.27.a.0.7.

    7. Action of Artillery.

    (a) The attack will be carried out under cover of an artillery barrage as follows:-

    Zero - Zero plus 5 mins. on ICELAND TRENCH.
    At Zero plus 5 mins. the barrage will make its first lift and will creep forward at the rate of 100 yds. in 3 mins. till it reaches a line 300 yds. E. of IONIAN TRENCH where it will rest till Zero plus 20 mins.

7. **Action of Artillery (Continued).**

At Zero plus 20 mins. it will again lift and creep back 100 yds. in 3 mins. to MORAY TRENCH where it will dwell till Zero plus 30 mins.

At Zero plus 30 mins. it will lift on to INDIAN TRENCH, remaining there till Zero plus 50 mins.

At Zero plus 50 mins. the barrage will lift on to ITALIAN TRENCH and continue as a protective barrage round the Right flank of the 2nd objective, the fire being carried out by bursts throughout the night.

(b) Heavy Artillery will bombard MORAY TRENCH, INDIAN TRENCH, ALABAMA TRENCH, RLY. Embankment with Safety limits, and all approaches for likely counter-attacks from Zero hour onwards.

8. **Action of M.Gs.**

(1) M.Gs. of 51st Division will fire as follows from positions N. of the SCARPE.

Zero - Zero, plus 40 mins. Enfilade INDIAN and ITALIAN TRENCHES.

Zero plus 40 mins. onwards. Bursts of fire between LANCER TRENCH and River SCARPE.

(2) "A" Coy., 57th Bn., M.G.Coy. will arrange to establish 2 M.Gs. in the vicinity of BROKEN MILL to cover the Right flank after the objectives have been taken.

9. **R.E. and Pioneers.**

(1) A party of R.E. will be attached to each attacking Coy. for the purpose of examining dugouts.

No dugouts will be entered by troops until reported safe by a sapper.

(2) 3 platoons 2/5th L.N.L.R. pioneers will establish themselves in RAILWAY AVENUE in H.20.d. by Zero hour, by which time the Officer i/c of the party will report to O.C. 1/5th Bn. L.N.L.Regt.

This party will be prepared to dig a C.T. between BROKEN LANE and ICELAND TRENCH under the orders of O.C. 1/5th L.N.L.Regt.

10. **Signal Arrangements.**

(1) O.C. 1/5th L.N.L. Regt. will arrange for a line to be run out to MORAY TRENCH as soon as the 2nd objective has been reached.

(2) Attacking Coys. will carry 4 pigeons.

(3) Bde. Signal Officer will arrange Visual Communication between Advanced Bde. H.Q. and Advanced H.Q. 1/5th L.N.L.Regt.

(4) Flares will be carried by attacking troops and will be lit by most Advanced troops whenever called for by contact aeroplane.

11. **Dress.** Fighting Order. Bombs, flares, tools and rations, according to instructions already issued.

12. Watches have already been synchronised.

13. ZERO HOUR will be at 1.0 a.m. August 19th.

14. R.A.P. of 1/5th L.N.L.Regt. will be at H.21.c.4.4.

15. Adv. Bde. H.Q. will open at LONDON CAVE (No. 14 tunnel entrance, G.29.d.0.8) at 12 mid-night, night 18/19th August.

Rear Bde. H.Q. will remain at G.22.c.9.7.

16. ACKNOWLEDGE.

W?!????.
Captain,
Brigade Major,
170th Infantry Brigade.

Issued through Signals
at 10 p.m. 18/8/18.

COPIES TO:-

1. 2/5th K.O.R.L. Regt.
2. 2/4th L.N.L. Regt.
3. 1/5th L.N.L. Regt.
4. 170th L.T.M.Bty.
5. "A" Coy., 57th Bn., M.G.C.
6. "A" Coy, 2/5th L.N.L.R.(P).
7. 502nd Fld. Coy., R.E.
8. 171st Inf. Bde.
9. 46th Inf. Bde.
10. 51st Division (G).
11. C.R.A., 51st Div.
12. Bde. Sigs. Offr.
13. Brigadier.
14. Bde. Major.
15. Staff Captain.
16. War Diary.
17. File.

Diary of Moves.
502 Wessex Field Coy. R.E. — APPENDIX B

12-2-17	502nd (Wessex) Field Coy., R.E. left Blackdown.
"	Arrived Southampton.
"	Embarked on 'Manchester Importer' (2 Offrs. 81 O.R. transport and 79 animals.
"	" 'Archangel.' (6 Offrs., 1 W.O., 5 Sgts., (4 Cpls., 4 2/Cpls. 114 Sappers
13-2-17	Disembarked Le Havre and proceeded to No. 5 Rest Camp.
14-2-17	Left Rest Camp at 8-30 a.m. and (Minus Spr. Burland evacuated proceeded by rail to Bailleul. (to No.2 Hospital, Le Havre.
15-2-17	Arrived Bailleul 6-0 p.m.
"	Left " 8-30 p.m.
"	Arrived Rue du Bois 12-0 p.m.
16-2-17	Arrived Vieux Berquin 7-00 p.m.
18-2-17	Left " " 5-30 a.m.
18-2-17	Arrived Sailly sur le Lys (G.22.a.7.3.) at 1-0 p.m. and proceeded to take over and carry on the work of the outgoing Unit (1st Fld.Coy., New Zealand Engrs.) Sections 1,2,3, and 4 occupied working billets near Fleurbaix - Sections 2 and 4 Barret Farm, corner of Rue de Bassieres and Rue Brache, and Sections 1 & 3 Rue de Quesne.
1-3-17	Lieut. Norman, with No. 1 Section, moved from working billets at Rue de Quesne to Rue de Bruges (G.24.a.5.1.)
5-3-17	Major Jane and Offrs. and Sections 1,3, and 4 rejoined Hdqtrs. Section at Sailly sur le Lys.
27-4-17	Moved to Port a Clou Farm (H.15.c.1.0.) - Hdqtrs. and Sections 2 & 3, leaving Section 4 and Hdqtrs. Details at Sailly.
28-4-17	Major Jane acting C.R.E.
4-5-17	Lt. Street and Section from Sailly to Port a Clou. Lt. Davison and Section 2 from Port a Clou to Sailly. Lt. Norman and Section joined Hdqtrs. at Port a Clou from advanced billet at H.26.a.0.2;
15-5-17	Major Jane returned to Hdqtrs. at Port a Clou Farm.
23-5-17	Major Jane left Unit sick.
1-8-17	Nos. 1 & 3 Sections under 2/Lieut. Fletcher moved to Armentieres (C.25.c.30.25.)
3-8-17	Headquarters and 2 & 4 Sections moved to Armentieres (C.25.c.45.35)
16-9-17)	Company, less No. 4 Section (Advance Party), left Armentieres
17-9-17)	for Fleschinelle, via Wacklands Camp.
18-9-17	Hdqtrs. and 3 Sections at L.32.b.7.6.
19-9-17	" " " U.6.a.0.0.
20-9-17	" " " Flechinelle (M.33.b.3.3.)
17-10-17	Coy. moved to Renescure area.
18-10-17	" " " Portland Camp. (Proven Area.)
20-10-17	Pioneer Coy. rejoined 502nd (Wessex) Fld. Coy. R.E.
23-10-17	Portland Camp to Canal Bank between Ypres and Langemarck.
"	Arrived Boesinghe.
8-11-17	Left "
9-11-17	Arrived Hocquingham.
10-11-17	Nos. 1 & 2 Sections left for Nortbecourt.
12-11-17	No. 3 Section left for Merckeghem
5-12-17	Nos. 1 & 2 Sections returned from Nortbecourt. No. 3 Section returned from Merkeghem.
9-12-17	Coy. moved to Pardo Camp (Proven Area).
10-12-17	" " " Elverdinghe (B.14.b.20.70.)
17-12-17	Hdqtrs. and 4 Sections Boesinghe (B.5.d.4.3.) Transport near De Wippe Cross Roads (A.11.a.9.6.)
1-1-18	Moved to Portland Camp for Armentieres (19X26.c.4.6.)
2-1-18	" " La Hays Farm " " (B.28.b.2.6.)
3-1-18	" " Armentieres (Jute Factory) (B.29.b.5.2.)
14-1-18	" " Nieppe (B.23.a.85.45.)
16-1-18	Nos. 3 & 4 Sections to La Rolanderie Farm (H.17.b.20.80.)

17-1-18	Section 2 The Farm (H.5.c.2.3.)
26-1-18	Hdqtrs. and No. 1 Section to Rue Dormoire (Huts). (H.8.b.90.20.)
29-1-18	No. 3 Section rejoined Hdqtrs.
8-2-18	Major Fox left for O.C's Course at Blendecques R.E. School of Instruction (A.P.O. S.2)
"	Captain Davison returned from - do -
13-2-18	Hdqtrs and Section 4 moved to Armentieres (B.30.d.0.3.)
"	Horse Lines " (B.29.a.5.1)
20-3-18	Bac St. Maur - Hdqtrs. and Sections (36 N-W) H.13.c.60.90.)
	Horse Lines " G.5.b.50.50.
31-3-18	Company moved from Bac St. Maur to L.32.b.7.6., beyond Estaires.
1-4-18	Arrived Steenbecque.
3-4-18	Left "
"	Arrived Warluzel F.4. 60.70.
8-4-18	Left "
"	Arrived Mendicourt F.4. 50.05.
9-4-18	Left "
"	Arrived (Orville) Amplier. E.5. 75.67.
10-4-18	Left " "
"	Arrived Halloy (57D.N-W) B.17.
12-4-18	Left "
"	Arrived Sus-St.-Leger.
13-4-18	Left "
"	Arrived Authie. (In woods).
16-4-18	Left "
"	Arrived Couin. (57D.) J.8.a.2.8. H.Q. pontoons and G.S. 4 Sections, limbers, and tool carts J.16.d.95.70.
19-4-18	Couin. Coy. with Transport arrived J.1.b.90.70.
6-5-18	Hdqtrs. with Sections 2 & 4 moved to Coigneux (J.3.b.3.4.) Sections 1 & 3 moved to Sailly-au-Bois. (J.18.d.65.40.)
20-5-18	No. 3 Section rejoined Hdqtrs. at Coigneux.
22-5-18	No. 1 " " " " "
5-6-18	Major Fox and 4 Sections to Gommecourt Wood (E.28.c.90.70.) Transport remained at J.3.b.3.4., moving out of huts for 505th Fld. Coy. and occupying others in same vicinity.
1-7-18	Coy. with transport moved to Bus. (J.20.c.3.9.)
29-7-18	" " " arrived Bouquemaison.
30-7-18	" " " " Wanquetin (K.32.b.5.0.) and spent one night in Cemetery Field.
1-8-18	Hdqtrs. and 1,3, & 4 Sections arrived Arras (Rue des Augustines and Grande Place) G.22.c.7.9. Horse Lines and No. 2 Section at Louez (L.10.a.8.5.)
22-8-18	Arrived Wanquetin. Hdqtrs. and 4 Sections with transport in Cemetery Field.
23-8-18	Arrived Warluzel. " " " " " " F.4.60.70.(51C)
25-8-18	" Basseux " " " " " " H.4.65.70.(51C)
27-8-18	After night march occupied old Gun positions at S.8.c.50.50. Arrived 2-30- a.m.
28-8-18	Arrived St Martins-sur-Cojeul area, occupying dugouts and any other shelters in area. (N.32.b.5.9.)

CONFIDENTIAL.

WAR DIARY

OF

502ND (WESSEX) FIELD COY. R.E.

FROM: SEPT. 1ST 1918   TO: SEPT. 30TH 1918.

VOLUME XX

WAR DIARY
of
INTELLIGENCE SUMMARY.
(Erase heading not required.)

Army Form C. 2118.

Place	Date	Hour	Summary of Events and Information	Remarks and references to Appendices
SHEET 7 LENS 11 ST MARTIN SUR COJEUL K.4.c.9.75	1/9/18		To FONTAINE-LES-CROISILLES with CRE inspecting proposed wells	
			being dug there (2 by two Coy.) in SENSEE RIVER bed.	
			Div¹ attacked this morning + reached broken outskirts of HENDECOURT +	
			BULLECOURT- Attacked again this evening + took HENDECOURT +	see CWD
			RIENCOURT.	
	2/9/15		Attacked again this morning + made further advance	
			O.C. Consolidation inspected wells in HENDECOURT. Met CRE who	
			approved finishing two sections forward - OC on to RIENCOURT	
			which wells are all blown in + dry. Wells in HENDECOURT	
			been - Got into touch with R.E. of 52nd on right + Canadian Engineers	
			on left, so as not to overlap. Two sections joined OC at U.17.a.o.3	see CWD
			with one tool cart + 2 limbers	
HENDECOURT 5½ SW U.17.a.6.3	3/9/18		Our Div⁹ took QUEANT, PRONVILLE, were then relieved by 63rd Div?/52nd	
			taking over their 2 villages. Reconnoitred wells + road + bridges	
			around these villages. Info from CRE called post MARTIN, inspecting	
			wells in SENSEE VALLEY en route - # Coy moved to U.17.a.o.3.	showery CWD

WAR DIARY
or
INTELLIGENCE SUMMARY.
(Erase heading not required.)

Army Form C. 2118.

Instructions regarding War Diaries and Intelligence Summaries are contained in F. S. Regs., Part II. and the Staff Manual respectively. Title pages will be prepared in manuscript.

Place	Date	Hour	Summary of Events and Information	Remarks and references to Appendices
51B SW. D.5.b.1 & 57c NE. HENDECOURT 51B SW. U.17.a.0.3	4/9/18		Reconnoitred roads, wells, bridges in valley of INCHY + PRONVILLE + then on to BUISSY + BARALLE. Got into touch with R.E. of 52nd Div on right, of 63rd Div line of INCHY) + with Canadian Inf on front line on left. Our line running 500x also behind CANAL DU NORD. Attempts to cross it last night failed. Valley near INCHY seems well watered. Should be a good place for transport, lines + troops when safer. At present pretty hot. C.R.E. called re open air bath made by us at FONTAINE, where water supply insufficient. E. r. Yn. Coy. installing plant at hot well in HENDECOURT, further enquire + hood tell.	
	5/9/18		Men doing sundry jobs on water supply. Cpl W. Bowen occurioated INCHY (which was lost but retaken by us last night) Si Blewy heavily shelled. Received orders to move to MERCATEL - These was counter-manded an hour later.	Jul Crd One Cas.
	6/9/18		During last night H.V. shells were arriving in vicinity of Camp every quarter of an hour or so. No casualties. Men working on odd jobs. All hands had a hot bath	

WAR DIARY or INTELLIGENCE SUMMARY

Army Form C. 2118.

Place	Date	Hour	Summary of Events and Information	Remarks and references to Appendices
HENDECOURT U.17.a.o.3	6/9/18		O.C. Capt. DAWSON went to 17th Bde. H.Q. A new Brigadier (Lt.Col. RANSOM) taken command in place of Brig. Genl. BOYD promoted to command 46th Div. Begun dugs to move forward on 8th following.	Showery CRJ
	7/9/18		63rd Div. relieved 52nd Div. during night. No. 295 Coy. (63rd Divl.) whom we relieve. CRE called. 6" FLETCHER to QUEANT to take over work supply from the Coy. (52nd Divl.)	
51-B V.28.c.o.9			Moved to V.28.C.o.9 in quarry with 2 Bde HQ o.c. I Section to QUEANT and one remaining at HQ2 Lines.	Showery CRJ
QUEANT D.7.6.4.9	8/9/18		Moved to QUEANT + joined Section there D.7.6.6.9. Working for 171-172 Bdes. HQ o.c. CRE called. HorseLines moved to V.26.d.6.8.	Showery cool day CRJ
	9/9/18		Working on water supply in QUEANT. CRE called. Drew stock of mat. bn.) Saw 171 Bde HQ re their requirements — also their three Bn. C.O.s who require too proping to many dug-outs — inspected 2 dug-outs 4/two 8 for pistol tractor W over turned by Boche on light railway.	
	10/9/18		Lt. DIXON visited Bde HQ, 172 Bde + all their Batts. Commandeer but found their requirements being attended to by his S.O.s Coy.	Showery CRJ

WAR DIARY or INTELLIGENCE SUMMARY

Army Form C. 2118.

Place	Date	Hour	Summary of Events and Information	Remarks and references to Appendices
QUEANT NE D7.b.49	10/9/18	(cont'd)	To CRE re crossing over CANAL DU NORD – New Coy had to marry to proceed with Bde acting as Div Advance Guard in case Bde White + first wave would probably be too far forward to transport across Canal.	showing that
	11/9/18	10.170	Bcd saw good photo of bridges + crossings. Canal is dry in most places, banks of varying height – only two crossings (causeways) appear to be intact if it falls in. Got to 5th Sqn (K.L.R.) to arrange parties for inspection of canal. Thus not possible as canal objective canal, but learnt that AWR is attacking at 6.15 p.m. to try to establish posts on the canal. Went to B Coy HQ + waited result of attack. Got info just canal as soon as posts established, but attack not successful on 171 Bde front. 170 Bde took MOEUVRES + established 2 posts 100x from Canal. Captured 62 prisoners + only had 50 casualties. Starting an open air bath in QUEANT. Work for repairs + so on	

Army Form C. 2118.

WAR DIARY
or
INTELLIGENCE SUMMARY.
(Erase heading not required.)

Instructions regarding War Diaries and Intelligence Summaries are contained in F. S. Regs., Part II. and the Staff Manual respectively. Title pages will be prepared in manuscript.

Place	Date	Hour	Summary of Events and Information	Remarks and references to Appendices
57 C.R.E. 51 B. QUEANT D.7.b.4.9.	11/9/18		Water bowsers procuring.	showery cld
	12/9/18		Reconnoitred MOEUVRES. Managed to get to causeway & demolished bridge at E.15.b.2.3. Found only a shell hole not a large crater in centre of causeway.	
			CAPT DAWSON and horselines moved to Coy HQ. Noon clear by an trench & behind bankers.	showery cld
	13/9/18		Collecting with some fire from M.G.s in neighbourhood with a view to retiring. Improving point at D1.d.6.5. Last night the enemy twice attacked 170 Bde. on the second time driving them to him	
			MOEUVRES	showery cld
	14/9/18		Yesterday 170 Bde retook MOEUVRES + their old post in LOCK ST. Am having a lot of significant for repairs in neighbourhood	shaggery
	¼		20 Officers & 412 Coy (relieving us) called. CRE called.	
	15/9/18		Finished off all jobs in hand - Handed over to 412 Coy's officer.	dull clear cld
CROISILLES T.30.B.5.5	16/9/18		Moved to the CROISILLES - Bivouacked.	
GOUY EN ARTOIS 51Q P.16.d.1.6	17/9/18		A hurricane during last night soaked everyone - Transport proceeded	

WAR DIARY or INTELLIGENCE SUMMARY

Army Form C. 2118.

Place	Date	Hour	Summary of Events and Information	Remarks and references to Appendices
GOUY EN ARTOIS P.18.d.1.6.	17/9/18		On road to GOUY. Sappers marched to BOYELLES. Horses turned to BOYELLES & marched to GOUY where are in billets thurs.	See Ch.3
	18/9/18		Cleaning up + drying wet things - Inspections	See Ch.3
	19/9/18		Squad drill &c - Hot bath all ranks. Buying new books for canteen	See Ch.3
	20/9/18		from AVESNES LE COMTE. Squad mill. Lewis gun instruction. Received orders to move to RIVIERE. Reconnoitred billets there.	See Ch.3
RIVIERE - GROSVILLE R.25.d.65.15	21/9/18		Moved to RIVIERE (GROSVILLE). Coy billets in town hubs & PEARCE and showery farm (an hour from lion)	See Ch.3
	22/9/18		Clean Inspection. Parade and address by O.C. on recent higher. Attended CRE's conference at BAVINCOURT re expected operations.	showery Ch.3
	23/9/18		CAPT. DAVISON & 4 O.R. to BULLECOURT to take over communication equipment from Corps. Men doing physical training, pontoon drill (without equipment) re football v. R.E.'s	See Ch.3
	24/9/18		To SAULTY to see 170th Inf. Bde. re proposed operations - Lt. DIXON to BULLECOURT with 17 O.R. + pontoon wagons - to load bridging equipment in wagons. Leave there ye of 2 men - other details arranging Transport going with men.	See Ch.3

Army Form C. 2118.

WAR DIARY
or
INTELLIGENCE SUMMARY.
(Erase heading not required.)

Instructions regarding War Diaries and Intelligence Summaries are contained in F. S. Regs., Part II. and the Staff Manual respectively. Title pages will be prepared in manuscript.

Place	Date	Hour	Summary of Events and Information	Remarks and references to Appendices
57. RIVIERE R2a&b5a&b	24/9/18 (cont)		Sections being organised into 2 structures with, both w/s carried fixed up, so that each section can tackle a stunt on any bridging, fitting, carpentering or demolition job. Each Section practiced firing with Lewis guns on airplane sights today.	Sgd. C.E.S.
RIVIERE 25/9/18			Transport moved with Bde. Group to NEROEUIL Sappers " " " "	
57C.N.W. NEROEUIL 26/9/18			via BAPAUME — arrived 1.0 a.m. by train to NOREUIL. 26/9/18. O.C. to C.R.E.'s conference re Bourlons interests. The Coy. is to forward with 170 Bde to help exploit success & help cross CANAL DE L'ESCAUT.	Sgd. C.E.S.
57C. N.E. 27/9/18			Moved to sunken road N.E. 29.d.2.2. with Bde Group. Left at 6.30 A.M. arrived 11.30 P.M. very tortuous journey. No. 52 & Coy living both objectives but too late for S.58.t pierced — Slept in dark — very cold & miserable — Road track v.good to refer.	Sgd. C.E.S.

WAR DIARY or INTELLIGENCE SUMMARY

Army Form C. 2118.

Place	Date	Hour	Summary of Events and Information	Remarks and references to Appendices
57 c N.E. & E.29 d 22.25			2 Sections moved up on north bank toward CANAL DE L'ESCAUT hoping to assist in crossing CANAL DE L'ESCAUT at 4 a.m.	
		02.00	2/K.O.Y.L.I. observed on towing at L of E.29 d.7.5	
		6	Small accurate ? enemy shell fire at E.24 c.5.7 but Boche on opposite bank in strength. Reported to O.C. Force. Officers & men of "D" moved up R. of	
		10.30	"D" with "D" Coy "M"K. Coy went forward to bridge rec built by 62nd F. Coy R.E. at E.29 d.16 c. one hour one with ours (wording for Pet to build) was heavy	shewing end
29/9/18			O.C. 1st Division & 20 Sappers in CANAL DE L'ESCAUT erected & nearly completed Cribber Trestle bridge over ESCAUT at F.30 a.2.4 Boche heavy suddenly opened rifle and arriving within the hour on the spot. Repaired a bridge received or today trip, to enable a cavalry troop to cross at another point. Returned to pump & truck nearby —	
			No. 1, 14 Section returned to Coy H.Q. 6th Div. went through & some enemy beyond canal	true
			one Section	R.E.S.

WAR DIARY or INTELLIGENCE SUMMARY

Army Form C. 2118.

Place	Date	Hour	Summary of Events and Information	Remarks and references to Appendices
BRANCOURT	Sep 29/18		Instructions received to put a bridge over the CANAL DE ST. QUENTIN and RESCAUT. Lt PEARCE left at twenty with 30 men & reported to CAPT MARSHALL 309 Co RE with orders to make a roadway & get a large pontoon to the canal. Two lorries to make a roadway. By 11 AM the three lorries went to Canal du F24a & constructed a pontoon bridge across Canal and MINOR traffic began. No 2 R.ESCAUT, cut down & carry up to 10 new lined baulks — lifted up by 10 Pioneers lined to truck for R.X.A. across the bridge and onward down & to PROVILLE. Completed bridge started by Lt PEARCE on range but daylight. Whole run over before surplus went north Skeltzee & M.E. fire — Had one casualty — Sapper HARRIS wounded. Reconnoitred bridges at PROVILLE etc.	

CONFIDENTIAL.

-- WAR   DIARY --

OF

502nd. (WESSEX) FIELD COMPANY R.E.

From October 1st.1918   To October 31st. 1918.

VOLUME XX1.

WAR DIARY
or
INTELLIGENCE SUMMARY.

Army Form C. 2118.

Place	Date	Hour	Summary of Events and Information	Remarks and references to Appendices
57° N.E. GRAINCOURT E.29.b.2.2	1/10/18		L/ PEARCE started a bridge over CANAL DE ST QUENTIN at lock in	
			A.13.d.22 but was shelled off. Enemy apparently have observation	
			down canal from spurs of CAMBRAI. L/ DIXON recco'd secret	
			to pontoon bridge &c.	O.2.66 C.R.C.
	2/10/18		L/ FLETCHER + STREET. clined footpath shewing recce of md locks	
			at A.13.d.22 + raised saddleback of pontoon bridge or church watershed	
			has dropped 2 to 9 ft. Trying to find bridge which if found but	Fire S.A.D.
			without success.	
	3/10/18		Two Sections of CANAL recce'd – Pearce recco'd after reconnaissance	
			by C.R.E. r.O.C. intending to build trestle bridge over R. ESCAUT.	
			at A.20 a & q were twice got at by M.G. from wood to east of them +	31/46 C.E.
			were lucky to escape being hit, bridge could not be built	
	4/10/18		Two sections repairing pontoon bridge Pontoon Bridge has been cleared	Sine die
			by M/ WILPRED.	
	5/10/18		CAPT DAWSON absented absent. O.C. & H.Q. R.E. to A.D.R.E. CAPT DAWSON assumed command	
			of Coy.	

WAR DIARY or INTELLIGENCE SUMMARY

Army Form C. 2118.

Instructions regarding War Diaries and Intelligence Summaries are contained in F. S. Regs., Part II. and the Staff Manual respectively. Title pages will be prepared in manuscript.

(Erase heading not required.)

Place	Date	Hour	Summary of Events and Information	Remarks and references to Appendices
54 C N.E. & 54 B N.W.				
GRAINCOURT	6/10/18		Capt Davies & Lt Spence to PROVILLE to reconnoitre site for bridge at A20.b.20.99.	
E.29.B.2.2.			Found they started work soon to perfect the 10ft sections but were nearly about to [...]	
			2 mile above CANAL, he came up to also away the [...] of the bridge, demolished	
			by Bosch. Attempts to erect 2 trestles were made but delay ensured for dark [...]	
			bridge by with 20m. glass piles [...] bridge at F.24.b.20.60. Shore [...] on [...]	
			and [...] to [...] the [...] men [...]. Drivers too [...].	
	7/10/18		No.1. section to F.24.b.20.60 to relieve [...] equipment No.3 [...] repair	
			bridge [...] and at L.T. STREET [...] all the [...] to take [...] over, [...]	
			52nd Divs. No.2 section [...] to build up at WESTERN approach to bridge	
			at F.29.d.5.8. No.4 section [...] [...] buffer approach to [...] at F.24.b.	
			20.60 [...] [...] [...] after [...] the A.20.b.20.99 trestle bridge	
			[...] returning [...] to [...]. Borehole [...] [...] by [...].	
	8/10/18		No.1 section [...] up @ 2 (SERVICE) TRESTLE bridge at A.20.b.20.99 [...]	
			to [...] [...] [...] [...] [...] [...] [...], this was about the 1st attempt	
			to put @ bridge [...] in the vicinity. SHORE [...] on bridge at F.24.b.20.60	
			[...] [...] No.4 [...] put 2 SERVICE TRESTLES in place	

WAR DIARY
or
INTELLIGENCE SUMMARY.

(Erase heading not required.)

Army Form C. 2118.

Place	Date	Hour	Summary of Events and Information	Remarks and references to Appendices
57 c N.E. GRAINCOURT E.29.c.2.2	9/10/18		No 3 section to PROVILLE to clear roads to & from bridge at A.20.c.25.95 formed by Nek of RIVER ESCAUT. 12" bridge of C.E. VII Corps. Received information from C.R.E. CAMBRAI definitely reversing orders No 1 & 4 orders to prepare roads	
57 B.N.W. PROVILLE A.20.c.20.50			to PROVILLE & establishes HQ there. OC reconnoitred all roads from PROVILLE to CAMBRAI & entered CAMBRAI, which was now practically clear. Found that	
			all 4 of the numbers of the Company to come to PROVILLE (excluding transport). OC again ordered one section with Lt PEARCE and Jones all ranks from PROVILLE to CAMBRAI. Orders to transport to follow arrive & test traps Dec at A.16.c.20.25 across the whole width of the road area 30' deep × 15' across.	
		18.00 Lon.	the Coy were busy transport establishes at A.20.c.20.50. Received orders from C.R.E. to withdraw to F.21. (57 c NE) to road on leaving south answer to intersection.	Fine but very short very short attempts for moving
			Direct where shall we are nearly shelled gas 5 minutes until for where seems HE & gas two hundred amongst transport lightly no casualties. Bullets entered [?] by aeroplane actually came to lie at F.21.d.95.30	
		20.45 Lon.	Coy establishes at F.21.d.95.30. Rocket killing Jones. 9 Jan the rest are 2 men.	
			The everyone had back to fairly Hard day	

Army Form C. 2118.

WAR DIARY
or
INTELLIGENCE SUMMARY.
(Erase heading not required.)

Instructions regarding War Diaries and Intelligence Summaries are contained in F. S. Regs., Part II. and the Staff Manual respectively. Title pages will be prepared in manuscript.

Place	Date	Hour	Summary of Events and Information	Remarks and references to Appendices
54 C.N.E.				
FONTAINE F21 d 9630	10/9/18		Received orders to move forward also by support at F.19.0.2.9 at 13.30 hours	
		1645	Arrived at D.29.C.50.30. Have no arrangements to make for men till next day.	
D.29 c 50.30	11/9/18	0315	Received orders from C.R.E. to collect Lieut. Barker's battery & proceed to Light Cap F21 d 9630. Lt. Barker to lead up. Lt. Pearce i/c Barker's party to follow.	
			QUENTIN. Lt DIXON detached i/c wagons. Lt PEARCE i/c Barker's party to follow.	
		0430	Barker's wagons left. Lt DIXON will proceed direct from CAMBRAI to APPRES.	
			BDE. transport will be located in vicinity of ... time tonight.	
		0830	Lt FLETCHER i/c transport moved off for APPRES and dismounted party & Coy with civilians proceeded via Cruille, 12/10/18 Junck etc. MARLES LES MINES area (old LENS II).	Survey 1500 hrs Lours
		1200	Lt STREET 9H OR proceeded as advanced party.	anvedo mp.D/
		1000	Lt PEARCE's party arrived back from Coudry (advanced section) C.R.E. arrived.	
	12/9/18		R Coy. C. completed the entraining last (HERMIES) Lt. PEARCE, 6 men & 2 wagons travelled the other route (entraining at FREMICOURT) See 170-2nd/Field bde B.C. arrived 158 & 159 stopped Company entrained at 1645 hours; train proceeded	to eta 84

(A-834) Wt. W8091/M1672. 350,000. 4/17. Sch. 32a. Forms C.2118/14. D(D). & L., London, E.C.

Army Form C. 2118.

WAR DIARY
or
INTELLIGENCE SUMMARY.
(Erase heading not required.)

Place	Date	Hour	Summary of Events and Information	Remarks and references to Appendices
MARLES LES MINES MAZEBROUCK	13/10/18		Cpl By Reward at LHARLES LESMINES at 0800 turns after railway journey from Ib. arrived at 1930 taken lorries billets for the men within 500 liters.	Very close
			Horses to be shipped, stables 1/2 mile from billets. Officers (CO & 2 in C) & Reader up the Line.	I.O.A.
16.2.1.			2nd C/ Bm. to more to the base about DEVILLE LES LOUVEMER	29/10/18
		1900	Reserves polics for 172 2/f Bm. to more to the base about DEVILLE LES LOUVEMER	
			(See L/ 346 diste 1/10/18)	
BETHUNE	14/10/18		By reces received a copy at new billets at 1600 hours there are hundreds	
728,000 R12, H 28			I have instructed were to hold line & following my own reckon...	Love 29/10/18
			...under the order of this above formed	
			Received orders to relieve 517 Wks Coy RE & 47 Div on 15/10/18 then outposts	
			The Coy RE of M24 & 28 on 16/10/18.	
			Lt Crawley & C & GE Powell W awarded M.M (see Coy orders attached) Braves & Cox	
			will carry on operational work.	
	15/10/18		CO & A.O. STREET to N3 & 6.28 to see 517 520 Coys R.E. last after arrival of Lens.	Look but
			That M21 Elt Hy RE has been ordered to relieve us 6.20. Reached spec. Yesterday	or very bad
			however for the storming on 3 men were sent up on 15/10/18, C.R.E. to arrange that	
			these men will shortly be told night transport, top also to be indem C.R.E. of 7th Div.	

CRE 47th Div

Army Form C. 2118.

WAR DIARY
or
INTELLIGENCE SUMMARY.
(Erase heading not required.)

Instructions regarding War Diaries and Intelligence Summaries are contained in F.S. Regs., Part II. and the Staff Manual respectively. Title pages will be prepared in manuscript.

Place	Date	Hour	Summary of Events and Information	Remarks and references to Appendices
BETHUNE 1:40,000 M.12.a.2.8	16/10/18		Men as C.A.P. to duties overleaf of messgaurd. Inspection of S.B.Rs, rifles, equipment etc.	Roster wk of 9.4.41
M.2.H.6.27.	17/10/18		Moved to M.2.H.6.2.7. taking over billets from 510 Co. R.E. Ho. moved forward on same day with W.2.H.6.2.7. Proceed to reconnoitre roads and bridges etc. at CANAL at LILLE, as C. in C. forward with Lt. Pearce to reconnoitre to LILLE.	Two
Sheet 36 1:40,000 HALLENES P.30.c.5.7.	18/10/18	0070	into Western suburbs of LILLE. Everything quiet, HOLMDEL, Pat Bradburn saw Lt Pearce with Hd. 102 complete moved forward to HALLENES, to await instructions for bringing the CANAL HAUTE DEULE. Lt Fletcher with H.5 section proceeded to Div HQ at ENGLOS (used as kit dep.), thence to LONNE & LE MARAIS, nearby as much Lt STREET reconnoitred roads, Lu. Kersey new dump area, Pot & Pow at CARNOYS Div to relieve D.C. to CANAL, Lo reconnoitre new Jap bridges on again P.II.A.9.B, P.10.B.9.D.	so Oct 21 Bridge Q memorandum Jav O.4.
		1500	Remainder of Coy. moved to HALLENES, another Lt. BURRELL, who reported to Coy. from leave.	
HELLEMES Q.18.O.0.70	19/10/18	18.00	Lt Pearce with Ho. 102 section to CANAL at P.10.C.8.2, to construct bridge for field guns. Lt BURRELL & Ho.1 section moved forward to HELLEMES from HQ of Div. H.Q. engineers C.R.E., O.C. 9 & Lt. FLETCHER reconnoitres demolition damages at PONT LOUIS XIV Q.4.C.5.13. Bridge to be constructed by Ho. Coy. 8 Ho.2 section to 3 sections with material somewhere Lille to fire. Ho. 4 section ordered to report at 0.4.d.0.0 to Devonville to rebuild new bridge in middle	

1577 Wt.W10791/1773 500,000 1/15 D.D.&L. A.D.S.S./Forms/C. 2118.

WAR DIARY or INTELLIGENCE SUMMARY

Army Form C. 2118.

Place	Date	Hour	Summary of Events and Information	Remarks and references to Appendices
SHEET 36 1:40,000 HELLEMMES Q.18.a.2.8.	19/9/18	11.50	Lt PEARCE finishes field gun bridge at P.10.c.8.2., offers wooden all night. Goes and sees good time, trestle bridge 75 ft span. (made probably good) Monthifferes 8. (In LILLE today, unless the 3 sectors with bridging transport, parade cheer't, the people were very excited, cheery, shouting, throwing men, throwing flowers, the flags & in any case are having the mee. It becomes all new men agreed appearing to no vestige founded by style and against them.) Remainder of company moves to HELLEMMES, Q.18.a.2.8. No H. section at monitor bridge at Q.4.c.5.1.	Cheery 19/9/18
Sheet 37 1:140,000 H.17.a.5.4.	20/9/18 21/9/18	10.00	No sections en bridge, others later by Mon 103. Bridge finished by 08.00 hours on 21/9/18. Quart & wK.Of finished. 8 trestles, H2' span to carry 8 ton aub loads. No. & of Mon. 18. Company moved forward to TEMPLEUVE area, billetted in a farm, 500 yards to where the H.67 F.C H.64 & R.E. 59 Div had billy that moved to this morn. Unclimowns very meager.	21/9/18
	22/10/18		O.C. & Lt FLETCHER went forward to reconnoitre RIVER D'ESCAUT, on both front, O.C. willing to mend the demolished Pont à CHIN road bridge, which had not yet been reconnoitred. The infantry were crossing the river at 08.00 lower Pt PONT À CHIN	

1577 Wt. W10791/1773 500,000 1/15 D. D. & L.   A.D.S.S./Forms/C. 2118.

Army Form C. 2118.

WAR DIARY
or
INTELLIGENCE SUMMARY.
(Erase heading not required.)

Instructions regarding War Diaries and Intelligence Summaries are contained in F. S. Regs., Part II and the Staff Manual respectively. Title pages will be prepared in manuscript.

Place	Date	Hour	Summary of Events and Information	Remarks and references to Appendices
Sheet 37-1-40,000				
H.21.c.6.4	24/10/18	0930	Enemy had retired to canal to fludge. We were shelled and came under heavy M.G. rifle fire, some casualties. Attacks were reformed & reinforced by the companies in support. Two companies were detailed to go forward again as Escort, but returned to near the encampment was prevented in every way from going forward.	Report J.V. 81
			Lt FLETCHER & 40 Zouaves went forward to PONT à CHIN, and attempted to pass BOSCNE level bridge at I 32 a 9.1. Enemy was very active; a number of over 3 men were withdrawn, so that, inspite of repeated attempts nothing was done.	
			Company moved to CAZEAU, H.33.a.6.6.	
GAZEAU H.33.c.6.6	24/10/18		OC at conference with Div Commander & GOC 170 Bde. Two platoons going along ling to Pot. front. OC to RAMEGNIES-CHIN to see CO Belle - me (New PERLE) to arrange. Intelligence negative. Reconnaissance showed it cannot be made except for cavalry pass or etc. etc. Div. tels on CDNE South, significant delay.	
		18.00	Lt BURRELL with 40 Vouches went forward to foot bridge area at I 26 a.8.5. Successfully	
			Show by 2300 Leave	
		18.00	Lt PEARCEY & 40 Zouaves went forward to foot bridge area at I 33 central. Successfully	
		00.30	Leave 24/10/18	

WAR DIARY or INTELLIGENCE SUMMARY

Army Form C. 2118.

Place	Date	Hour	Summary of Events and Information	Remarks and references to Appendices
GIZEAU				
H.33.c.6.6	23/10/18		2 Lt S.E.L. HUNT from BASE, reported for duty.	
			In text cases there had been enemy aeroplanes very busy MG fire. The situation was that there was no warning posts on E. either of river. Enemy kept in certain 50 + 60 x yards but shot smartly at our observations from time to time. (Time lot of work.)	2/Lt. H. 81
		18.00	2nd Lt. MUIR, 6 & party of 8 moved forward to I.32.a.9.1.9 against the sand ridge. One stallion & H.Ga. It exploded job earlier to casualties. (forbidden to use horses.) Was having a sit-out, enemy came into camp. Appear to be unaware of advance, not see-ever. The cave into the caps we have a continually shots day & night & yelling. Slightly nightly. Spent day indoors in any kit. MAJOR FOX on leave to U.K. Section at work on FOURCROIX, nothing onward to BEA.Q.I.8.2.9 onles by morning. O.E.H.S. Party got day forward.	2/Lt. Muir 81
	24/10/18	07.15	Beats & billeting recces in TEMPLEUVE. Head shirt kit on a cattle, use sent 2 men, 8 to MOORE & BENSON, Dental Surgery infirmed, about 6 miles. (Cottless.) Excellent opportunities. Two spare horses. All the miles came from England sent to no.	E.C. 2/Lt. Muir 81
	26/10/18	10.00	Motor-lorry-pot Lieut. to SAILLY-LEZ-LANNOY, G.34.a.8. 2 miles Lt BURRELL. Lt STREET reported from 51 C.C.S. Still very much unwell, unwind at HORSE LINES. Finally at I.32 & I.32.a.9.1 reported damage by shell fire and out Lt PEACE	

Army Form C. 2118.

WAR DIARY
or
INTELLIGENCE SUMMARY.
(Erase heading not required.)

Place	Date	Hour	Summary of Events and Information	Remarks and references to Appendices
Sheet 37		1:40,000		
CAZEAU H33.c.2.6	26/10/18		with No 2 section went up to reorganise new decoy steels at CAMPS, fix smoke and floating lights. Surplus bridge materials to pushing plank for engineers.	See Apx. 81
	27/10/18		Lieut HAYRES with No 9 party of 8 men from No 1 section did repair bridge at I 26.c.4.5. Bridge next abutmt o Pushe Siever, but work was finished by 0080 hours 28/10/18. Lt FLETCHER 9 Co. 1/5 L.N.L.R (2/Lt GOODWIN R.E.) reconnoitred new bridge in I 32 d. reg.com. The bridge is not to be put down until everything is ready. Lt HUNT & 8 men of No 4 section to go to Batta HQ. H36.c.8.1 to do the bridge. Site closes I 32 d. 3.8. Material for this bridge taken up & dumped at I 32.c.5.4.	See Apx. 81 / See Apx. 81
	28/10/18		Dust from CRE Corps to turn 2 as henceforth to reconnect Role in case of enemy retirement. Lightly spent learning new army from instructions. Hostilities ceased by Lt. _____ CO to love tins. Think we can now arrange transport & Coy lorry & truck mules & harness NCO's horses aright.	Tool set Indented for 29/10/18
	29/10/18		Dust of CRE and 117th Div. 107th & CRE 117th Div. ref. relief by 518 Fld Co R.E. henceforth. CHEETHAM, OC 518 Co. R.E. arrived to take over motif. 1 section of his Co. also arrived to where services needed. Relief of forward sections complete at 2100. Lieut No 1 section to HORSE LINES. Lt PEACE attached to LEZENNES Sheet 36 R13 a.00.70.	See Apx. 81

… **WAR DIARY** *or* **INTELLIGENCE SUMMARY** …

Army Form C. 2118.

Place	Date	Hour	Summary of Events and Information	Remarks and references to Appendices
Sheet 36 LEZENNES R.13.d.05.45	31/10/18	1:40,000 06 45	Coy. moved in accordance with CRE's instructions order No. 29 (attached) & arrived at destination 1600 hours. Billeting accommodation appears good.	Copy of Ins Ors 29

W.J.M. Dowsett, Major.

SECRET.

Copy No .....

170TH INF. BDE. ORDER NO. 158.

Ref. Maps Sheets 57c.N.E. 1:20,000.
             LENS.1:100,000.
             HAZEBROUCK. 1:100,000.
                                          10th October 1918.

1. Part of the transport of 170th Inf. Bde. Group (as laid down in para. 2 below) will move to ARRAS on October 11th, and will move thence to MARLES LES MINES on October 12th.
    For this purpose 170th Infantry Brigade Group will be composed as follows:-

        170th Inf. Bde.
        502nd Fld. Coy., R.E.
        3/2nd W.L.Fld.Ambce.
        No.2 Coy., 57th Divl.Train.
        Mobile Veterinary Secn.

2. (a) The following transport will proceed by Road on October 11th and 12th :-

170th Bde.H.Q.	less 1 G.S.Wagon, 1 L.G.S.Wagon 7 Riders.
Bde.Signal Secn.	less 1 L.G.S.Wagon and 4 Riders.
Battalions.	less 2 Cookers, 1 Water Cart, 1 Mess Cart, 1 Baggage Wagon, 4 Riders.
Fld.Coy.,R.E.	less 1 L.G.S.Wagon, 1 Mess Cart, 2 Riders.
Field Ambce.	less 1 L.G.S.Wagon, 1 Mess, Cart, 1 Water Cart, 2 Riders.
Mobile Vet.Secn.	All Transport.
Coy., Divl.Train.	All Transport less Baggage Wagons.

(b). All Transport not going by Road, and personnel, will move by train on October 12th under orders to be issued later.
    Billeting parties will be required to proceed by lorry to the new area on October 11th; Instructions for this will be issued later.

3. Transport (as shown in para. 2.) will move as follows on October 11th 1918.:-
    Starting Point: CROSS ROADS J.9.b.7.2.

No.2 Coy. Div.Train pass starting point at		0910 hrs.
170th Inf.Bde.H.Q.	-do-	0915 "
2/5th Bn.K.O.R.L.R.	-do-	0920 "
2/4th Bn.L.N.L.R.	-do-	0925 "
1/5th Bn.L.N.L.R.	-do-	0930 "
502nd Fld.Coy.R.E.	-do-	0935 "
3/2nd W.L.Fld.Ambce.	-do-	0945 "
Mobile Vet.Secn.	-do-	0950 "

    ROUTE:) Road Junction D.19.c.3.1. - LAGNICOURT - CROISILLES - HENIN - BEAURAINS.

4. (a) Lt.Col. H.W.F.Stokes,D.S.O., Commanding 57th Divl.Train will command all the Div. Transport moving by road and will be responsible for issuing orders and co-ordinating march of transport of Brigade Groups.
    (b). Transport of 170th Inf.Bde.Group will be under the command of Captain LEAHY, Commanding No.2 Coy., 57th Divl. Train., during the move.

5. Orders for the move of Transport from ARRAS to MARLES LES MINES will be issued by O.C. 57th Divisional Train.

6. Distances of 200 yds. between Transport of Units and 25 yds. between Sections of 6 vehicles will be maintained on the march.

7. ACKNOWLEDGE.

                                                                  Captain,
                                                             Brigade Major,
                                                     170th Infantry Brigade.

Issued through Signals at
2330, 10th October, 1918.
(Distribution shown overleaf).

1-2. 2/5th Bn. K.O.R.L.R.
3-4. 2/4th Bn. L.N.L.R.
5-6. 1/5th Bn. L.N.L.R.
7. 170th L.T.M.B.
8-9. 502nd Fld.Coy., R.E.
10-11. 3/2nd W.L.Fld.Ambce.
12-13. No.2 Coy., 57th Div. Train.
14. 57th Mobile Vet. Secn.
15. 57th Division 'G'.
16. 57th Division 'Q'.
17. O.C. 57th Divl. Train.
18. Staff Captain.
19. War Diary.
20. File.

SECRET.

170TH INF. BDE. ORDER NO. 159.

Copy No. 10

11th Octr. 1918.

Reference Shts:- 57C.N.E.) 1-20,000.
57C.N.W.)
LENS.) 1-100,000.
HAZEBROUCK.)

::

1. 170th Inf. Bde. Group (less portion of transport which has already proceeded by road) will move by tactical trains to the MARLES-LES-MINES Area on Octr. 12th, and will be transferred to I Corps, Fifth Army.

2. March to entraining stations and entrainment will be carried out in accordance with the attached Tables 'A' and 'B'. Table 'C' shows detail of troops and transport to proceed by Train No. 5.

3. On arrival at LAPUGNOY (detraining station) units will proceed to billets as follows:-

```
Bde. H.Q...       ...     ... )
2/4th L.N.L.R...          ... )
170th L.T.M.B.    ...     ... ) MARLES - LES - MINES.
502nd Fld. Coy., R.E. ...     )
3/2nd (W.L.) Fld. Ambce.      )
No.2 Coy., 57th Div. Train.   )

2/5th K.O.R.L.Regt.....    LUZINGHEM.

1/5th L.N.L. Regt......    CALONNE - RICOUART.
```

Units will march to billets from the detraining station in the order of their serial Nos. in Tables 'A' & 'B'.

4. (a) Quartermasters of battalions and 1 Officer from each other unit proceeding by train No. 5 will report to the Staff Captain at FREMICOURT STATION at 14.00 hours Octr. 12th.
   (b) One officer from each unit proceeding by train No. 4 will report to the Bde. Major at HERMIES STATION at 15.00 hrs. Octr. 12th to assist in entrainment.
   These officers will know the entraining strengths of their unit.
   (c) The above officers will be required to assist in detraining at LAPUGNOY.

5. No detrainment will take place until definite orders have been given to that effect.

6. Intervals of 100 yds. between Coys. and 100 yds. between transport of units will be maintained during all marches.

7. Arrival in billets in the new area and location of new H.Q. will be reported to Bde. H.Q.

8. Bde. H.Q. will close at D.29.c.8.8 at 12.30 hrs. Octr. 12th and will be on No. 5 train, re-opening at MARLES-LES-MINES on completion of move.

9. ACKNOWLEDGE.

Issued through Sigs.
at 17.30 hours. 11/10/18.

Captain,
Brigade Major,
170th Infantry Brigade.

COPIES TO-
1-2. 2/5th K.O.R.L.R.   7-8. 170th L.T.M.B.   13. 57th Div. 'G'.
3-4. 2/4th L.N.L.R.   9-10. 502nd Fld.Coy.R.E. 14.   do.   'Q'.
5-6. 1/5th L.N.L.R.   11-12. 3/2nd (W.L.) F.A. 15. Brigadier.
16. Bde. Major. 17. Staff Capt. 18. Bde. Sigs.Offr. 19. W.D. 20. File.

TABLE "A" for personnel moving by Train No. 4.

SERIAL NO.	UNIT.	FROM.	TO.	STARTING POINT.	TIME PASSING S.P.	ROUTE TO STATION.
1.	Part of 170th Bde. H.Q.	D.29.c.	HERMIES STA:	Rd. junc. J.5.b. 3.4.	13.00.	Track to J.6.a. 7.1 -DEMICOURT- HERMIES J.30.a. 3.3-J.30.b.2.4- J.30.c.8.3 -K. 31.a.0.3.
2.	1/5th L.N.L.	do.	do.	do.	13.03.	do.
3.	2/5th K.O.RL.	do.	do.	do.	13.12.	do.
4.	2/4th L.N.L. (less 1 Coy.)	do.	do.	do.	13.21.	do.
5.	502nd Fld.Co.	do.	do.	do.	13.27.	do.
6.	3/2nd (W.L.) Fld. Ambce.	do.	do.	do.	13.35.	do.

NOTE - The above train will convey PERSONNEL ONLY. Time of entrainment - 15.15. Time of arrival at LAPUGNOY=-20.20.

TABLE "B" for personnel moving by Train No. 5.

SERIAL NO.	UNIT.	TO.	STARTING PT.	TIME PASSING S.P.	ROUTE.	REMARKS.
1.	170th Bde.H.Q. (less portion travelling by Train No.5)	FREMI- COURT STA:	Rd. junc. J.4.b.3. 1.	11.15.	LOUVERVAL- LEUGNY - FREMICOURT	-
2.	1 Coy.2/4th L.N.L.R.	do.	do.	11.20.	do.	Loading & unload- ing party.
3.	1/5th L.N.L.R. (T'pt. only)	do.	do.	11.25.	do.	
4.	2/5th K.O.R.L. (T'pt. only)	do.	do.	11.30.	do.	
5.	2/4th L.N.L.R. (T'pt. only).	do.	do.	11.35.	do.	
6.	170th L.T.M.B.	do.	do.	11.40.	do.	
7.	502nd Fld.Coy. R.E.(T'pt.only)	do.	do.	11.45.	do.	
8.	3/2nd (W.L.)Fld. Ambce.(T'pt.only)	do.	do.	11.50.	do.	

NOTE - This train will convey transport and such personnel as is laid down in Table 'C'.
Time of entrainment - 14.15. Time of arrival at LAPUGNOY- 21.20.

TABLE 'C'. Detail of transport proceeding by Train No. 5.

UNIT.	PERSONNEL Offrs. O.Rs.		HORSES.	4-WHEELED VEHICLES.	2-WHEELED VEHICLES.
Bde. H.Q.					
1 G.S. & 1 L.G.S.	6	14	7	-	-
wagon.	-	4	4	2	-
Bde. Sig. Scn.	1	27	9	1	-
(L.G.S. wagon).					
Battns. (each).	1	-	-	-	-
2 cookers.	-	2	4	2	-
1 water cart.	-	2	2	-	1
1 baggage wagon.	-	2	2	1	-
1 mess cart.	-	1	1	-	1
4 riders.	-	4	4	-	-
1 L.G.S.	-	1	2	1	-
502nd Fld. Coy., R.E.	1	-	-	-	-
1 L.G.S. wagon.	-	1	2	1	-
1 mess cart.	-	1	1	-	1
4 riders.	-	4	4	-	-
3/2nd (W.L.) Fld.A.	1	-	-	-	-
1 G.S. Wagon.	-	2	2	1	-
1 L.G.S. Wagon.	-	1	2	1	-
1 mess cart.	-	1	1	-	1
3 riders.	-	3	3	-	-
170th L.T.M.B.	4	50	-	-	-
1 Coy. 2/4th L.N.L. (loading and unloading party).	4	100.	-	-	-

SECRET.

Copy No. 5.

170TH INF. BDE. ORDER NO. 160.

13.10.18.

Ref: BETHUNE Combined Sheet 1:40,000.

1. (a) 170th Inf. Bde. Group will move to the FOSSE - BOUT DEVILLE Area on Oct. 14th in accordance with the attached March Table.
    (b) For this purpose 170th Inf. Bde. Group will be composed as follows:-

    170th Inf. Bde.
    502nd Fld. Coy. R.E.
    3/2nd W.L. Fld. Amb.
    No.2 Coy. 57th Divl. Train.
    57th Bn. M.G.C. less 2 Coys.

2. Billeting areas will be allotted by the Staff Captain who will inform units when and where billeting parties are required, and will arrange for guides from these billeting parties to meet units on entering the new area.

3. A halt will be made for dinners at 11.50 hrs, the march being resumed at 13.00 hrs.
    During this halt units will keep the road clear, and will halt outside villages.

4. Distances of 500 yds between Battalions, 100 yds between other units, Coys., and a unit and its transport, will be maintained on the march.

5. Arrival in billets and location of new H.Q. will be notified by units, who will send the usual runners, to Bde. H.Q.

6. Bde. H.Q. will close at MARLES - LES - MINES at 08.45 hrs. and will reopen in the new area at a place to be notified later, on completion of the march.

7. ACKNOWLEDGE.

Issued at 20.00 hrs,
13.10.18.

Captain.
Brigade Major,
170th Infantry Brigade.

COPIES TO:-

1. 2/5th K.O.R.L.R.
2. 2/4th L.N.L.R.
3. 1/5th L.N.L.R.
4. 170th L.T.M.B.
5. 502nd Fld. Coy. R.E.
6. 3/2nd W.L. Fld. Amb.
7. No.2 Coy. 57th Divl. Train.
8. 57th Bn. M.G.C.
9. 57th Div. 'G'.
10. 57th Div. 'Q'.
11. Brigadier.
12. Brigade Major.
13. Staff Captain.
14. Bde. Sig. Offr.
15. War Diary.
16. File.

March Table to accompany 170th Inf. Bde. Order No. 160.

Serial No.	Unit.	From.	To.	Starting Pt.	Time passing Starting Pt.	Route.
1.	Bde. H.Q.	MARLES-LES-MINES.	FOSSE - BOUT DEVILLE Area.	Level Crossing, D.19.d.6.1.	09.00 hrs.	CHOCQUES - CHAT. L'ABBAYE - W.14.d.4.6. - HINGES - Q.28.d. 9.2. - Q.30.b.5.3. - R.21.d.1.7.
2.	2/5th K.O.R.L.	LOZINGHEM.	do	do	09.05 hrs.	do
3.	2/4th L.N.L.R.	MARLES-LES-MINES.	do	do	09.17 hrs.	do
4.	1/5th L.N.L.R.	CALONNE-RICOUART.	do	do	09.29 hrs.	do
5.	170th L.T.M.B.	MARLES-LES-MINES.	do	do	09.41 hrs.	do
6.	502 Fld.Coy.RE.	do	do	do	10.05 hrs.	do
7.	3/2 W.L.Fld. Ambce.	do	do	do	10.08 hrs.	do
8.	No.2 Coy. 57th Divl. Train.	do	do	do	To clear Starting Pt. by 08.30 hrs.	do
9.	57th Bn. M.G.C. (less 2 Coys).	BRAQUEMONT.	do	As ordered by Div. H.Q. To join 170th Inf. Bde. Group in FOSSE – BOUT – DEVILLE Area.		

CONFIDENTIAL.

WAR DIARY.

OF

502nd. (WESSEX) FIELD COMPANY R.E.

From November 1st.1918 - To November 30th.1918

(Volume 22)

Army Form C. 2118.

WAR DIARY
or
INTELLIGENCE SUMMARY.
(Erase heading not required.)

Instructions regarding War Diaries and Intelligence Summaries are contained in F. S. Regs., Part II. and the Staff Manual respectively. Title pages will be prepared in manuscript.

Place	Date	Hour	Summary of Events and Information	Remarks and references to Appendices
SHEET 36, 37	1 – 40/10/18			
LEZENNES. (FINE) R.13.d.05.	1.11.18 (wet)		Coy cleaned its Installation equipment & checked its deficiencies.	
"	2.11.18 (wet)		Coy commenced its training programme, working from 0900 — 1500 hrs.	
"	3.11.18 (wet)		Coy. carried on with its training as above.	
"	4.11.18 (wet)		Ditto	
"	5.11.18		Ditto. Lieut Burnell departed on 5 days leave to Boulogne	
"	6.11.18 (wet)		(7.11.18 to 12.11.18) Training carried on. Major W.J.M. DAVISON. left coy to command 505th Field coy R.E.	
"	7.11.18 (fine)		Training carried on as per programme; LIEUT. I. DIXON. left for leave to U.K.	
"	8.11.18 (showery)		Training carried on as per programme. Painting of Mob. vehicles commenced.	
"	9.11.18		Major FOX returned from leave. Received orders to be prepared to move at short notice. Major D. Hundriatch in Sist. Assoc. Leogue - still unsuccessful.	Func. CH?
TEMPLEUVE 10/11/18 27. H.33	10/11/18		Left LEZENNES 0500 hrs. Arrid in old billet "HOSPICE" TEMPLEUVE 1300. O.C. with	

Army Form C. 2118.

WAR DIARY
or
INTELLIGENCE SUMMARY.
(Erase heading not required.)

Instructions regarding War Diaries and Intelligence Summaries are contained in F. S. Regs., Part II. and the Staff Manual respectively. Title pages will be prepared in manuscript.

Place	Date	Hour	Summary of Events and Information	Remarks and references to Appendices
TEMPLEUVE 37. H. 33.	10/11/18		Officers to PONT-A-CHIN to reconnoitre bridge built there by 147th Div'n. a very poor bit of work.	2nd Cav?
	11/11/18		1 Section to PONT-A-CHIN working on approaches to above bridge. OC and CRE 147. & 37. at MONT GARNI on road to TOURNAI where diversion is blocked by bridge. Sent Lt FLETCHER & STREET & sections to MT GARNI to make road ford, police there, billets at FROYENNES.	2nd Cav?
	12/11/18		LIEUT. G. RAYNER M.C. No 1 H 21 Co. promoted to CAPT. in This Coy vice CAPT. DAVISON who has been promoted to be SO to Coy. Lt HUNT left this Coy for no H21. Capt RAYNER arrived. DAVISON has been in this Coy since its formation, joined when it went to CHRISTCHURCH in October 1915. Has been second in command since June 1917 & others acted as OC. a painstaking keen & energetic officer. Has made a great success of HQ Section & mounted personnel. OC to MONT GARNI - PONT-A-CHIN. Received orders to send 2	

WAR DIARY or INTELLIGENCE SUMMARY

Army Form C. 2118.

Place	Date	Hour	Summary of Events and Information	Remarks and references to Appendices
TEMPLEUVE 37 H 33	12/11/18		Sections tomorrow to O.C. 505 Coy for work on bridge in TOURNAI also to take over maintenance of bridge r.c. at PONT-A-CHIN	505 Coy.
	13/11/18		O.C. with Lt BURRELL & Capt RAYNER rode to MONT ST AUBERT to see enemy lines, r.c. (and view). Armistice with Germany officially declared. O.C. to PONT A CHIN where Lt PEARCE taking over from 515 Co. thence to TOURNAI to 505 Coys bridge. Saw four other bridges in TOURNAI, two of them INGLIS bridges. Back along river bank reconnoitring for breached obstructions r.c. CAPT RAYNER to MONTGARNI	505 Coy
	14/11/18		Work as yesterday. Lt PEARCE replacing broken trestle bridge over soft credit in Causeway at PONT A CHIN by heavy trestles. Material drawn from a fine Boche dump at X.1.IV. O.C. to Brigs Coy in afternoon. Wireless telegrams from Germany State 7 minus equivalent to go off in TEMPLEUVE today. Be reconnoitred ground, billets where No 3 & Sections have been for 2 days.	9/153
	15/11/18		At FROYENNES Coy moved there. Lt FLETCHER went to Paris on leave. O.C. started writing history of Coy. Hourly frost weather fine & scarcely.	9.vi O.P.

Army Form C. 2118.

WAR DIARY
or
INTELLIGENCE SUMMARY.
(Erase heading not required.)

Instructions regarding War Diaries and Intelligence Summaries are contained in F. S. Regs., Part II. and the Staff Manual respectively. Title pages will be prepared in manuscript.

Place	Date	Hour	Summary of Events and Information	Remarks and references to Appendices
FROYENNES Sheet 37. O.14.	16/11/18		2nd Lieut PEARCE'S section finished a pontoon trestle bridge at PONT A CHIN across a 50ft crater - work on bridge in TOURNAI progressing; difficulties encountered owing to silt & great height of trestles.	2nd CRE
	17/11/18		Bridge in TOURNAI finished - About 15 Q work done by the Coy -	2nd CRE Lieut Colo CRE
	18/11/18 19/11/18		Several visits to TOURNAI on pass. Gave men a rest as they have been working long hours lately.	
			Moved to LEZENNES. Keys 1st day march - 30 miles per hour average. Back in old billets. Called on 25 KORLR. Captain Journey Wounded. Coy away & Tournai full of Italian returned prisoners.	
	20/11/18		2 officers at LEZENNES i.e. officer attached looking by new C.O. I. W/All 2nd Lt. KC. D.S.O. on dismobilization	Lieut Colo
	21/11/18		OC to C.R.E on various matters - Warned [that] R.M. probably moving shortly.	CRE
	22/11/18		OC left on French leave	
	23/11/18		Church Parade and Educational training.	
	24/11/18		Capt Knyvett went on Paris leave. Church Parade with 2/5 KORLR	
	25/11/18		Education Scheme now properly comprehensive & time.	

Army Form C. 2118.

WAR DIARY
or
INTELLIGENCE SUMMARY.
(Erase heading not required.)

Instructions regarding War Diaries and Intelligence Summaries are contained in F. S. Regs., Part II. and the Staff Manual respectively. Title pages will be prepared in manuscript.

Place	Date	Hour	Summary of Events and Information	Remarks and references to Appendices
LEZENNES Sheet 36 A.13.d.05.45	26/10/18 27/10/18		Training and Evacuation lectures but Pothelesi will train 1/yr.	
	25/10/18		Training and Evacuation Route March.	
	29/10/18		Lecture by Sir Francis Younghusband KCSIE&c — on INDIA and the war, was most interesting, all officers attended	
	30/10/18		Eshquin preparatory to moving on more	

COMMANDING 500
WESSEX FIELD Co. R.E.

CONFIDENTIAL

WAR DIARY

of

509nd (WESSEX) FIELD COY." R.E.

From: December 1st 1918   To: December 31st 1918.

Volume XXIII.

Army Form C. 2118.

WAR DIARY
or
INTELLIGENCE SUMMARY

(Erase heading not required.)

Instructions regarding War Diaries and Intelligence Summaries are contained in F.S. Regs., Part II. and the Staff Manual respectively. Title pages will be prepared in manuscript.

Hour, Date, Place	Summary of Events and Information	Remarks and references to Appendices
CARVIN (MINE). LENS 11 40.85 1/12/18	Marched from huts LEZENNES to CARVIN & were inspected en route by G.O.C. Arrived to date in coal mine. Men billetted in old Boche huts.	Majority C/S CWD
LOUEZ. LENS 11 3 T 57.75 2/12/18	Marched from CARVIN to LOUEZ & marched through LENS en route. Men arrived in camp chilled to the bone - cooked and frozen to their huts.	Fine PW3
3/12/18	Men rested after march. Camp fatigues only were carried out. No 4 Section moved to AGNEZ LES DUISANS.	Wet PW3
4/12/18	LIEUT STREET & No 4 Section commenced work at on 17 of 13 de Groupe. Capt RAYNER returned from PARIS Rages No 1, 2 & 3 Sections worked in camp & Rendering huts & fire proof etc.	Fine CWD

1247 W 3299 200,000 (E) 8/14 J.B.C. & A.   Forms/C.2118/11.

WAR DIARY
or
INTELLIGENCE SUMMARY
(Erase heading not required.)

Army Form C. 2118.

Hour, Date, Place	Summary of Events and Information	Remarks and references to Appendices
LOUEZ. (ENS.II. 3 J 57.75) 5/12/18	MAJOR FOX returned from leave in France	Auth. C.I.O.
6/12/18	50 Chinese students road up to Camp. C.R.E. called. No.2 Section at work on earthquake.	Auth C.I.O.
7/12/18	All hands busy on various works. Adjutant J.S.S. C.I.O. called	
8/12/18	O.C. to M.S.R. R.E. H.Q. + Detachment at AGNES-LEZ-DUISANS	J.S.S. C.I.O.
9/12/18	To R.E. H.Q. I received another copy of another report from Capt L.O. Davies ref. to where he was reported as casualty from Blangies where he was attached on 3/12/18. He also missing near GRAINCOURT at 4.30 a.m. 26/9/18 + believed to be a casualty.	J.S.S. C.I.O.
10/12/18	No.2 Section left for AGNES yesterday to work with Tp. H.	Auth C.I.O.
11/12/18	Mjr Str Davies taken to C.C.S. No APM for enquiry re K AGNES Inch Supply	Auth C.I.O.

Army Form C. 2118.

WAR DIARY
or
INTELLIGENCE SUMMARY
(Erase heading not required.)

Instructions regarding War Diaries and Intelligence Summaries are contained in F. S. Regs., Part II. and the Staff Manual respectively. Title pages will be prepared in manuscript.

Hour, Date, Place	Summary of Events and Information	Remarks and references to Appendices
LOUEZ 12/1/18	O.C. + H.Q. Section also reported on recent operations.	wet C.H.?
13/1/18	Received orders O.S.O.1 (Lt. Col.) V.C. J. ARQMS (B.S.M.G. Cpl.) Manual through Wales - O.S.O.3 - Cpl. Lieutenants [illegible] brought improvements. Arrangements have been made in camp.	dull
14/1/18	Major FOX moved to Div. H.Q. to take up duties of C.R.E. during absence of Lt.Col. JORDAN.	dull G.R.
15/1/18	The men of company had whole day off works & parades except small party working on Baths at [illegible].	fine G.R.
16/1/18	MAROEUIL. Lt. BURRELL moved to H.Q.R.E. to take up duties of Stores Officer. 2/Lt. LEDSON on leave. 2/Lt. DIXON moved to AGNEZ-les-DUISANS to relieve 2/Lt. STREET who proceeded on leave to U.K.	wet G.R.
17/1/18	O/O.C. wrote to 314 P.O.W. Coy & 139 A.T. Co. R.E. to arrange for work to be done in Corps Dump, Road Company.	Heavy showers G.R.

WAR DIARY or INTELLIGENCE SUMMARY

Army Form C. 2118.

Place	Hour, Date	Summary of Events and Information	Remarks and references to Appendices
LOUEZ	18-12-18	No. 1 Section (Sergt. SILVESTER in charge) proceeded to AUBIGNY in afternoon, to take over duty for reception in that area.	Showery. G.R.
"	19-12-18	A/O.C. went to AUBIGNY before the parade occupies of hut had not been warned & were unwilling to part with them. Asked to return back to Coy.H.Q. — O.R.E. concerned. Lt. PEACE & 5 O.R. proceeded to GOMMECOURT area.	Dull. G.R.
"	20-12-18		Wet. G.R.
"	21-12-18	Half company employed in running hotels & stables & making tables & benches for use of Division at Xmas.	Fine G.R.
"	22-12-18	SUNDAY. Spent as a rest day.	Wet. G.R.
"	23-12-18	2nd Lts DIXON & SELKIRK 3 & 4 rejoined Company from AG-NEZ – ex- DUISANS	Dull. G.R.
"	24-12-18	Men of company busy making special menu tables etc & decorations for Xmas. Officers of company were entertained at Sergeants Mess in the evening.	Wet. G.R.

Army Form C. 2118.

WAR DIARY
or
INTELLIGENCE SUMMARY

(Erase heading not required.)

Instructions regarding War Diaries and Intelligence Summaries are contained in F. S. Regs., Part II. and the Staff Manual respectively. Title pages will be prepared in manuscript.

Hour, Date, Place		Summary of Events and Information	Remarks and references to Appendices
LOUEZ	25-12-18	CHRISTMAS DAY. N°s 1, 2, 3 & 4 Section messes had Christmas Dinner at 1pm. The chief items being Turkey, pork & plum-pudding, with beer to finish. The O/C. R.E., O.C. & officers visited all the sections at dinner. Each section had a sing-song in evening.	Wet. gR.
	26-12-18	BOXING DAY. H.Q's Section had Christmas Dinner at which they entertained MAJOR FOX M.C. & CAPT. RAYNER M.C., 2nd Lt. PEARCE M.C., 2nd Lt. DIXON. C.S.M. BARLOW & 5 O.R. followed by a supper & sing song in the evening.	Wet. gR.
	27-12-18	The above party returned from LILLE. Company returns for C.R.E.'s unloaded trainloads of timber etc.	Wet. gR.
	28-12-18	Company work much curtailed on account of very bad weather. Men scrubbed equipment etc.	Wet & Stormy gR.
	29-12-18 30-12-18	SUNDAY. Day off. Company repaired Nissen huts on camp improvements etc & Mica works party. Lt. & 2nd Lt. Dix. accompanied by G.S.O.I. C.R.E. inspected trenches G.O.E. S.S.K. and 7 O.R. proceeded on Lorry trip to LILLE.	Wet & Stormy gR.
	31-12-18	2nd Lt. DIXON delivered 1st series of lectures on telegraphy etc. Major FOX returned from leave.	Wet. gR.

CONFIDENTIAL

WAR DIARY

OF THE

505TH (WESSEX) FIELD Co R.E.

FROM

JANUARY 1st to 31st 1916.

VOLUME TWELVE

Jan 31st 1916

CONFIDENTIAL

WAR DIARY

OF

502nd. (WESSEX) FIELD COY. R.E.

From: 1st January 1919   To: 31st January 1919

VOLUME 28.

WAR DIARY
or
INTELLIGENCE SUMMARY

(Erase heading not required.)

Army Form C. 2118.

Hour, Date, Place	Summary of Events and Information	Remarks and references to Appendices
1/1/19. LOUEZ near ARRAS.	O.C. returned to Bry. Lt.Col. Goodwin taking over as C.R.E. First day of 57 Div. Racemeeting. Lt.Burrel's horse fell during steeplechase. Lt.B. taken to C.C.S. suffering from concussion.	Fine Ch?
2/1/19	Second day of Race Meeting	Showery Ch?
3/1/19	Bacher for Inspection by G.O.C.	Showery Ch?
4/1/19	Inspected & inspected boots C.R.E. wagons newly painted, turned out over a pretty good show.	Fine Ch?
6/1/19	Inspection by G.O.C. van MARDEUIL - was very pleased with men. Cups returned. Lieut Skuts rehabilitation team.	Fine Ch?
7/1/19	421 Coy. going to LIGNY. S&S training. Third Coy. handing over all work for the Brig. to Div.H.Q. Agreed to be distributed with which 2 Platoons under Lieut Pearce to AGNES. One to WARLUS.	showery Ch?
8/1/19	To WARLUS BERNEVILLE. Out CPL "R" Baker rapidly this poor. Manual work on cinema To DIV HQ AGNES	Fine Ch?
10/1/19	To HANQUETIN - saw Co. 2/f/ LR. Work on rifle range proceeding	Fine Ch?

Army Form C. 2118.

WAR DIARY
or
INTELLIGENCE SUMMARY
(Erase heading not required.)

Instructions regarding War Diaries and Intelligence Summaries are contained in F. S. Regs., Part II. and the Staff Manual respectively. Title pages will be prepared in manuscript.

Hour, Date, Place	Summary of Events and Information	Remarks and references to Appendices
LOUEZ near ARRAS		
11/1/19	15 O.R. demobilized	one C.A.P. clean C.A.P.
12/1/19	14 " "	"
13/1/19	19 " "	2nm C.A.P.
14/1/19	7 " "	Ann. C.A.P.
17/1/19	5 " "	2nm C.A.P.
18/1/19	3 " "	fine C.A.P.
19/1/19	8 " "	fine C.A.P.
20/1/19	O/C to HQ to take over from C.R.E. procedure on leave & Lt. St Pierre warned for Demobilization	rain C.A.P.
21/1/19	2/Lt. J.E. Reeves leaves write for Demobilization. 2. O.R. Demobilized. Detachment (No 3 Section) return to Coy Hd.Q. from WARLUS. 505 Fld Coy relieve us on work for C.R.E.'s HQ & 172nd Bde.	Frosty. Frost
22/1/19	Re Classification of Horses X.192.	Frosty fog
23/1/19	45 Horses & mules malinged.	Frosty. fair
24/1/19	7. O.R. Demobilized	Frosty. fair
25/1/19	2. O.R. Demobilized	Frosty. fair
26/1/19		Frosty Frost & a little snow fell

WAR DIARY
or
INTELLIGENCE SUMMARY
(Erase heading not required.)

Army Form C. 2118.

Hour, Date, Place	Summary of Events and Information	Remarks and references to Appendices
LOUEZ near ARRAS.		
27/1/19.	Nothing to record. Capt RAYNER rejoined the company from duty with 4.11th Fd. Co.	Frosty, slight thaw. Fuss
28/1/19.	Remainder of Horses & vehicles realigned & Classified	Frosty. Fuss
29-1-19 "	X, Y & Z Received instructions to send detachment from AGNEZ LES DUISANS	Frosty g/R
30-1-19 "	The two sections — detachments at AGNEZ LES DUISANS rejoined the company in afternoon.	g/R
31-1-19 "	Lt Start accompanied G.S.O.1 & others to BERNEVILLE to make arrangements for transport at proposed film demonstration.	g/R

CONFIDENTIAL.

WAR DIARY

OF

502nd.(WESSEX) FIELD COMPANY R.E.

From Feb.1st.1919 - to - Feb.28th. 1919.

Volume. 25.

Army Form C. 2118.

WAR DIARY
or
INTELLIGENCE SUMMARY

(Erase heading not required.)

Instructions regarding War Diaries and Intelligence Summaries are contained in F. S. Regs., Part II. and the Staff Manual respectively. Title pages will be prepared in manuscript.

Hour, Date, Place	Summary of Events and Information	Remarks and references to Appendices
ZOUEZ Nr ARRAS.		
1/2/19.	6y[?] Regmn[?] schme[?]	Fine
2/2/19.	One O.R. Demobilized	Fine.
3/2/19.	One O.R. Demobilized	"
	Nothing to Record.	

WAR DIARY
or
INTELLIGENCE SUMMARY

(Erase heading not required.)

Army Form C. 2118.

Instructions regarding War Diaries and Intelligence Summaries are contained in F. S. Regs., Part II. and the Staff Manual respectively. Title pages will be prepared in manuscript.

Hour, Date, Place	Summary of Events and Information	Remarks and references to Appendices
LOUEZ near ARRAS		
4/2/19	CAPT. RAYNER left on leave. LIEUT DIXON left in connection with citizenship at OXFORD, due to return 19/3/18	in cold & fine car
5/2/19	CRE returned from leave. MAJOR FOX rejoined unit.	u. cold & fine car
6/2/19	On praying Sgt. RICHARDS & Cpl KNIGHT to man float at R.E. Shops MARQUEIL	V. cold c/s
9/2/19 11/2/19	OC. to DUISANS, AGNES at work on fencing around cemeteries at DAINVILLE AIX NOULETTE	u cold & fine v cold c/s
13/2/19	LIEUT. STREET to TINCQUES	
14/2/19	2nd Lt. F. SKINNER attached for duty from 505 Rd by RE	V. Cold. Fine
15/2/19	2 men Demobilized. Major Fox handed over Coy accounts & Imprest to Lieut. T.W.T. STREET	V. Cold. Fine
16/2/19	Major Fox left Unit for Demobilization. 4.O.R.	Thaw. Fine
17/2/19.	12 O.R. reSD on Detachment to TINQUES. 4.O.R. Demobilized.	Thaw Fine & Rainy.
18/2/19.	Conference attended by O.C. & CRE 5 T.G. on mobilization equipment.	Divorce & Fine Cold. Cold. Fine.
19/2/19	Nothing to Record.	

1247 W 3299 200,000 (E) 8/14 J.B.C. & A. Forms/C. 2118/11.

Army Form C. 2118.

WAR DIARY
or
INTELLIGENCE SUMMARY

(Erase heading not required.)

Instructions regarding War Diaries and Intelligence Summaries are contained in F. S. Regs., Part II. and the Staff Manual respectively. Title pages will be prepared in manuscript.

Hour, Date, Place	Summary of Events and Information	Remarks and references to Appendices
ZOUEZ Near ARRAS.	C.O.R. to Detachment at TINQUES.	Showery. TOB
20/2/19.		
21/2/19.	Nothing to Record.	Showery. R108
22/2/19.		Showery. R08
23/2/19.	Work 2. Arrivals to Staging Camp.	
24/2/19.	Work at Halte Repas, TINQUES. Erection of huts etc. Lt. Walther & T.O.R. proceeded to huts at BRETENCOURT. To carry out a film demonstration. Lt. J.G. Buller took over Command of Company	Fine Fine
25/2/19.	Work at HALTE REPAS TINQUES.	Showery
26/2/19.	" "	Showery
27/2/19.	Work at HALTE REPAS TINQUES. C.R.E. - inspected Animals, Transport, MT Transport Lines, Drivers & Batmen. He gave instructions for improvements to Drivers huts - to be carried out.	Wet

1247 W 3209 200,000 (E) 8/14 J.B.C. & A. Forms/C. 2118/11.

Army Form C. 2118.

WAR DIARY
or
INTELLIGENCE SUMMARY

(Erase heading not required.)

Instructions regarding War Diaries and Intelligence Summaries are contained in F. S. Regs., Part II. and the Staff Manual respectively. Title pages will be prepared in manuscript.

Hour, Date, Place	Summary of Events and Information	Remarks and references to Appendices
ZOUEZ N. ARRAS. 28/2/17.	Work @ HALTE REPAS, TINQUES, B. TILSENT. 2nd/Lt. 7.O.R. returned from B. RETENCOURT. 2nd Lt. Stuart took over from 2nd L.G. Rutter, who returned to C.R.E's H.Q.	S. Ginny (Tubs)

Vol 26

CONFIDENTIAL.

War ▲ Diary

OF

502nd.(WESSEX) FIELD COMPANY R.E.

March 1st.1919   -   To   -   March 31st.1919

Volume 27.

Army Form C. 2118.

WAR DIARY
or
INTELLIGENCE SUMMARY

(Erase heading not required.)

Instructions regarding War Diaries and Intelligence Summaries are contained in F. S. Regs., Part II. and the Staff Manual respectively. Title pages will be prepared in manuscript.

Hour, Date, Place	Summary of Events and Information	Remarks and references to Appendices
ZOUEZ N. ARRAS		
1/3/19.	Went to VINQUES.	Stormy. Fair
2/3/19.	Nothing to Record.	Frost. T.O5.
3/3/19.	Went to VINQUES.	Frost.
4/3/19.	O.C. to VINQUES.	Stormy. T4H
5/3/19.	Went to Rest Camp at VINQUES (men down to ZOUEZ.)	Frost. T6ff.
6/3/19.	Capt. Marshall D.C.M. R.E. taken over by from 2a T.R.Scool.	Stormy. T6ff.
7/3/19.	Nothing to Record.	W.D. T6ff.
8/3/19.	Sapper Davies on Suspended Sentence returned to unit. Final lists of Cadre A prepared.	Fine. T10.
9/3/19.	Church Parade.	Stormy. T10.
10/3/19.	Draft of 10 O.R. left for 24th Div. 4 arrivals for Deafness. Total arrivals in Charge only 17.	Dull. T10.

WAR DIARY or INTELLIGENCE SUMMARY

Army Form C. 2118.

(Erase heading not required.)

Instructions regarding War Diaries and Intelligence Summaries are contained in F.S. Regs., Part II. and the Staff Manual respectively. Title pages will be prepared in manuscript.

Hour, Date, Place	Summary of Events and Information	Remarks and references to Appendices
LOUEZ 11-3-19	Capt G. RAYNER rejoined unit from leave after 14 days extension on medical grounds	fine g/r
" 12-3-19	Capt RAYNER took over command from Capt MARSHALL & visited H.Q. R.E. as to work in hand in afternoon.	Showery g/r.
" 13-3-19	O.C. visited party at TINCQUES with C.R.E. also to see new job dismantling hut at SAVY	fine g/r. still g/r.
" 14-3-19	Routine	full g/r Showery g/r
" 15-3-19	Party at TINCQUES completes work & rejoined unit.	
" 16-3-19	SUNDAY Church Parade, no works	
" 17-3-19	Cpl. STRATTON & 6 O.R. proceeded to SAVY to dismantle SASKATOON CLUB hut for M.J. BANGRINE. O.C. visited them & arranged for returning by 57 Div. M.T. lay	Showery g/r
" 18-3-19	Officers & O.R. attended Band concert by R.E. Band (from CHATHAM) at SUISANS in afternoon. The Band also gave concert to the 3 Field Cos of the	

WAR DIARY or INTELLIGENCE SUMMARY

Army Form C. 2118.

(Erase heading not required.)

Hour, Date, Place	Summary of Events and Information	Remarks and references to Appendices
LOUEZ 16-3-19 (a.m.)	Garrison in hut of 505 Fd Co R.E., wk. 15 instruments.	Showing g.R.
" 19-3-19	1st STREET M.C. R.E. (The last remnant of Officers who came to France with the Company) & 11 O.R. left the Company (for demobilisation). O.C. visited FREVIN CAPELLE (with C.R.E.) & SAVY	give g.R. give g.R.
" 20-3-19	Preparing & checking stores & equipment for visit of A.D.O.S.	give g.R.
" 21-3-19	ditto	Nil g.R.
" 22-3-19	All stores & equipment arranged, deficiencies noted & signature of A.D.O.S. XI Corps obtained to amended A.F.G.1098. Officers & vehicles unserviceable &c.	give g.R.
" 23-3-19	SUNDAY V Voluntary Church Service	give g.R.
" 24-3-19	Stores & equipment repacked in ToN carts.	Still g.R.

Army Form C. 2118.

WAR DIARY
or
INTELLIGENCE SUMMARY

(Erase heading not required.)

Instructions regarding War Diaries and Intelligence Summaries are contained in F.S. Regs., Part II. and the Staff Manual respectively. Title pages will be prepared in manuscript.

Hour, Date, Place	Summary of Events and Information	Remarks and references to Appendices
LOUEZ 25-3-19	Lost remaining 13 animals (grade 'X' Mules) Despatched to railhead enstuched by L/C Hicks & 7 drivers. Receive two mules attached from 57 K Div P of (B AC)	Fine gr.
" 26-3-19	Cleaning up wagons & equipment	Dull gr.
" 27-3-19	Completed transfer of stores from LOUEZ dump to 1st Army Dump ETRUN	Showing gr.
" 28-3-19	Cleaning up wagons & reinforcement	Fine gr. Snow storms gr.
" 29-3-19	Ditto	Ditto
" 30-3-19	SUNDAY. No church parade. WSGT HUNT joined the party from leave in UK.	
" 31-3-19	Cpl Shatton & 6 Rs proceeded by lorry to AUBIGNY & dismantle a hut in lieu of 57" RAMT 6. Vehicles maintained from Sugar factory at LOUEZ and parked in the company lines.	Fine gr.

No. 626
Date 30/4/19

CONFIDENTIAL WAR DIARY

OF

502 (Wessex) FIELD COMPANY R.E.

From 1st April 1919 to 30th April 1919.

Volumn No. 27.

WAR DIARY
or
INTELLIGENCE SUMMARY

Army Form C. 2118.

(Erase heading not required.)

Instructions regarding War Diaries and Intelligence Summaries are contained in F. S. Regs., Part II. and the Staff Manual respectively. Title pages will be prepared in manuscript.

Place	Date	Hour	Summary of Events and Information	Remarks and references to Appendices
LOUEZ	1/4/19		Routine	fine gr.
"	2/4/19		11th Simon rejoined from leave in UK.	
	3/4/19		O.R. left unit for army of occupation	
	4/4/19		1st Skinner & 9 O.R. left unit for demobilization	fine gR
	5/4/19		11th Simon & parties to H.Q. R.E. Works party returned from AUBIGNY	
	6/4/19		Sunday. Works party 60 O.R. proceeded to AUBIGNY.	
	7/4/19		Company visited & quarters inspected by Brig. Genl. Meynell, Cdg 57th Div 91 Indus	
	8/4/19		Routine	
	9/4/19		Works party returned from AUBIGNY.	
	10/4/19			
	11/4/19		Routine	dull with showery gR
	12/4/19			
	13/4/19			
	14/4/19		Easter Holiday	21st & 23rd fine
	21/4/19			
	22/4/19		Routine	dull with heavy showery gR
	30/4/19			

- CONFIDENTIAL -

WAR   DIARY

509nd (WESSEX) FIELD COMPANY, R.E.

1st May 1919.   to   31st May 1919.

VOLUME No. 28

Army Form C. 2118.

WAR DIARY
or
INTELLIGENCE SUMMARY

(Erase heading not required.)

Instructions regarding War Diaries and Intelligence Summaries are contained in F. S. Regs., Part II. and the Staff Manual respectively. Title pages will be prepared in manuscript.

Hour, Date, Place	Summary of Events and Information	Remarks and references to Appendices

Instructions regarding War Diaries and Intelligence Summaries are contained in F. S. Regs., Part II. and the Staff Manual respectively. Title pages will be prepared in manuscript.

WAR DIARY
or
INTELLIGENCE SUMMARY
(Erase heading not required.)

Army Form C. 2118.

Hour, Date, Place		Summary of Events and Information	Remarks and references to Appendices
LENS. 11.	17.5.19.	5 O.Rs. left for demobilization.	Weather fine. [initials]
3 T. Coy. B.	18.5.19.	Routine	Fine [initials]
	19.5.19.		
	20.5.19.		
	21.5.19.	Lt. HUNT left for demobilization.	Fine [initials]
	22.5.19.	Routine	Fine [initials]
	23.5.19.	Capt. G. RAYNER left for repatriation (UK) - Lieut. S. J. R. SAUNDERS took over command of the Coy.	Fine [initials]
	24.5.19.	Routine.	Fine. [initials]
	25.5.19.	Routine.	Fine [initials]
	26.5.19.	Authority received to reduce cadre by 75% of numbers as in [illegible] Instructions Part 3 - [illegible] IIA. [illegible] only 12 O.Rs.	Fine [initials]
	27.5.19.	Routine	Fine [initials]
	28.5.19.	1 O.R. left for demobilization	Much colder. [initials]
	29.5.19.	Routine	Fine [initials]
	30.5.19.	Routine	Fine [initials]
	31.5.19.	Routine	Fine [initials]

[signature]
A/O.C. [illegible] Field Coy. R.E.

1247 W 3299 200,000 (E) 8/14 J.B.C. & A. Forms/C. 2118/11.

WAR DIARY
or
INTELLIGENCE SUMMARY.
(Erase heading not required.)

Army Form C. 2118

502 (WESSEX) FIELD COMPANY

Instructions regarding War Diaries and Intelligence Summaries are contained in F. S. Regs., Part II. and the Staff Manual respectively. Title pages will be prepared in manuscript.

Hour, Date, Place	Summary of Events and Information	Remarks and references to Appendices
LENS #1 31 Jan. 18		
1 p.m.	Orders received to be in readiness to move to U.K. An advance party of 1 officer and 3 O.R's to leave on learn to 3 Below Bridge	Weather fine. M.O.
2 p.m.	Remainder of Coy to follow on and entrain. Coy to report approximately 1 hundred.	Less M.O.
3 p.m.	Orders received that upon relieved Coy to entrain at 3.7.19	Moved M.O.
	Coy entrained at MARLES L DUNKERQUE.	
No 2 EMBARKATION at 5 p.m. CAMP DUNKERQUE	Coy MARLES at 3 am proceeded DUNKERQUE from Marles to No 2 Embarkation Camp Marched to No 2 Embarkation Camp	Fine M.O.
5 p.m.	Awaiting orders to embark.	" M.O.
6 p.m.	Coy transport flooded on board vehicle. One Pontoon Wagon accidentally damaged going from alongside.	" M.O.
7 p.m.	Awaiting orders to embark.	" M.O.
8 p.m.	"	" M.O.
9 p.m.	"	" M.O.
10 p.m.	Orders received to embark at once.	" M.O.
	Coy breakfasted and on no CLUMB. Coy boarded (less transport in charge of Lieut S.A. KENYON R.E.) at DUNKERQUE for SOUTHAMPTON ENGLAND about 11 pm	

M. Buchanan Lieut RE
O.C. 502 Field Coy RE

Forms/C. 2118/10.

www.ingramcontent.com/pod-product-compliance
Lightning Source LLC
Chambersburg PA
CBHW081132220426
43649CB00038B/3329